Street by St

C000301269

BRIGHTON
WORTHING
HOVE, LEWES, NEWHAVEN

Ferring, Lancing, Peacehaven, Portslade-by-Sea, Rottingdean, Seaford, Shoreham-by-Sea, Sompting, Southwick, Steyning, Upper Beeding, Woodingdean

4th edition September 2007
© Automobile Association Developments Limited 2007

Original edition printed May 2001

 This product includes map data licensed from Ordnance Survey® with the permission of the Controller of Her Majesty's Stationery Office. © Crown copyright 2007. All rights reserved. Licence number 100021153.

Published by AA Publishing (a trading name of Automobile Association Developments Limited, whose registered office is Fanum House, Basing View, Basingstoke, Hampshire RG21 4EA. Registered number 1878835).

Produced by the Mapping Services Department of The Automobile Association. (A03383)

A CIP Catalogue record for this book is available from the British Library.

Printed by Oriental Press in Dubai

Key to map pages — ii-iii

Key to map symbols — iv-1

Enlarged map pages — 2-5

Main map pages — 6-73

Index – towns & villages — 74

Index – streets — 75-89

Index – featured places — 89-92

Acknowledgements — 92

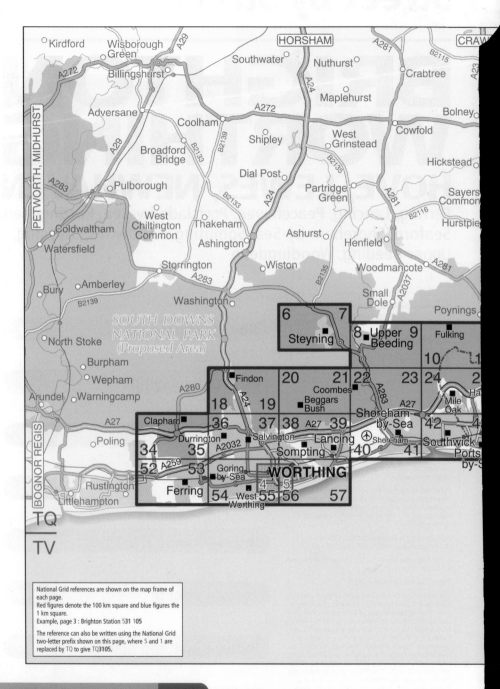

Kirdford · Wisborough Green · Billingshurst · Adversane · Coolham · Shipley · Southwater · HORSHAM · Nuthurst · Crabtree · Maplehurst · Bolney · A272 · West Grinstead · Cowfold · Hickstead · Broadford Bridge · Dial Post · Partridge Green · Sayers Common · Hurstpier · Pulborough · West Chiltington Common · Thakeham · Ashington · Ashurst · Henfield · Woodmancote · Coldwaltham · Watersfield · Storrington · Wiston · Small Dole · Poynings · Bury · Amberley · Washington

SOUTH DOWNS NATIONAL PARK (Proposed Area)

North Stoke · Burpham · Wepham · Arundel · Warningcamp · Clapham · Findon · Durrington · Salvington · Poling · Rustington · Littlehampton · Ferring · West Worthing

PETWORTH, MIDHURST

BOGNOR REGIS

CRAW

6	7		
Steyning	8 Upper Beeding	9	Fulking
20	21	22	23 24
18 19	Coombes Beggars Bush	Shoreham-by-Sea	42
36 37	38 39	40 41	Southwick
34 35	Sompting Lancing		
52 53	Goring by-Sea	WORTHING	
Ferring 54	55 56	57	

10
Mile Oak
Shoreham
Ports by-S

TQ
TV

National Grid references are shown on the map frame of each page.
Red figures denote the 100 km square and blue figures the 1 km square.
Example, page 3 : Brighton Station 531 105

The reference can also be written using the National Grid two-letter prefix shown on this page, where 5 and 1 are replaced by TQ to give TQ3105.

Enlarged scale pages 1:10,000 6.3 inches to 1 mile

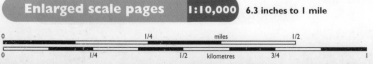

0   1/4   miles   1/2
0   1/4   1/2   kilometres   3/4   1

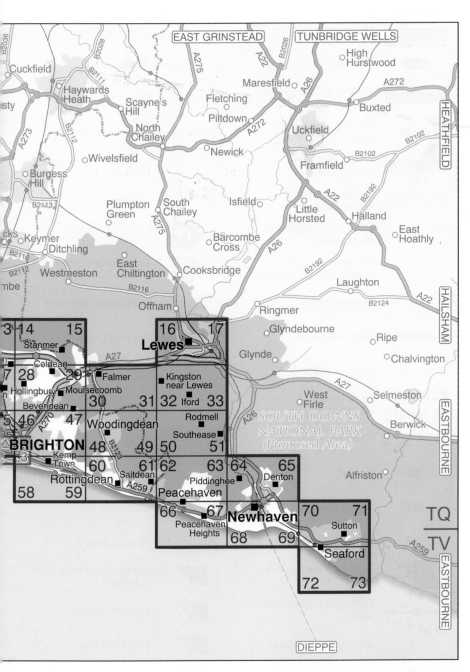

EAST GRINSTEAD

TUNBRIDGE WELLS

HEATHFIELD

High
Hurstwood

Cuckfield

Haywards
Heath

Maresfield

A272

Scayne's
Hill

Fletching

Buxted

Piltdown

North
Chailey

Uckfield

Wivelsfield

Newick

Framfield

Burgess
Hill

Plumpton
Green

South
Chailey

Isfield

Little
Horsted

Halland

East
Hoathly

Keymer

Barcombe
Cross

Ditchling

Westmeston

East
Chiltington

Cooksbridge

Laughton

Offham

Ringmer

Glyndebourne

Ripe

Chalvington

HAILSHAM

Lewes

Glynde

Selmeston

Stanmer

Falmer

Kingston
near Lewes

West
Firle

Berwick

EASTBOURNE

Coldean

Hollingbury

Moulsecoomb

Iford

Rodmell

SOUTH DOWNS
NATIONAL PARK
(Proposed Area)

Bevendean

Woodingdean

Southease

BRIGHTON

Kemp
Town

Alfriston

Rottingdean

Saltdean

Peacehaven

Denton

Piddinghoe

TQ

Newhaven

Sutton

TV

Peacehaven
Heights

Seaford

EASTBOURNE

DIEPPE

3	14	15		16	17	
7	28	29		32	33	
5	46	47	48	49	50	51
58	59	60	61	62	63	64	65
		66	67	68	69	70	71
				72	73	

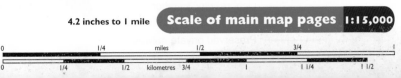

| 0 | 1/4 | miles | 1/2 | 3/4 | 1 |
| 0 | 1/4 | 1/2 | kilometres 3/4 | 1 | 1 1/4 | 1 1/2 |

iv

Junction 9	Motorway & junction
Services	Motorway service area
	Primary road single/dual carriageway
Services	Primary road service area
	A road single/dual carriageway
	B road single/dual carriageway
	Other road single/dual carriageway
	Minor/private road, access may be restricted
← ←	One-way street
	Pedestrian area
	Track or footpath
	Road under construction
	Road tunnel
P	Parking
P+	Park & Ride
	Bus/coach station
	Railway & main railway station
	Railway & minor railway station
⊖	Underground station
⊖	Light railway & station
+++++++++	Preserved private railway

LC	Level crossing
●—●—●—●	Tramway
----------	Ferry route
....	Airport runway
— · — · · — · · —	County, administrative boundary
▼▼▼▼▼▼▼▼▼	Mounds
17	Page continuation 1:15,000
3	Page continuation to enlarged scale 1:10,000
	River/canal, lake, pier
	Aqueduct, lock, weir
465 ▲ Winter Hill	Peak (with height in metres)
	Beach
	Woodland
	Park
	Cemetery
	Built-up area
	Industrial/business building
	Leisure building
	Retail building
	Other building

⊓⊓⊓⊓⊓	City wall	♜	Castle
A&E	Hospital with 24-hour A&E department	🏛	Historic house or building
PO	Post Office	Wakehurst Place (NT)	National Trust property
📖	Public library	Ⓜ	Museum or art gallery
_i_	Tourist Information Centre	♞	Roman antiquity
_i_	Seasonal Tourist Information Centre	⚱	Ancient site, battlefield or monument
▮ ▮	Petrol station, 24 hour Major suppliers only	🏭	Industrial interest
†	Church/chapel	✻	Garden
🚻	Public toilets	◉	Garden Centre Garden Centre Association Member
♿	Toilet with disabled facilities	🌳	Garden Centre Wyevale Garden Centre
PH	Public house AA recommended	🌲	Arboretum
🍴	Restaurant AA inspected	🛒	Farm or animal centre
Madeira Hotel ⌐	Hotel AA inspected	🦌	Zoological or wildlife collection
🎭	Theatre or performing arts centre	🐦	Bird collection
🎥	Cinema	🦆	Nature reserve
⚑	Golf course	🐟	Aquarium
▲	Camping AA inspected	**V**	Visitor or heritage centre
🚐	Caravan site AA inspected	⚘	Country park
▲🚐	Camping & caravan site AA inspected	☉	Cave
🎢	Theme park	✸	Windmill
🏚	Abbey, cathedral or priory	🛢	Distillery, brewery or vineyard

Congreve

St Andrews CE High School for Boys

Springfield First School

56

Ruskin Rd

Thackeray Rd

Kingsley Cl

Ham Bridge Trading Estate

F **G** **H** **J** **K**

Marston Rd

Warner

Meredith

East Worthing Station

Ham Close

Ham Way

16

HAM ROAD

Oakleigh Cl

Pages Lane

Mansfiel

Sackville Way

Road

King Edward Avenue

Ashwood

Chesswood Close

Stuart Cl

1

B2223

The Quashetts

King Edward Close

Chesswood Road

Road

Chesswood Middle School

Selborne Rd

Davison CE High School for Girls

Chester Av

2

Chester Avenue

HAM

Archbald

Chatfield

King Edward Avenue

Works

Chesswood Road

Halsbury Close

Halsbury Rd

Ladydell

Lyndhurst First School

ROAD

Road

Station

Thurlow Rd

Sugden

Alverstone Rd

Ten Acres

B2223

Newland

Homefield Park

Homefield

Park Av

Cranworth Road

Cottenham Rd

Dawes Av

Dawes Cl

Colebrook

3

Pendine venue

Dagmar St

Upper High St

Park

Worthing Hospital

Eldon Rd

Lyndhurst Road

Windsor

56

Navarino Road

Ashdown Rd

Sussex Road

Tower Rd

Road

A&E

Selden

Gannon Road

Road

Hotel

4

Markwick Ms

High Street

St George's Road

Road

Gordon

Ltl High Street

Providence Ter

Lyndhurst Road

Farncombe

Church

Alexandra Rd

CAB

Madeira Avenue

PO

Selden Road

Selden Lane

NORTH STREET

HIGH

Superstore

Park Road

English Bowling Association

Beach House Park

The Esp

5

Town Hall Annexe all Museum llery

West Sussex Coll of Design

P

STREET

P

Charlotte Rd

Ash Gv

Warwick Pl

Sandhurst School

ROAD

PO

Police Station

P

Chatsworth Rd

Elm Rd

Warwick Gdns

Wyke Av

Warwick

BRIGHTON

Merton

New Pde

Northbrook Coll Sussex eatre & Cinema

Environment Agency

Guildbourne Centre

Aquarena Swimming Pool

6

Market

Warwick St

York Road

Alfred Pl

P

Beach

Parade

Chapel Rd

Ann St

Stanford Square

Bus Depot

Steyne Gdns

Ardington Hotel

Parade

Montague Shopping Centre

South St

Marine Pl

Bedford Row

Library

The Steyne

Marine Parade

Bath Pl

Dome

7

Marine

uncil Building

Pavilion Theatre

Worthing Pier

HING

F **G** **H** **J** **K**

15 16

02

6

515 | 16

A **B** **C** **D**

Wiston Park

Great Barn Farm

Mouse Lane

†

1

112

BM

2

Wiston Barn

Charlton Co

Mouse

3

111

Peppe

4

South Downs Way

5

110

515 | 16

A **B** **C** **D**

Monarch Way

Road

No Man's Land

Bostal

1 grid square represents 500 metres

New Hill

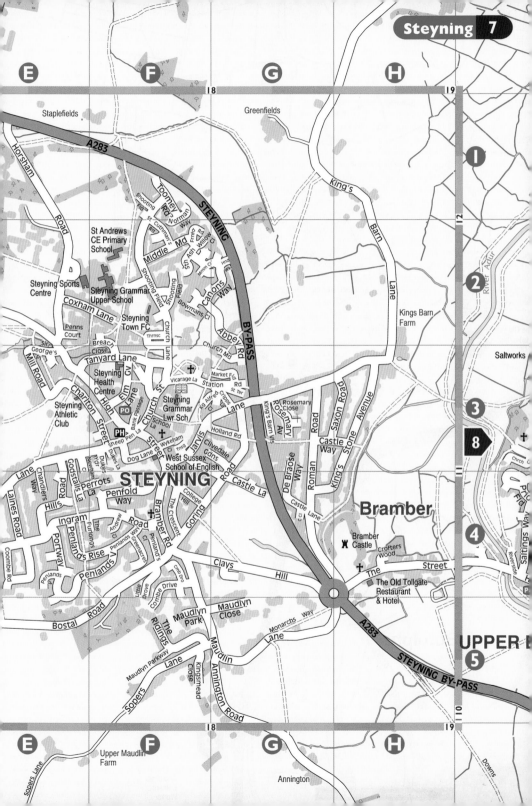

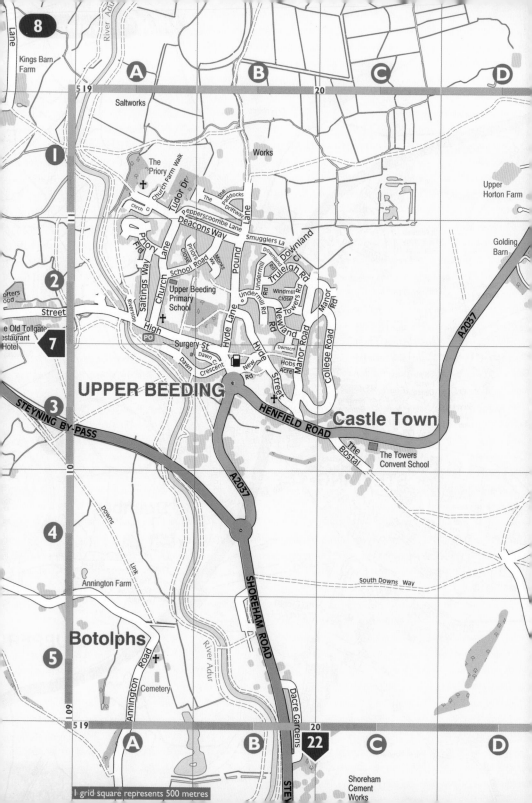

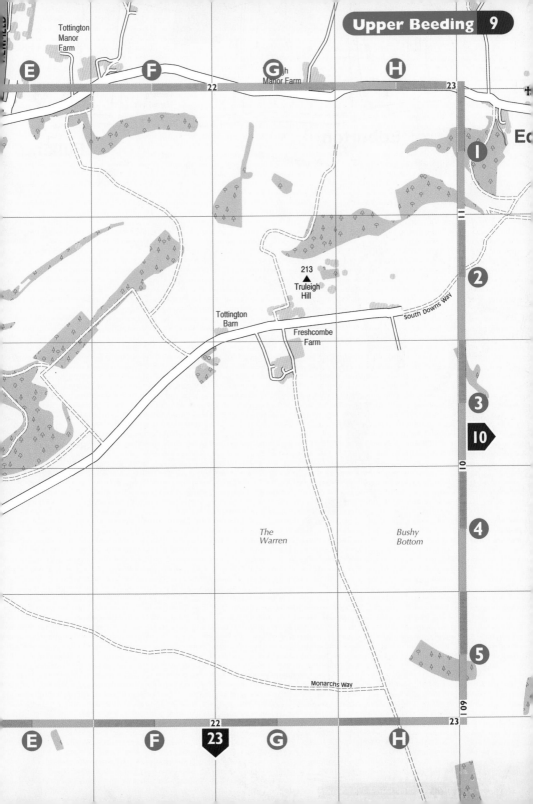

Tottington
Manor
Farm

E

F

G
Manor Farm

H

22

23

I

Ec

213
▲
Truleigh
Hill

South Downs Way

2

Tottington
Barn

Freshcombe
Farm

3

10

10

The
Warren

Bushy
Bottom

4

5

09

Monarchs Way

E

F

22
23

G

H

23

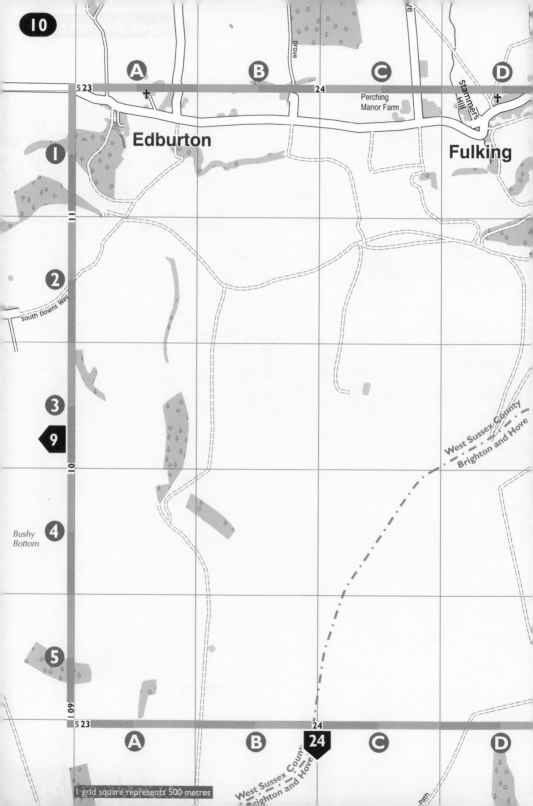

10

A **B** **C** **D**

S 23 24

✝

Perching
Manor Farm

Edburton

Fulking

✝

Stammers Hill

Drove

1

2

South Downs Way

3

9

0

West Sussex County

Brighton and Hove

4

*Bushy
Bottom*

5

S 09

S 23 24

A **B** **C** **D**

24

West Sussex County

Brighton and Hove

Path

1 grid square represents 500 metres

Wickhurst
Barns

E   F   G   H

26   27

Sa

I

Devil's
Dyke

Devil's Dyke Road

South Downs Way

2

Border Path

Devils

Dyke

3

12

Devil's
Dyke Farm

Road

10

4

109

5
Skeleton
Hovel

Brighton &
Hove Golf Club

E   F   26   G   H

25

Monarchs Way

27

Saddlescombe

West Sussex County
Brighton and Hove

Sussex Border Path

Brighton and Hove
West Sussex County

Sussex Border

Golf Course

Skeleton
Hovel

Brighton &
Hove Golf Club

Waterhall
Golf Club

Brighton
RFC

I grid square represents 500 metres

E   F   G   H

30   31

Pangdean Farm

West Sussex County
Brighton and Hove

I

South Hill Farm

Sussex Border Path

2

3

14

A23

Sussex Border Path

4

LONDON ROAD

Braypool Lane

Waterhall

A27

Avenue

Braeside

Kenmure Av

Bengairn Av

Thornhill Av

Plainfields Av

Baranscraig Av

5

Solway Av

Sanyhills Av

Heston Av

Craignair Avenue

60

LONDON ROAD

Court Close

Vale

The Village Barn

Church Hill

Ashley Cl

Barrhill Av

Mackie Av

31

Patcham Place

30

PATCHAM

Innkeeper's

PO

Highview Av North

Highvw Rd

Highview Way

Wrmd Av

Miles Cl

Ladies' Mile Road

Stoneleigh Close

Dharma School

Ladies' Mile Road

Singleton Road

Sunnydale Av

Sunnydale Close

Patcham Junior School

Winf

14

A   Lower   B   C   D
           Standean

531   32

1

New
Barn

2

3

13

10

4

Ditchling Road

Coldean Lane

5   Heston Av 601
                                                        Superstore
Avenue   Eastwick Cl
       Kenmure   Glenfalls   Mackie Avenue
Bengairn   Av   Av   Eskbank   Hollingbury
Thornhill Av   Plainfields Av   Av   BN1   Carden Avenue   Industrial
Baranscraig Av   The Deeside   Crowhurst Road   Estate
Solway Av   Sanyhils Av   Clovers
Ladies'   Mackie Aven 531   End   Old Boat
Mile   Craignair   Dharma   Wk
Cl   School   Windmill   Buttercup
                          A   Vw   B   28   C   D
Ladies' Mile   Singleton   Portfield Av   Tangmere   Petworth Road
Stoneleigh   Road   Sunnydale   Rd   Morecambe Rd   Midhurst Rd
Close   Sunnyd   Close   Haywards   Cuckmere
                                                        Way

Ditchling Road

Saunders Hill

Crawley
Road

Hawkhurst

1 grid square represents 500 metres

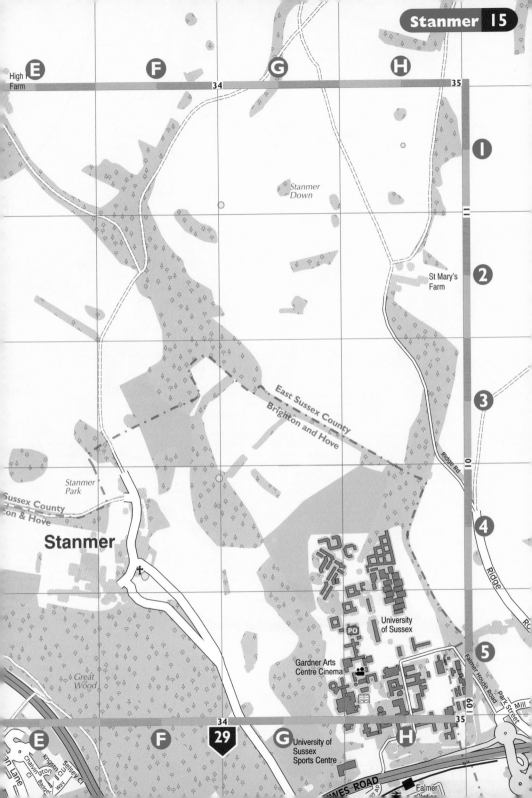

High
Farm

E **F** **G** **H**

34 35

I

Stanmer
Down

St Mary's
Farm

2

East Sussex County

Brighton and Hove

3

Ridge Rd

Stanmer
Park

Sussex County
on & Hove

4

Stanmer

University
of Sussex

Gardner Arts
Centre Cinema

PO

Ridge
R

5

Falmer House Road

Park Street

Mill

Great
Wood

E **F** **29** **G** **H**

34 35

University of
Sussex
Sports Centre

Kingston
Bagger

Chalvington
Way

Selsey Cl

n Lane

LEWES ROAD

Falmer

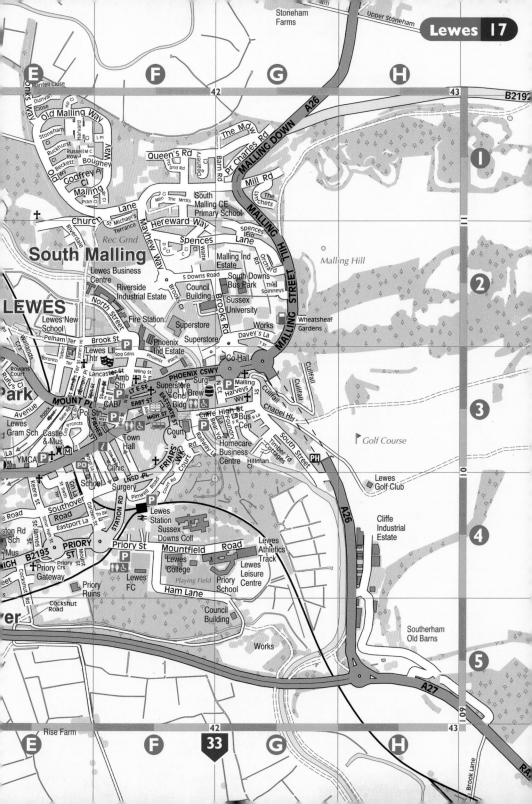

Stoneham Farms

Upper Stoneham

B2192

E Mantell Close

F

G

H

I

Old Malling Way

Old Malling Way

Stoneham

Harvey Dr

L Pl

Buckhurst Cl

Russell Row

M C

Beckett Cl

Boughey Cl

Godfrey Pl

Malling

Pckh Cl

Malling

Lane

Church

Riverdale

St Michael's Terrance

Rec Grnd

South Malling

Queen's Rd

Grid Rd

Deanery

Barn Rd

Pt Charles Rd

The Mdw

MALLING DOWN

A26

Mill Rd

The Lynchets

The Lynchets

MALLING HILL

Malling Hill

Mlln

The Mrtlts

South Malling CE Primary School

Mayhew Way

Hereward Way

Spences Lane

Waite

Spences Fl Rd

MALLING STREET

Lewes Business Centre

Riverside Industrial Estate

Brooks Cl

Council Building

Sussex University

Malling Ind Estate

Orchard

South Downs Bus Park

The Spinneys

LEWES

Lewes New School

Pelham Ter

North Street

Fire Station

Superstore

Superstore

Works

Davey's La

T St

Wheatsheaf Gardens

Culfall

Culfall

Culfall

Culfall

Walands

Talbot Ter

Ashmen Ter St John's Ter

Toronto Ter

Brook St

Lewes Lit Thtr

Spg Gdns

Phoenix Ind Estate

Phoenix Place

Co Hall

Malling WV Harveys

2

Lancaster St

Amb Stn

CAB

Surg

PHOENIX CSWY

Superstore

Chel Brew Bdg

N Ct

Chapel Hly

South Street

3

Rowans Court

Rufus Cl

Avenue

Lewes

New

Pol Stn

MOUNT PL

Castle & Mus

FISHER ST

EAST ST

HIGH ST

Court

Cliffe High St

Bus Cen

Bear La

Foundry

Timber Yd Cottages

PH

Lewes Golf Club

ark

YMCA

Gram Sch

M

Prcncts

Town Hall

PO

Clinic

FRIARS'

LWR

Court

Railway La

Court Rd

Homecare Business Centre

Hillman Cl

Golf Course

School

LNSD PL

Surgery

Pinwell Road

Court Rd

Southover Road

Keere St

Eastport La

STATION RD

Garden St

Tn BK

Lewes Station Sussex Downs Coll

Lewes Athletics Track

Cliffe Industrial Estate

4

Priory St

St James

PRIORY ST

Mount St

Priory Crs

Lewes College

Mountfield

Road

Lewes Leisure Centre

B2193

Priory Gateway

Priory Ruins

Lewes FC

Playing Field

Ham Lane

Priory School

Southerham Old Barns

Cockshut Rd

Cockshut Road

Council Building

Works

A26

A27

Rise Farm

E

F

33

G

H

Brook Lane

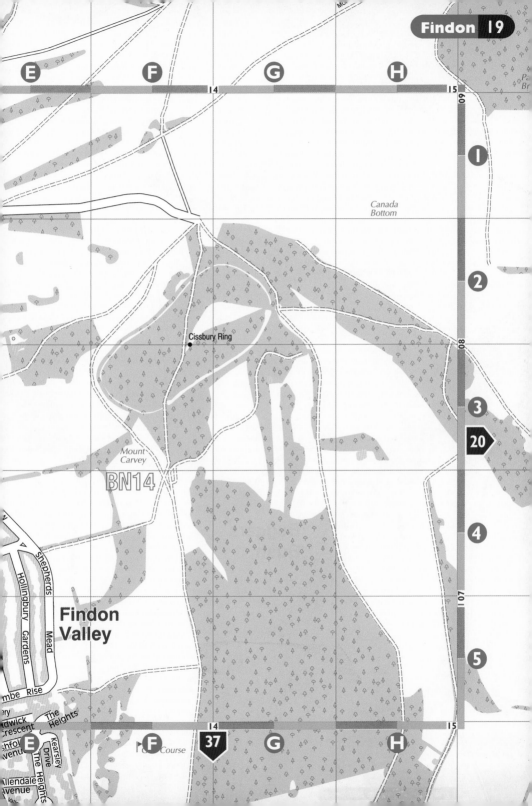

E　　F　　G　　H

14

15

60

I

Canada Bottom

2

08

Cissbury Ring

3

20

Mount Carvey

BN14

4

07

Findon Valley

5

Shepherds Mead

Hollingbury Gardens

...mbe Rise

The Heights

...dwick Crescent

...shfo... Avenue

Kearsley Drive

The Heights

...llendale Heights

E　　F　　**37**　　G　　H

...f Course

14　　　　　　15

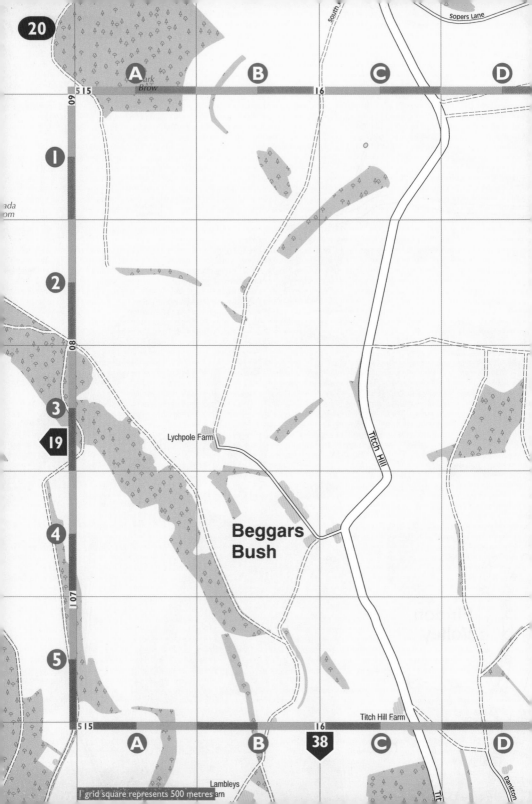

20

A · ark · Brow

B

C

D

Sopers Lane

South

1

2

3

19

4

5

60 515

08

1 07

516

Lychpole Farm

Beggars Bush

Titch Hill

A 515

B

38

C

D

Titch Hill Farm

Lambleys

Dankton

ada om

Tit

1 grid square represents 500 metres

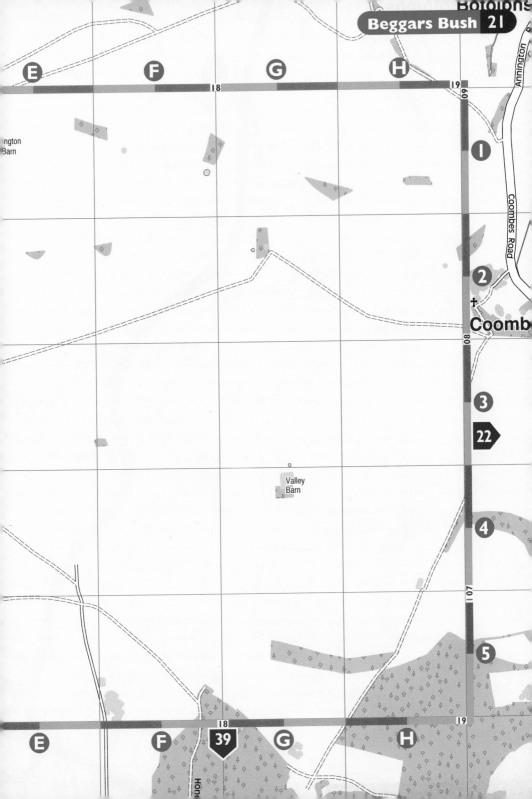

E F G H

18 19

Annington

Coombes Road

1

2

✝

Coomb

60

80

07

19

3

22

4

5

ngton
Barn

Valley
Barn

E F G H

18 19

39

Hon

Monarchs Way

E F **9** G H

22 **23** 60

I

New Erringham Farm

2

80

BN43

3

24

4

107

Buckingham Barn

Slonk Hill Farm

5

Mill Hill

SHOREHAM BY-PASS

Chanctonbury Drive

Saxons

Slonk Hill Road

22 **23**

E F **41** G Downside H

Shoreham

Mill Hill Drive

Mill Hill Gdns

Edburton Gdns

Ann Cdn

Amb Cl

Ravensbourne Av

Cypress Cl

Rvnsbr Cl

Truleigh Wy

Athlings Wy

Th Wy

New Barn Rd

Greenways Crescent

M Pl

Lavender BC Wy

Rosemary Drive

Bergamot

japonica

F C L

tarragon

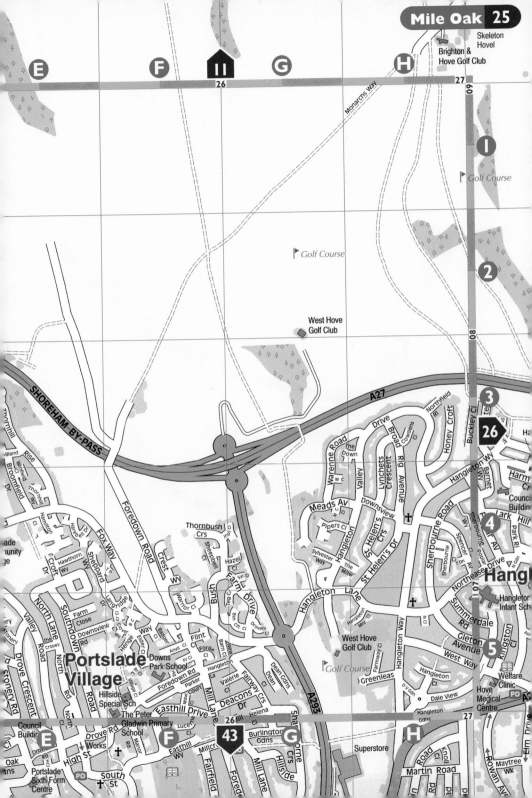

Skeleton Hovel

Brighton & Hove Golf Club

E F **H** 26 G H

27

60

Monarchs Way

Golf Course

I

Golf Course

2

West Hove Golf Club

A27

SHOREHAM BY-PASS

Foredown Road

Northfield Rd

3

26

Buckley Cl

Hangleton Way

Barnet Wy

Harm Cr

Council Buildin

Warenne Road

Drive

Broad Rig Avenue

Cowdens Cl

Honey Croft

The Down

Valley

Lynchets Crescent

Park Hill

Park Rd

Meads Av

Downsview

St Helen's Crs

Sherbourne Road

Sherbourne

Spencer Cl

Northease Drive

Pk Av

4

Thornbush Crs

Hazel Cl

Sheepfell Cl

Farm drive

Bush

Pipers Cl

Hangleton

Sylvester Way

St Helen's Dr

The Mews

107

Hang

Thornhill Rise

Broomfield Dr

Thornhill Cl

Fox Way

Crest Wy

Manor Wy

Hangleton Lane

Summerdale Rd

Hangleton Infant Sch

Hawthorn Wy

Sheppard

Lang Bridge

Flint Cl

Forge

Drovers

West Hove Golf Club

Hangleton Way

Hangleton Cl

Gleton Avenue

5

Kingston

Valley Road

North Lane

Southdown Rd

Farm Close

Downsview Rd

The Crssway

Henge Way

Anvil Cl

Barn Cl

Alden Cl

Dean Gdns

Fairway Crs

Dean Cl

Greenleas

D V Gdn

West Way

Welfare Clinic

Portslade Village

Downs Park School

Foredown Rd

Parker

Valérie Court

Deacons Dr

Hangleton Gdns

Dale View

Hove Medical Centre

PO

Drove Crescent

Greenery Rd

Hillside Special Sch

The Peter Gladwin Primary School

Easthill Drive

Mill Lane

Helena Cl

Burlington Gdns

Sharpthorne Crs

A293

Hangleton Gdns

27

Council Buildin

E

Drove Rd

High St

F

Easthill Wy

Fairfield

Millcr

43

G

Superstore

H

Martin Road

Rowan Av

Maytree Wk

Portslade Sixth Form Centre

PO

South St

Oak Ins

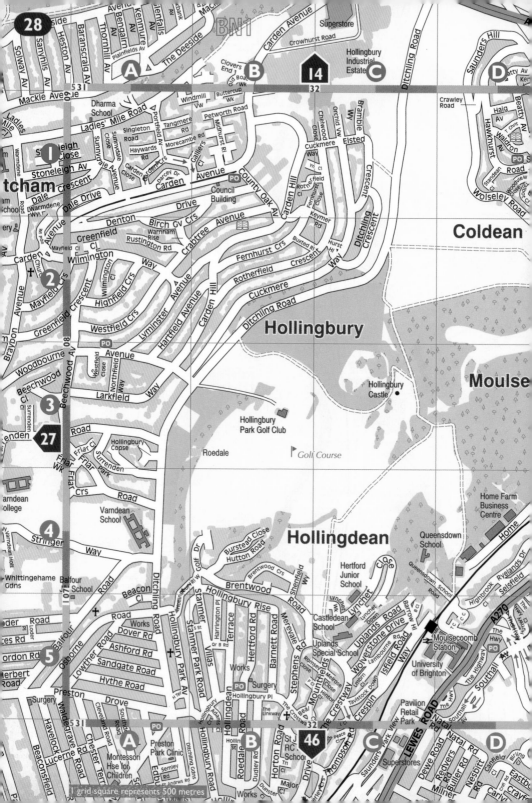

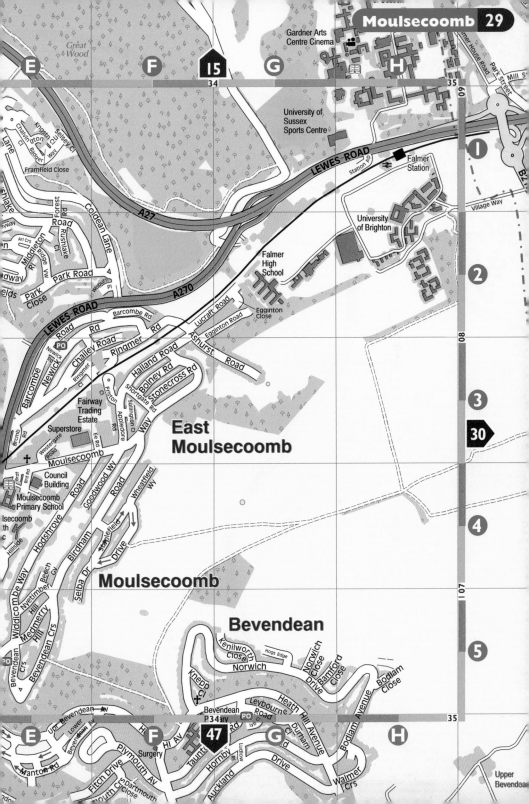

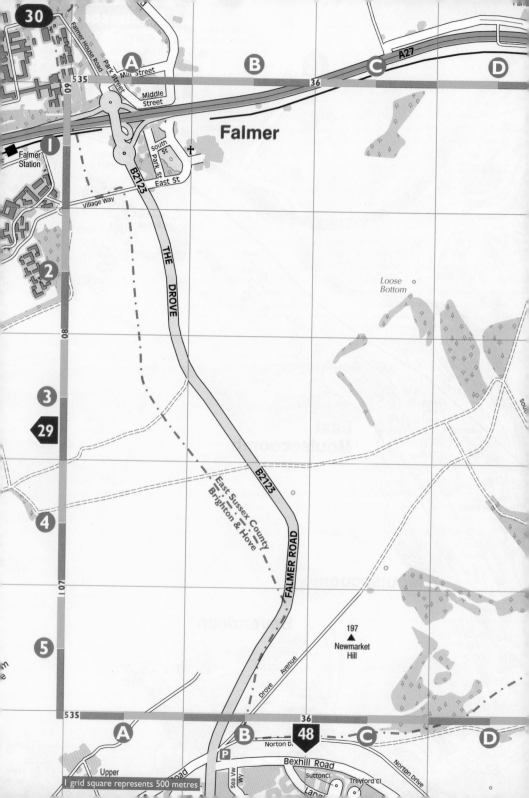

A27

38   39

Ashcombe Hollow

Kingston Hollow

1

Kingston Ridge

Ridgway Paddock

Ashcombe

The Avenue

Church

La

The Flints

Church Lane

Lockitt Way

Monckton Way

Cordons

Bramleys

Thyroom

St Pancras

Ba
Cl
Stre

2

The

80

K
n

South Downs Way

South Downs Way

3

32

South Downs Way

4

Dencher

107

Wildfowl
Reserve

5

38   39

49

A   B   16   C   D

Works

Juggs Road

Cranedown

Kingston Road

Lewes
Sports
Club

39
60

Ashcombe Hollow

Kingston Hollow

Kingston Ridge

Ridgway
Paddock

1

Ashcombe Lane

Church La

The Avenue

Lockitt Way

Cordons

St. Pancras Gn

Monckton Way

Bramleys

Mushroom

The Flints

Kent
Flds

Iford & Kingston
CE Primary School

Snednore

Kingston Hollow

40

2

PH

Barn
Cl

St. Pancras Gn Fld

Hyde Cft

Church Lane

Gows
Cft

The Holdings

Wellgreen Lane

Swanborough Hollow

Wyevale
Garden
Centre

The

80

**Kingston
near Lewes**

3

31

South Downs Way

107

Swanborough Drove

4

Dencher Road

Swanborough Hollow

†

5

39

South Downs Way

A   B   50   C   D

40

White

E   F   **17**   G   H

Works

Old Barns

A27

Rise Farm

Brook Lane

42   43   60

I

Northease
Manor
School

Rise
Barn

The
Brooks

River Ouse

2

80

3

4

107

5

E   **F**   **51**   G   H

42   43

Northease Farm

Swanboro

Monk's
House (NT)

Rodmell

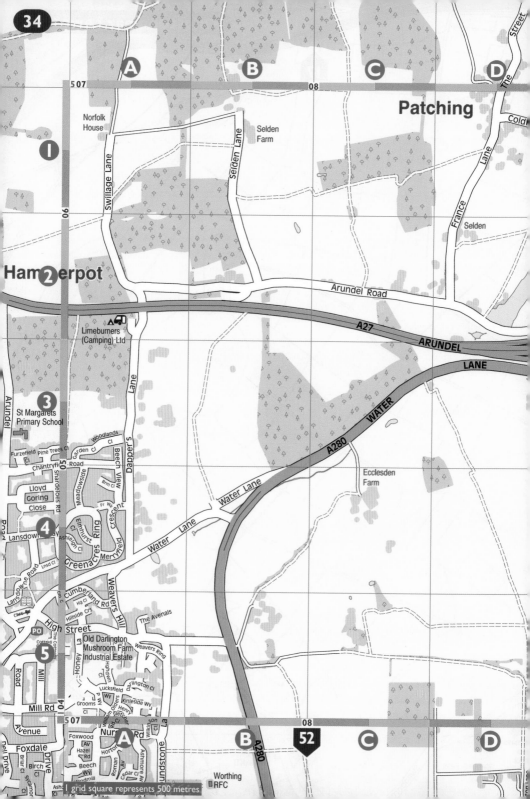

Clapham

A280

LONG FURLONG

The PO
Clapham & Patching CE Prim Sch
Clapham Common

Church Cl
Street

Holt Farm

A27

Titnore Lane

Woodlands

Forest Barn

ARUNDEL

Cherwell Road

Humber Avenue

36

Humber Close
Hobart Cl
Adelaide Rd
Brisbane Close
Canberra Road
Shopping Ce
store

Adur

Loxton

Highdown Hill

Titnore Lane

Titnore Way

Fulbeck Avenue
Moore
Varey Road
squad
Essenh
Eriskay Cl
Rchstr
Apsley Way
Saxifrage
Pennycress Av
Samphire Dr
Corfe Cl
Leeds Ct
Jevington
Carisbrooke Dr
Wy
Brignac
Romany Road

Lewis
Winterbourne Wy

County First School

Works
Winterbourne Wy
Birches Cl
Faraday Road

Romany
Whiteheam Rd

Poplar

The Ha
First Sc

5

Cypress
Juniper
Holly Cl
Silver Birch Dr
Laurel Close
Foxglove

Highdown Gardens

Works

Yeoman Rd

Yeoman Wy

A2032

Northbrook College Sussex

LITTLEHAMPTON ROAD

Kithurst
Kithurst Cl
Melville W
Limb
PO

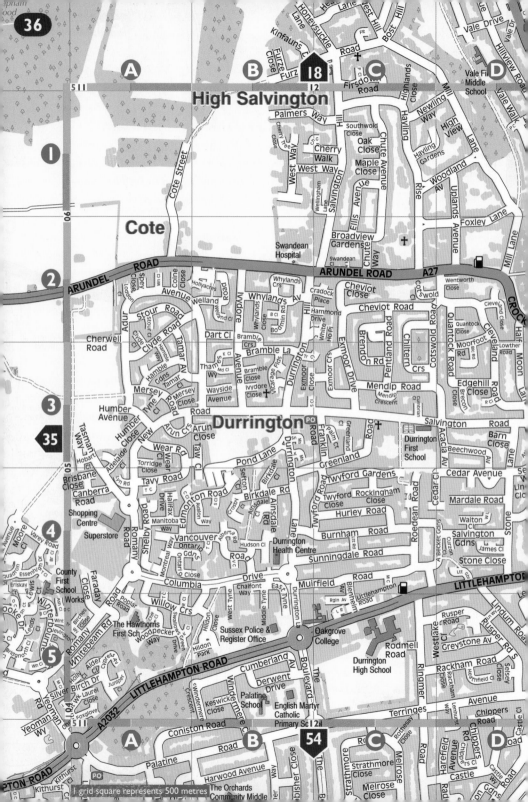

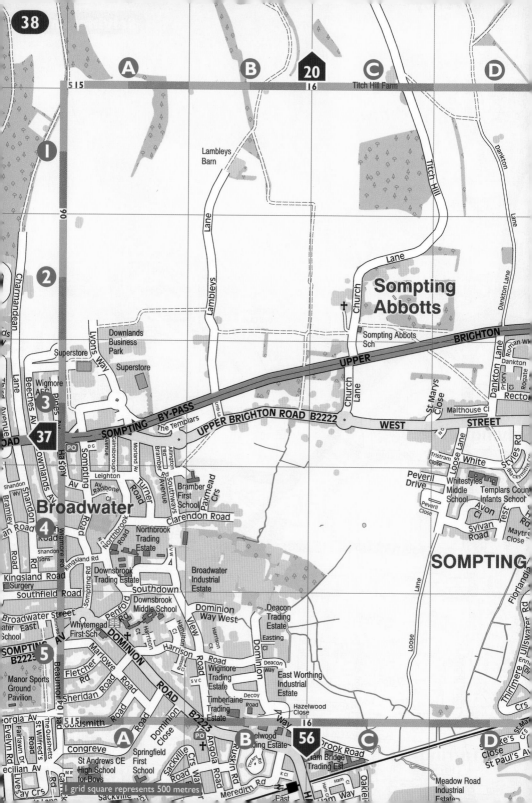

38

A   B   **20**   C   Titch Hill Farm   D

5 1 5   1 6

1

Lambleys
Barn

9 0

2

Sompting
Abbotts

† Church

Downlands
Business
Park

Lyons Way

Sompting Abbots
Sch

3

Superstore

Superstore

Wigmore
AFC

Pines
Av

Beeches Av

Charmandean Lane

Third Avenue

Dankton Lane

Titch Hill

Church Lane

Church Lane

Dankton Lane

BRIGHTON

UPPER

37

PO

Broadwater

SOMPTING BY-PASS   The Templars

UPPER BRIGHTON ROAD B2222

WEST   STREET

History Av

Cainsborough Avenue

DG

Sompting Av

Leighton Av

Redbone

Morland Av

Bramber Avenue

Southways

Turner Road

Allington Rd

Bramber
First
School

Paxmead
Crs

Clarendon Road

St Marys Lane

Malthouse Cl

Loose Lane

Dankton Lane

Roman Wk

Priory

Dankton

Rogate

Recto

White

Styles Rd

Blacksmiths Cl

Tristram
Close

Loose Lane

Peveril
Drive

Whitestyles
Middle
School

Templars Coun
Infants School

4

shandon
Wy

Shandon
Gdns

Bramley Road

Recilian Dr

Northbrook
Road

Kingsland Rd

Northbrook
Trading
Estate

Downsbrook
Trading Estate

S V W

Broadwater
Industrial
Estate

Avon
Cl

Peveril
Close

Sylvan
Road

Maytre
close

SOMPTING

Kingsland Road

Surgery

Southfield Road

Southdown

Dominion Way West

Florlandia
Rd

Thirlmere Rd

Ullswater Rd

Broadwater Street

water East
School

Penfold Road

Downsbrook
Middle School

View Road

Deacon
Trading
Estate

Easting Cl

5

SOMPTING
B2223

Whytemead
First Sch

Marlowe Road

DOMINION

Harrison
Road

Hamilton Cl

Russell Cl

Harrison Ct

Dominion Way

Deacon
Way

Crs

Ullswater Rd

Manor Sports
Ground
Pavilion

Beaumont Rd

Fletcher
Rd

Sheridan Rd

Dominion Road

ROAD

Harrison Road

S V C

Wigmore
Trading
Estate

Decoy Road

East Worthing
Industrial
Estate

Thirlmere Crs

Georgia Av

The Quashetts

St Wilfred's

Fairfawn Dr

Evelyn Rd

Lives Rd

Cecilian Av

ay Crs

Goldsmith Rd

Dominion
Close

Road

Sackville
Road

Angola Road

Ruskin Rd

Timberlaine
Trading
Estate

Way

Hazelwood
Close

Brook Road

St Luke's
Close

St Paul's Cl

A   **Congreve**   Springfield
First
School

St Andrews CE
High School
for Boys

PO

†

Crs Way

B2223

Meredith Rd

B   elwood
ding Estate   **56**   am Bridge
Trading Est   C   D

Trickety Rd

K Cl

Ham Bridge

East

Ham Way

Meadow Road
Industrial
Estate

1 6

1 grid square represents 500 metres

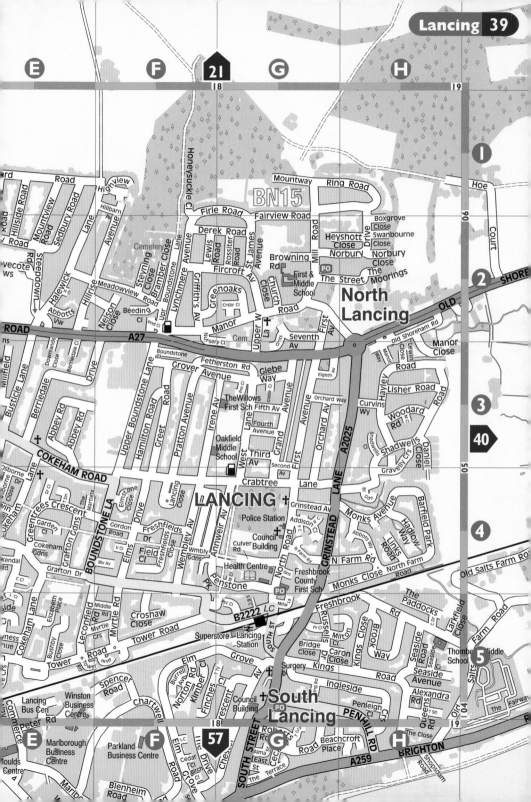

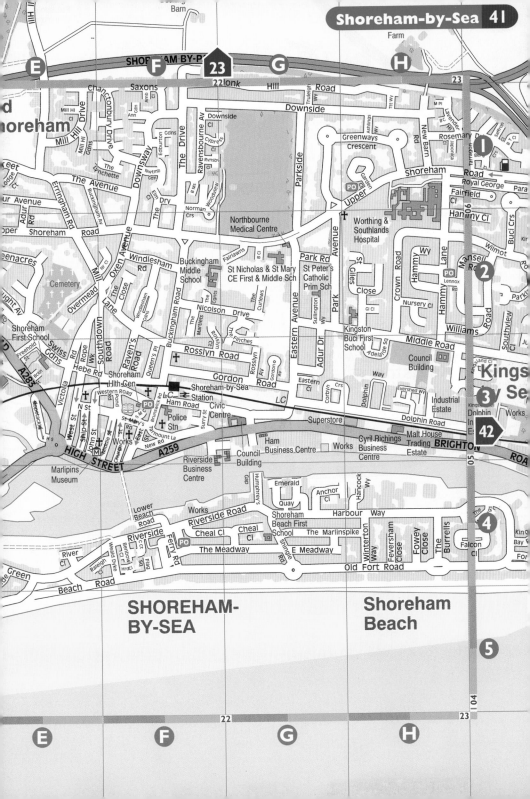

SHOREHAM-BY-PASS

Monk Hill

Downside

Downside

Greenways Crescent

Shoreham

Farm

Saxons

Mill Hi Cl

Mill Hill Drive

Chanctonbury Drive

Mill Hill Cl

Mill Hill Gdns

The Lynchette

The Cl

Ann Gdn

Edburton Gdns

Ravensbourne Av

Cl

Cypress

Parkside

Greenways Crescent

PO

Garden Wy

Upper Shoreham Road

Royal George

Para

Fairfield Cl

Hammy Cl

Ashlings

New Barn Rd

Lavender Dr

Rosemary Dr

Saffron

Taragon Cl

Japonica

MPI

BC

Bucl Crs

Wilmot

I

Northbourne Medical Centre

Worthing & Southlands Hospital

Mansell Rd

Hammy Wy

Hammy Lane

Southview Rd

2

Buckingham Middle School

Fairlawns

St Nicholas & St Mary CE First & Middle Sch

St Peter's Catholic Prim Sch

St Giles Close

Crown Road

Nursery Cl

Williams Road

The Drive

Downsway

Nwtmb Gdn

Woodview

The Dry

Norman Crs

The Giants

B Ms

Cl B

The Curlews

Sullington

Park Rd

Park Avenue

Eastern Avenue

Lennox Rd

PO

Shoreham First School

Oxen Avenue

Windlesham Rd

Windlesham Gdns

Nicolson Drive

The Martlets

The Finches

Rosslyn Rd

Rossel

Kingston Bucl First School

Middle Road

Council Building

Kingsland Cl

Kings by Se

Cemetery

Overmead

Mill Lane

Southdown Close

Raven's Road

Queen's Pl

Gordon Road

Rosslyn Road

Rossel Av

Gordon

Eastern Cl

Corbyn Crs

Way

Dolphin

Eversfield Wy

Industrial Estate

3

Greenacres

Adur Avenue

Erringham Rd

Swiss Gdns

Freehold St

Hebe Rd

Rope Wk

Shoreham Hlth Cen

Shoreham-by-Sea Station

Ham Road

Civic Centre

Adelaide Sq

Adur Dr

Dolphin Road

Kingsland Cl

Dolphin Ind Est

Works

42

A283

Victoria Rd

N St

West St

Ship St

John St

St Mary's

Western Road

Brunswick Rd

Surry St

Tarmount La

New Rd

Police Stn

Eastern Rd

Corbyn

Superstore

Malt House Trading Estate

Cyril Richings Business Centre

BRIGHTON

ROA

HIGH STREET

A259

Works

Riverside Business Centre

Council Building

Ham Business Centre

Works

05

Marlipins Museum

Lower Beach Rd

Riverside

Ferry Rd

PO

Riverside Road

Works

Cheal Cl

Cheal Cl

Humphrey's

Emerald Quay

Anchor Cl

Hancock Wy

Shoreham Beach First School

The Marlinspike

Winterton Way

Feversham Close

Fowey Close

The Burrells

Falcon Cl

King Bay

4

River Cl

Raleigh Rd

Weald Dyke

Benbow Ct

Flag

The Meadway

E Meadway

Shingle

Old Fort Road

Green

Beach Road

SHOREHAM-BY-SEA

Shoreham Beach

22

104

23

5

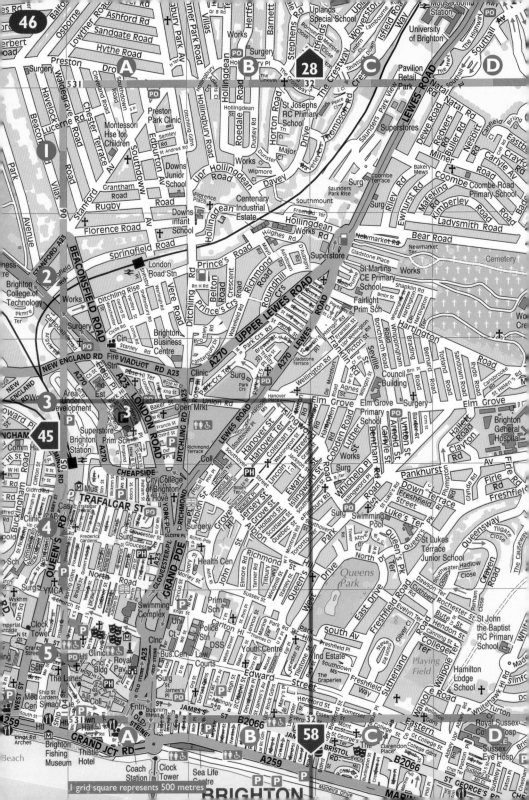

I grid square represents 500 metres

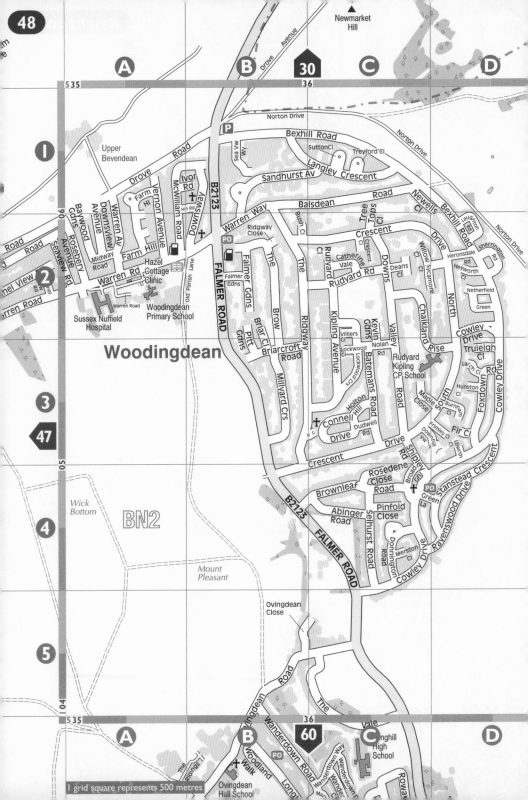

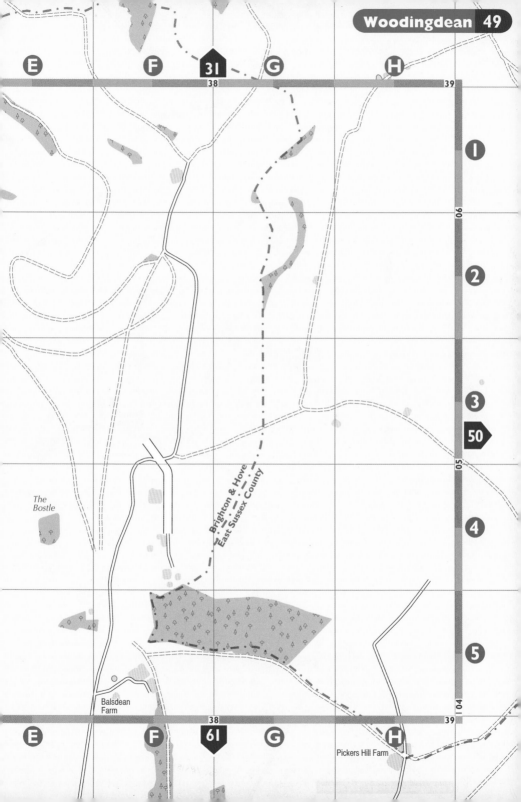

E F **31** G H

1

2

3

50

4

5

The
Bostle

Brighton & Hove
East Sussex County

Balsdean
Farm

E F **61** G H

Pickers Hill Farm

A   **B**   32   **C**   **D**

539   40

1

90

2

Whiteway
Bottom

3

49

05

Breaky Bottom
Vineyard

Breaky
Bottom

4

5

104

539   40

A   **B**   62   **C**   **D**

South Downs Way

South Downs Way

White Way

Hollo...

1 grid square represents 500 metres

E   F   **33**   G   H

42   43

I

90

2

Itford F

LC

Southease
Station

3

05

4

River Ouse

5

04   Durham Farm

E   F   **63**   G   H

42   43

Southease Maps Manor
ol

Northease Farm

Swanborough Hollow

Monk's
House (NT)

Rodmell
CE Primary
School

Rodmell

The Dicklands

Badgers
Dene

The
Paddocks

Mill Lane

Southease

Dean's Farm

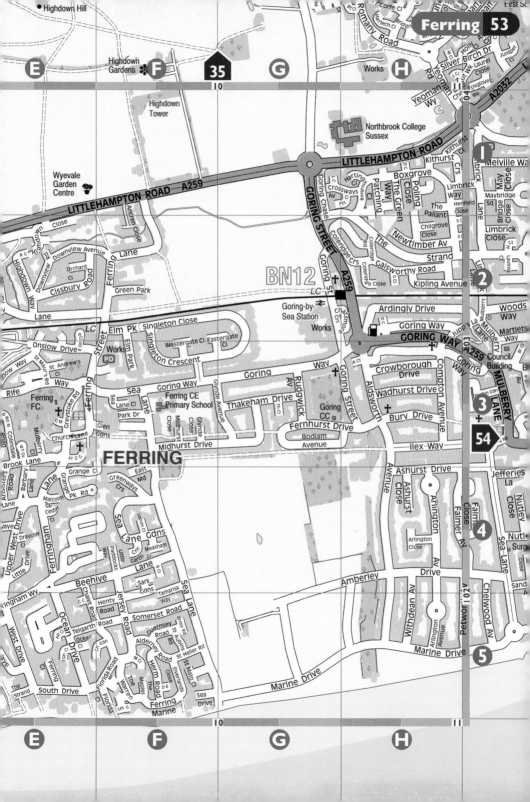

1 grid square represents 500 metres

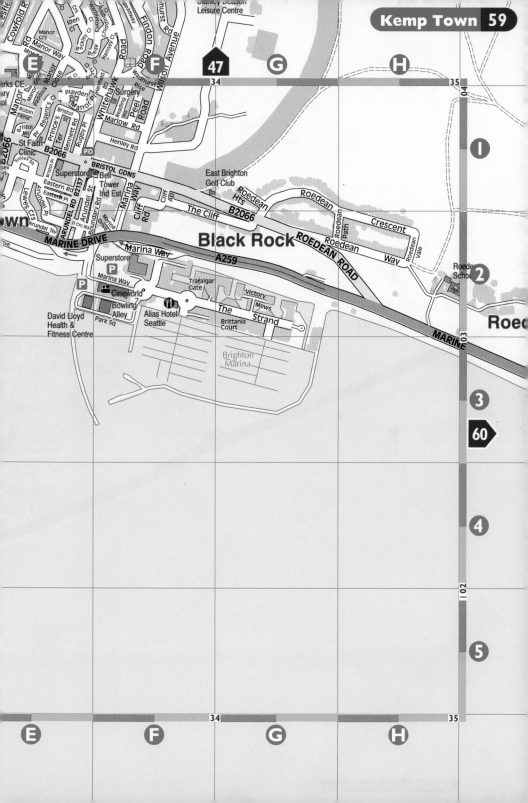

Kemp Town

Stanley Deason
Leisure Centre

Cowfold R
Manor
Way
Manor Way
Manor Crs
Iden
Meadow
Findon Road
Wilson Avenue
H

E
F
47
34
G
35
04

Manor
CE
Whitehawk
Surgery
Henfield
Wadhurst Rise
Reading
Rd
Playden
Cl
Peel Road
B2066

St Faith
Clinic
Prince's Ter
Pr. Regent's St
Marlow Rd
Henley Rd
Rugby Rd
Marina
Cliff
Cliff Apl
I

B2066
BRISTOL GDNS
Superstore
Bell
Tower
Ind Est
Marina
Way
Cliff
Rd
The Cliff
B2066
East Brighton
Golf Club
Roedean
Hts
Roedean
Crescent
Roedean
Path
Roedean
Roedean
Vale
Roede
Scho

Lewes Rd
ARUNDEL RD
B2137
Arundel
St
Boundary Rd
D Crc
Marine
MARINE DRIVE
Black Rock
ROEDEAN ROAD
Roedean
Way
2

own
Arundel Ter
Superstore
Marina Way
A259
MARINE
03
Roed

Superstore
P
Marina Way
Cineworld
Bowling
Alley
Trafalgar
Gate
Victory
Mews
The
Strand
MARINE

P

David Lloyd
Health &
Fitness Centre
Park Sq
Alias Hotel
Seattle
Brittania
Court
3

Brighton
Marina

60

4

02

5

34
35

E
F
G
H

A B 48 C D

535
04

Ovingdean Road

Vale
36

I

Wanderdown Road

Longhill High School

The Ridings
Woodland Walk
PO

Ovingdean Hall School

Rowan Way

B2123

Wanderdown Way
Wanderdown Drive
Wanderdown Close

Marvin's

Longhill Road

Elvin Crescent

Eley

+

Greenways

Roedean Vale

Dower Close
Ainsworth Close

Rowan Wy
New Barn Road

FALMER ROAD

Eley Drive

Court Farm Rd

2
Roedean School

Ainsworth Avenue

Eley Crs

Court Ord Rd

Meadow Pde

+

Beacon Hill

Ovingdean

Meadow Cl
Surgery

Wilkinson Close

Rott FC

Roedean

MARINE

DRIVE

Greenways

The Ridings
Burnes

Challoners Ms

3

A259

+

THE CRE

59

Our Lady of Lourdes RC Prim School

Olde Pl
Ms

Nevill Roa
Sheep
WK

4

Nevill Rd

CFS
Park
WK

Par

MARINE

5

535

36

535

36

A B C D

E   F   **49**   G   H

38

39

I

Pickers Hill Farm

Coor

Balsdean
Farm

2

Coombe Vale

Westfield
Av

Westfield   Westfield Av S

Stanmer Av

Coombe North

Coombe Vale

Stanmer Av

Westfield Rise

Welesmere
Rd

Gorham Avenue

Road

Falmer Av

Wivelsfield Road

Tumulus

Winton Av

Perry Hill

Ridgewood
Avenue

Vale Rd

Hallsham Av

Hallsham Av

Hilgrove Rd

Edward

Berwick

Hempstead Road

Coombe Rise

04

03

Court Road

Dean

Gorham
Close

Lustrells

Whiteway Lane

Bishopstone Dr

Saxon
Close

Crescent

Falmer Av

Chiltington
Way

Effingham

Chiltington
Cl

Vale

Glynde
Av

Hawthorn

Heathfield
Av

Arlington
Gdns

Mount
Dr

Avenue

3

62

nue

ROTTINGDEAN

Westmeston Avenue

Lindfield

Chorley Av

Ashdown Av

Lustrells

Lustrells

Tremola
Avenue

Vale
Drive

Clynebourne

School Lane

PO

Saltdean
Primary
School

Saltdean

Greenbank

Shepham Av

Saltdean

Homebush

Rodmell
Avenue

Crescent

Findon
Avenue

North

iteway
Road

Newlands
Road

Chailey
Av

Knole
Rd

Grand
Crescent

The
Park

The Pk

Cranleigh
Avenue

Founthill
Road

Lenham
Hill

Founthill
Av

Saltdean

Chichester Dr West

Arundel Drive West

Saltdean Park Rd

Arundel Drive East

West

Chichester D East

Linchmere

Oaklands

Bevendean
Avenue

Avenue

Cissbury

4

Avenue

Ashurst

vyn's
Md

Lenham Rd W

Romney
Rd

Little
Crs

Lenham Rd E

Lenham
Avenue

Eileen
Av

Marine Cl

A Cl

Withyham Av

Longridge

Chichester D

Surgery

Crowborough Rd

Nutley
Av

Ardingly
Rd

Cowden
Rd

Wicklands

Avenue

Brambletyne
Avenue

Avenue

Bannings Vale

Hamsey Rd

Av

5

DRIVE

A259

Lynwood Rd

PO

Waleascale Rd

SOUTH COAST ROAD

Tye Close

38

39

E   F   G   H

E F **51** G H

42

43

04

Durham Farm

Dean's Farm

I

Money Burgh

Bullock Down

2

The Lookout

Valley

Roderick Avenue North

Road

Halcombe Farm

Telscombe Road

Pidding

Gold Lane

Avenue

Heathdown Close

Wendale Drive

Highsted Park

Greenacres

3

Johns Cl

Grnh Wy

T P

Tlscmb

Ashmore

64

Road

Bretts Field

Mnt Cbrn Crs

Conel Furlong

Morestead

Nore Down

Roderick

Pelham

Swch Cl

Skyline Vw

4

Anzac Cl

Meridian Primary School

Cripps Av

Rise

T S

P Cl

Hoddern Farm

Badgers Field

Glynn

Trflgt Cl

Road

T Sycm

Avenue

Pelham

Clingwd

Rosemary Close

Cingleford

Rise

The Bricky

Edith Av N

Horsham Rd

Dorothy Av

Bramber Av N

View Road

Bee Road

5

Southview Avenue North

Dorothy Avenue

Br

BN10

Council Building

Meridian Leisure Centre

PEACEHAVEN

The Meridian Industrial Estate

42

43

Newton Rd

wich Way

Hoyle Road

Damon

Ryfrd Cl

Mason Cl

Arundel

Peacehaven Sports Centre

iff Pk ose

nue

102

03

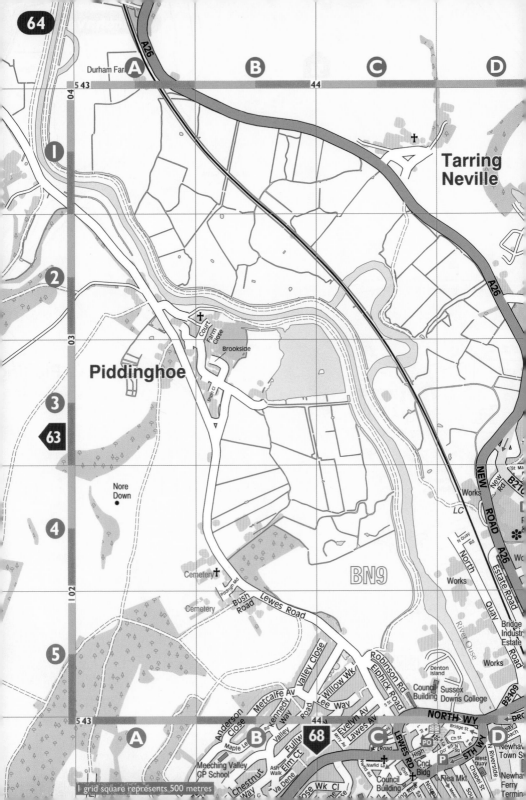

64

Durham Farm **A**

B

C

D

5 43

44

04

1

Tarring Neville

2

03

Court Farm Close

Brookside

Piddinghoe

Sun Cl

3

63

Nore Down

4

BN9

NEW ROAD

A26

B210

St Ma

New Rd

Works

LC

N Quay Rd

Works

North Quay

River Ouse

Bridge Industrial Estate

Works

Cemetery

Cemetery

Bush Road

Lewes Road

Robinson Rd

Elphick Road

Denton Island

Sussex Downs College

Council Building

Estate Road

A26

B2109

5

02

Metcalfe Av

Kennedy Way

Valley Close

Willow Wk

Lee Way

North Wy

A

Anderson Close

Maple Le

B

Fulling Valley

Fullway Rd

Elm Ct

Ash Walk

Va Dene

68

Evelyn Av

Lawes Av

C

Lewes Rd

High St

P

D

Newhav Town St

PO

Ch St

Bridge St

Chapel St

Newhaven Riverside

Newhav Ferry Termin

Meeching Valley CP School

Chestnut Way

Close Wk Cl

Nwfld La

Council Building

Flea Mkt

5 43

44

1 grid square represents 500 metres

E   F   46   G   H   47   04

I

2

03

South Heighton

Poverty Bottom

3

Hartfield Close
Leonard's Road
Wellington Road
The Close
Cantercrow Hill
Heighton Road
Rookery Way
Thompson Road
Cantercrow Hill
Lewis Close
St Leonards Cl
Rk. Cl
Denton Rise
Rectory
Acacia Road
The Grove
Denton Rd
Denton Road
Hill Rise
Hill Road
Park Drive
Vicrg Cl

Denton

community
Denton Drive
The Crescent
J D English Tuition
King's Avenue
Fairholme Road
Seaview Road
Crest Road
Palmerston Road
Palmerston Rd

Avis Close
Beresford
Arundel Road
Claremont Rd
Howey Close
Holmdale Road
Mount Road
Falaise Road

4

Norton

Rich Industrial Estate
Avis Rd
Station Rd
PO

Mount Pleasant

Premier Travel Inn

ROAD
Mount Road
Mount Close

02

THE DROVE
A259

5

Bishopstone Road

E   F   46   G   H   47

69 SEAFORD

WHAVEN

Stud Farm

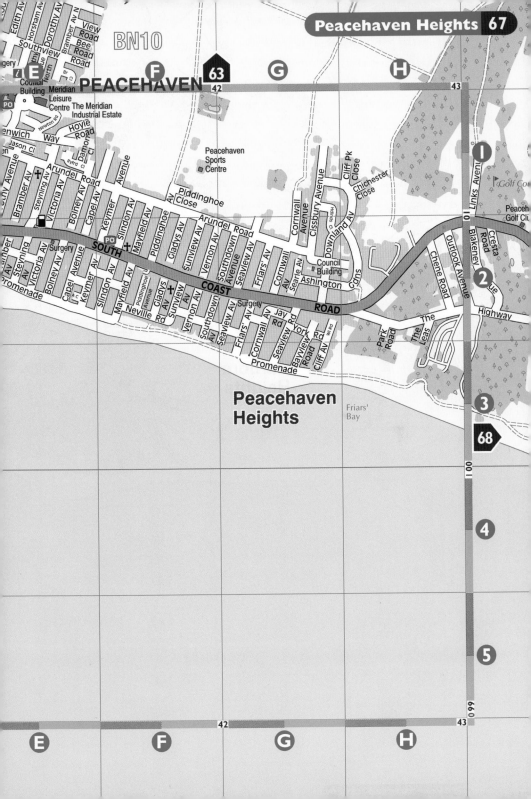

BN10

PEACEHAVEN 63

PEACEHAVEN HEIGHTS

Friars' Bay

E F 65 G H

46 47

SEAFORD

NEWHAVEN

A259 ROAD

Brightwell Industrial Estate

Ferryfield Industrial Estate

Works

Stud Farm

Elizabeth Close

Gleneagles Close

Freeland Close

Hurdis

Windsor Close

Holmes Close

St Andrew's

Hanover Close

Rosemount Close

St Margaret's Rl

Viking Close

Antony Close

Rookery Hill

Rochford Way

Rookery Way

Marine

Drive

NEWHAVEN ROAD A259

I

+

2

Bishopstone Road

Bishopstone Road

Beach Road

Road

Mill Creek

Mill Drove

LC

Tide Mills

Drive

3

Hill Rise

70

E BY-P

Hawth Crescent

Hawth Park Road

Hawth Cl

Hill

Station Road

Bishopstone Station

4

Works

Marine Parade

Buckle Rise

Buckle Cl

Buckle Dr

Kimberley Road

Cla

DIEPPE

5

46 47

E F G H

Rathfinny Farm

The Comp

E F G H

50 51

Cradle Hill

Alfriston Road

1

101

2

Balmoral Close
Snd Clo
Belvedere Gdns
Barn Cl
Queens Way
Barn Cl
Argent Close
Barn
Cradle Hill Road
T Pvit
Raymond Close
Cradle Hill Industrial Estate
Kammond Avenue
Old Nursery Rd
Alfriston Pk
Landsdown Rd
Hastings Avenue
Cemetery
Rise
Dover Cl
Alfriston Way
Winch Cl
Snd
Landsown Rd
Hillside Av
Battle Cl
Deal Av
Sandgate
3
Valley Drive
Quarry Lane
Vale Road
Vale Cl
East Dean Rd
Richington Way
Upp Chy Gdn
Dymchurch
Hythe Cl
100
West Dean
Rugby Rd
Bromley Rd
Upr Pevensey
Upr Chyngton Garden
Millberg Road
Hythe Crs
Hythe Crescent
Cinque Ports Way
Hythe Cl
Netherton
Harrow Way
Eton Rd
Rye Close
Hillside Avenue
H V
Alfriston Road
Bydown
Sandore Rd
Blue Haze
Greenwell
The Shepway
Chyngton Gardens
Saltwood Road
Walmer Road
Bodiam Close
BN25
4
Hindover Rd
Hanson Rd
Newlands Manor School
Preparatory School
Farm Close
Chyngton Av
PO
Dymock Farm
Downs Leisure Centre P
Sutton
Meadow Way
Stoke Cl
Nth Cl
Stirling Avenue
Elgin Gardens
Chyngton Lane North
D A259
Aql Pk W H P
Wellington
Sheep Pen La
Stoke Cl
Chesterton Av
Perth Close
S Cl
A259
EASTBOURNE   **ROAD**
99.0
Downs Pk
Road
Chesterton Drive
Badgers Copse
Stirling Avenue
Ash Drive
5
view Road
Manor Cl
Hazeldene
Sutton Avenue
Manor Rd
Kingston Cn
May Av
Middlefield
Juniper Close
Willow Drive
Birch La
Barcombeo Avenue
Chyngton Lane
dland Avenue
Oak Wall Dr
Links Cl
St Wilfred's
Kingston Way
Middlefield W
Kingston Rd
Pinn Cl
RW Cl
NC
Seaford Head Community College
Green WK
Arundel Road
Cuckmere Road
Rodmell Rd
Steyning Road
Old Chyngton Road
Hamsey Lane
E   **F**   **73**   **G**   **H**
nks Rd
her Rd
Bracken Road
Chyngton Pl
Fairways Road
Pinn Cl
Chyngton Farm
Chyngton Road
50 51

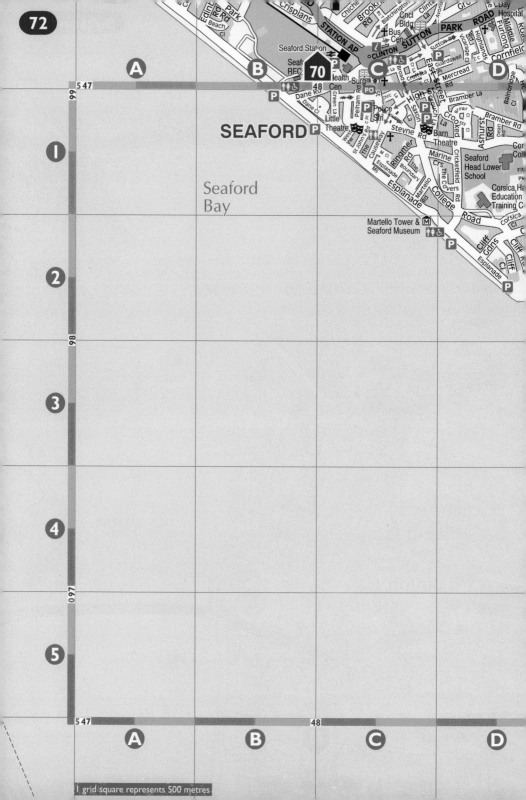

Aldrington 44 A3
Beggars Bush 20 B4
Bevendean 29 G5
Bishopstone 70 A1
Black Rock 59 F2
Botolphs 8 A5
Bramber 7 H4
Brighton 3 F6
Broadwater 37 H4
Castle Town 8 C3
Clapham 35 F1
Coldean 28 D2
Coombes 22 A2
Cote 36 A2
Denton 65 F4
Durrington 36 B3
East Blatchington 70 C4
East Kingston 52 C4
East Moulsecoomb 29 F3
East Preston 52 B3
East Worthing 56 D2
Edburton 10 A1
Falmer 30 B1
Ferring 53 F3
Findon 18 D1

Findon Valley 19 E5
Fishersgate 42 D3
Fulking 10 D1
Goring-by-Sea 54 B2
Hangleton 26 A4
Hangleton 52 C1
Harbour Heights 68 B3
High Salvington 36 A1
Hollingbury 28 B2
Hollingdean 28 B4
Hove 44 D5
Iford 32 D4
Kemp Town 58 D2
Kingston by Sea 42 A3
Kingston Gorse 52 D5
Kingston near Lewes 32 A2
Lancing 39 F4
Landport 16 D1
Lewes 17 E2
Mile Oak 24 D5
Moulsecoomb 29 F4
Mount Pleasant 65 G4
Nepcote 18 D2
Newhaven 69 E1
North Lancing 39 H2

North Moulsecoomb 28 D3
Norton 65 H4
Old Shoreham 41 E1
Ovingdean 60 C2
Patcham 27 H1
Patching 34 C1
Peacehaven 63 E5
Peacehaven Heights 67 G3
Piddinghoe 64 A3
Portslade-by-Sea 43 F4
Portslade Village 25 E5
Preston 45 G1
Rodmell 51 E2
Roedean 60 A2
Rottingdean 61 E3
Saddlescombe 12 A1
Saltdean 61 H3
Salvington 37 E3
Seaford 72 B1
Shoreham Beach 41 H5
Shoreham-by-Sea 41 F5
Sompting 38 D4
Sompting Abbotts 38 C2
Southease 51 G3
Southern Cross 43 E2

South Heighton ....
South Lancing ....
South Malling ....
Southover ....
Southwick ....
Stanmer ....
Steyning ....
Sutton ....
Tarring Neville ....
Telscombe ....
Telscombe Cliffs ....
Upper Beeding ....
Wallands Park ....
West Blatchington ....
Westdene ....
West Kingston ....
West Tarring ....
West Worthing ....
Whitehawk ....
Withdean ....
Woodingdean ....
Worthing ....

USING THE STREET INDEX

Street names are listed alphabetically. Each street name is followed by its postal town or area locality, the Postcode District, the page number, and the reference to the square in which the name is found.

Standard index entries are shown as follows:

Abbey Cl *LAN/SOMP* BN15 ....**40** B4

Street names and selected addresses not shown on the map due to scale restrictions are shown in the index with an asterisk:

Adur Valley Ct *STEY/UB* BN44 * **8** B2

GENERAL ABBREVIATIONS

ACC ....ACCESS	EMB ....EMBANKMENT	LK ....LOCK	RDG ....
ALY ....ALLEY	EMBY ....EMBASSY	LKS ....LAKES	REP ....RE
AP ....APPROACH	ESP ....ESPLANADE	LNDG ....LANDING	RES ....RESE
AR ....ARCADE	EST ....ESTATE	LTL ....LITTLE	RFC ....RUGBY FOOTBALL
ASS ....ASSOCIATION	EX ....EXCHANGE	LWR ....LOWER	RI ....
AV ....AVENUE	EXPY ....EXPRESSWAY	MAG ....MAGISTRATE	RP ....
BCH ....BEACH	EXT ....EXTENSION	MAN ....MANSIONS	RW ....
BLDS ....BUILDINGS	F/O ....FLYOVER	MD ....MEAD	S ....
BND ....BEND	FC ....FOOTBALL CLUB	MDW ....MEADOWS	SCH ....
BNK ....BANK	FK ....FORK	MEM ....MEMORIAL	SE ....SOUT
BR ....BRIDGE	FLD ....FIELD	MI ....MILL	SER ....SERVICE
BRK ....BROOK	FLDS ....FIELDS	MKT ....MARKET	SH ....
BTM ....BOTTOM	FLS ....FALLS	MKTS ....MARKETS	SHOP ....SHO
BUS ....BUSINESS	FM ....FARM	ML ....MALL	SKWY ....S
BVD ....BOULEVARD	FT ....FORT	MNR ....MANOR	SMT ....S
BY ....BYPASS	FTS ....FLATS	MS ....MEWS	SOC ....SO
CATH ....CATHEDRAL	FWY ....FREEWAY	MSN ....MISSION	SP ....
CEM ....CEMETERY	FY ....FERRY	MT ....MOUNT	SPR ....S
CEN ....CENTRE	GA ....GATE	MTN ....MOUNTAIN	SQ ....
CFT ....CROFT	GAL ....GALLERY	MTS ....MOUNTAINS	ST ....
CH ....CHURCH	GDN ....GARDEN	MUS ....MUSEUM	STN ....S
CHA ....CHASE	GDNS ....GARDENS	MWY ....MOTORWAY	STR ....S
CHYD ....CHURCHYARD	GLD ....GLADE	N ....NORTH	STRD ....S
CIR ....CIRCLE	GLN ....GLEN	NE ....NORTH EAST	SW ....SOUTH
CIRC ....CIRCUS	GN ....GREEN	NW ....NORTH WEST	TDG ....TR
CL ....CLOSE	GND ....GROUND	O/P ....OVERPASS	TER ....TE
CLFS ....CLIFFS	GRA ....GRANGE	OFF ....OFFICE	THWY ....THROU
CMP ....CAMP	GRG ....GARAGE	ORCH ....ORCHARD	TNL ....T
CNR ....CORNER	GT ....GREAT	OV ....OVAL	TOLL ....TO
CO ....COUNTY	GTWY ....GATEWAY	PAL ....PALACE	TPK ....TUR
COLL ....COLLEGE	GV ....GROVE	PAS ....PASSAGE	TR ....
COM ....COMMON	HGR ....HIGHER	PAV ....PAVILION	TRL ....
COMM ....COMMISSION	HL ....HILL	PDE ....PARADE	TWR ....T
CON ....CONVENT	HLS ....HILLS	PH ....PUBLIC HOUSE	U/P ....UNDE
COT ....COTTAGE	HO ....HOUSE	PK ....PARK	UNI ....UNIVI
COTS ....COTTAGES	HOL ....HOLLOW	PKWY ....PARKWAY	UPR ....U
CP ....CAPE	HOSP ....HOSPITAL	PL ....PLACE	V ....
CPS ....COPSE	HRB ....HARBOUR	PLN ....PLAIN	VA V
CR ....CREEK	HTH ....HEATH	PLNS ....PLAINS	VIAD ....VIA
CREM ....CREMATORIUM	HTS ....HEIGHTS	PLZ ....PLAZA	VIL ....
CRS ....CRESCENT	HVN ....HAVEN	POL ....POLICE STATION	VIS ....
CSWY ....CAUSEWAY	HWY ....HIGHWAY	PR ....PRINCE	VLG ....
CT ....COURT	IMP ....IMPERIAL	PREC ....PRECINCT	VLS ....
CTRL ....CENTRAL	IN ....INLET	PREP ....PREPARATORY	VW ....
CTS ....COURTS	IND EST ....INDUSTRIAL ESTATE	PRIM ....PRIMARY	W ....
CTYD ....COURTYARD	INF ....INFIRMARY	PROM ....PROMENADE	WD ....
CUTT ....CUTTINGS	INFO ....INFORMATION	PRS ....PRINCESS	WHF ....
CV ....COVE	INT ....INTERCHANGE	PRT ....PORT	WK ....
CYN ....CANYON	IS ....ISLAND	PT ....POINT	WKS ....
DEPT ....DEPARTMENT	JCT ....JUNCTION	PTH ....PATH	WLS ....
DL ....DALE	JTY ....JETTY	PZ ....PIAZZA	WY ....
DM ....DAM	KG ....KING	QD ....QUADRANT	YD ....
DR ....DRIVE	KNL ....KNOLL	QU ....QUEEN	YHA ....YOUTH H
DRO ....DROVE	L ....LAKE	QY ....QUAY	
DRY ....DRIVEWAY	LA ....LANE	R ....RIVER	
DWGS ....DWELLINGS	LDG ....LODGE	RBT ....ROUNDABOUT	
E ....EAST	LGT ....LIGHT	RD ....ROAD	

STCODE TOWNS AND AREA ABBREVIATIONS

EP......... Angmering/East Preston	HFD......................... Henfield	PEAHV....................Peacehaven	STEY/UB ....Steyning/Upper Beeding
...........................Brighton	HOVE...........................Hove	PTSD.......................Portslade	STHW.........................Southwick
ROTT..............Brighton east/	LAN/SOMP.......Lancing/Sompting	SALV......................Salvington	WTHG...........................Worthing
Rottingdean	LEWES.........................Lewes	SEAF........................Seaford	
.............................Ferring	NEWHV.....................Newhaven	SHOR......................Shoreham	

Index - streets

Abb - Bea

A

en Cl LAN/SOMP BN15	40 B4
HV BN10	63 E4
Rd BRIE/ROTT BN2	58 D1
/SOMP BN15	39 E3
Y/UB BN44	7 G2
HG BN11	4 B7
sbury Cl BRIE/ROTT BN2	61 F4
s Wy LAN/SOMP BN15	39 H4
ts Cl WTHG BN11	4 D4
ts Vw LAN/SOMP BN15	39 E2
ket Gdns SALV BN13	36 D4
een Rd BRIE/ROTT BN2	46 B2
er Pl LEWES BN7	17 E3
er Rd BRIE/ROTT BN2	48 C4
D BN41	43 F2
a Av HOVE BN3	44 B1
V BN13	36 D3
cre Cl WTHG BN11	4 A5
s Cl BRI BN1	46 B1
on Cl LAN/SOMP BN15	39 G4
on Rd HOVE BN3	26 E5
ide Cl SALV BN13	36 A4
SALV BN13	36 A4
R BN43	41 E1
Cl LAN/SOMP BN15	40 C5
or SHOR BN43	41 G3
Rd SHOR BN43	41 E2
Valley Ct STEY/UB BN44 *	8 B2
Vw STEY/UB BN44 *	8 A2
sane Rd SALV BN13	37 F5
s Rd WTHG BN11	54 D4
ie Rd BRIE/ROTT BN2	46 C3
ale Cl SALV BN13	36 B4
ale Cl SALV BN13	36 B4
orth Av BRIE/ROTT BN2	60 B2
ta Rd SALV BN13	36 B4
BRI BN1 *	3 F4
e Rd LAN/SOMP BN15	39 E2
Wy BRIE/ROTT BN2	47 F5
y Cl WTHG BN11	55 E4
y Ms HOVE BN3	44 D4
y Rd SEAF BN25	70 A5
y Vls HOVE BN3	44 D5
bemarle BRIE/ROTT BN2 *	3 H6
ta Rd SALV BN13	36 B4
t Man HOVE BN3 *	45 E4
t Ms HOVE BN3	44 D4
t Rd BRI BN1	2 E2
BN42	42 B3
HI BRIE/ROTT BN2	3 K3
t St BRIE/ROTT BN2	3 J2
VES BN7	17 F3
D BN41	43 F3
W BN42	42 B4
ie Rd BRIE/ROTT BN2	47 E3
Cl SALV BN13	36 A5
ey Rd FERR BN12	53 F5
t Rd FERR BN12	47 F4
gton Av HOVE BN3	44 C2
gton Cl HOVE BN3	43 H3
orth Av FERR BN12	53 H3
orth Ct FERR BN12	53 H3
orth Pde FERR BN12	53 H3
ck Crs SALV BN13	37 E1
nder Ter WTHG BN11 *	5 F5
ndra Ct SEAF BN25	70 C3
ndra Ct FERR BN12	54 A2
ndra Rd LAN/SOMP BN15	39 H5
HG BN11	5 K4
ndra Vls BRI BN1	2 E2
Cl SALV BN13	37 E3
PI WTHG BN11	5 H5
Rd BRI BN1	2 E2
on Cl BRIE/ROTT BN2	47 F4
V BN13	37 F5

Alfriston Pk SEAF BN25	71 G3
Alfriston Rd SALV BN13	37 F5
SEAF BN25	71 F3
Alice St HOVE BN3	2 A4
Alinora Av FERR BN12	54 B3
Alinora Av FERR BN12	54 B3
Alinora Crs FERR BN12	54 B4
Alinora Dr FERR BN12	54 A4
Allendale Av SALV BN13	37 E1
Allington Rd SALV BN13	38 A3
Alma St LAN/SOMP BN15	57 G1
Almond Av SHOR BN43	40 C2
Alpine Rd HOVE BN3	44 B2
Alverstone Rd WTHG BN11	5 J2
Amberley Cl SHOR BN43	41 F1
Amberley Dr FERR BN12	53 H4
HOVE BN3	26 A4
Ambleside Av PEAHV BN10	66 C1
Ambleside Rd LAN/SOMP BN15	39 E3
Ambrose Pl WTHG BN11	4 E4
Amelia Rd WTHG BN11	4 D4
Amesbury Crs HOVE BN3	44 A3
Amherst Rd HOVE BN3	44 B2
Anchor Cl SHOR BN43	41 G4
Anchor Ct FERR BN12 *	54 C4
Ancren Ct FERR BN12	53 F1
Anderson Cl NEWHV BN9	68 B1
Andrew Cl STEY/UB BN44	7 F4
Anglesea St WTHG BN11	4 D3
Angola Rd SALV BN13	56 B1
Angus Rd FERR BN12	54 C3
Annington Gdns SHOR BN43	41 F1
Annington Rd STEY/UB BN44	7 H5
STEY/UB BN44	22 A1
Ann St BRI BN1	3 G1
WTHG BN11	5 F5
Annweir Av LAN/SOMP BN15	39 G4
Anscombe Cl WTHG BN11	54 D4
Anscombe Rd WTHG BN11	54 D4
Ansisters Rd FERR BN12	53 E4
Anson Cl FERR BN12 *	54 A1
Anson Rd FERR BN12	54 A1
Ansty Cl BRIE/ROTT BN2	47 E5
Antioch St LEWES BN7	17 E4
Antony Cl SEAF BN25	69 H2
Anvil Cl PTSD BN41	25 F5
Anzac Cl PEAHV BN10	63 E4
Appledore Rd BRIE/ROTT BN2	29 F3
Applesham Av HOVE BN3	26 A5
Applesham Wy PTSD BN41	43 E1
Appletrees ANG/EP BN16	52 B5
The Approach BRI BN1	27 G4
April Cl FERR BN12	53 E5
Apsley Wy SALV BN13	35 G5
Aquarius Cl PEAHV BN10	67 E2
Aquila Pk SEAF BN25	71 E5
Arcade Buildings WTHG BN11 *	5 F6
Archibald Rd WTHG BN11	56 C2
Ardale Cl WTHG BN11	54 D3
Ardingly Ct BRIE/ROTT BN2 *	3 J3
Ardingly Dr FERR BN12	53 H2
Ardingly Rd BRIE/ROTT BN2	61 H5
Ardingly St BRIE/ROTT BN2	3 J5
Ardsheal Cl SALV BN13	37 G5
Ardsheal Rd SALV BN13	37 G4
Argent Cl SEAF BN25	71 E3
Argyle Rd BRI BN1	45 H3
Ariadne Rd WTHG BN11	4 A7
Arlington Av FERR BN12	53 H3
Arlington Cl FERR BN12	53 H4
Arlington Crs ANG/EP BN16	52 B2
BRI BN1	29 E2
Arlington Gdns	
BRIE/ROTT BN2	61 H3
Arnold St BRIE/ROTT BN2	46 C3
Arnside Cl LAN/SOMP BN15	39 E4
Arthur St HOVE BN3	44 C2
Arun Cl LAN/SOMP BN15	39 E3
SALV BN13	36 B3
Arun Ct ANG/EP BN16 *	52 A4
Arun Crs SALV BN13	36 A3
Arundel Cl SHOR BN43	42 A3
Arundel Dr East	
BRIE/ROTT BN2	61 G4

Arundel Dr West	
BRIE/ROTT BN2	61 G4
Arundell Gn LEWES BN7	16 D2
Arundel Ms BRIE/ROTT BN2 *	59 E1
Arundel Pl BRIE/ROTT BN2	59 E1
Arundel Rd Central	
PEAHV BN10	66 D1
Arundel Rd BRIE/ROTT BN2	59 E2
NEWHV BN9	65 F4
PEAHV BN10	67 E1
SALV BN13	34 C3
SEAF BN25	71 E5
Arundel Rd West PEAHV BN10	62 C5
Arundel St BRIE/ROTT BN2	59 E2
Arundel Ter BRIE/ROTT BN2	59 E2
Ashacre La SALV BN13	36 D3
Ashacre Ms SALV BN13	36 D3
Ashacre Wy SALV BN13	36 D4
Ashburnham Cl BRI BN1	29 E2
SALV BN13	35 H5
Ashburnham Dr BRI BN1	28 D1
Ash Cl HOVE BN3	27 E4
BN13	18 C1
Ashcombe La LEWES BN7	32 A1
Ashcroft Cl SHOR BN43	42 B3
Ashdown Av BRIE/ROTT BN2	61 F4
Ashdown Rd BRIE/ROTT BN2	46 B2
WTHG BN11	5 F2
Ash Dr SEAF BN25	71 G5
Ashfold Av SALV BN13	37 E1
Ashford Rd BRI BN1	28 A5
Ash Gv WTHG BN11	5 G4
Ashington Gdns PEAHV BN10	67 G2
Ashley Cl BRI BN1	13 G5
Ashlings Wy HOVE BN3	26 A4
SHOR BN43	41 H1
Ashmead Wy ANG/EP BN16	52 A1
Ashmore Av SALV BN13	52 A1
Ashmore Cl PEAHV BN10	63 F3
Ashton Ri BRIE/ROTT BN2	3 J3
Ashurst Av BRIE/ROTT BN2	62 A5
Ashurst Cl FERR BN12	53 H4
Ashurst Dr FERR BN12	53 H4
Ashurst Rd BRIE/ROTT BN2	29 F2
SEAF BN25	72 D1
Ashurst Wy ANG/EP BN16	52 A2
Ash Wk NEWHV BN9	68 B1
Ashwood Cl WTHG BN11	5 K1
Aspen Ct LAN/SOMP BN15 *	57 E1
Athelstan Rd SALV BN13	55 E1
Atlingworth St BRIE/ROTT BN2	3 K6
Attree Dr BRIE/ROTT BN2	46 C4
Auckland Dr BRIE/ROTT BN2	47 F1
Audrey Cl BRI BN1	27 G2
SEAF BN25	70 B3
Augusta Pl WTHG BN11	4 E6
Avalon Wy SALV BN13	36 B4
The Avenals ANG/EP BN16	34 A5
The Avenue BRIE/ROTT BN2	28 D5
FERR BN12	54 A1
LEWES BN7	31 H2
SHOR BN43	41 E5
Avery Cl PTSD BN41	24 D3
Avis Cl NEWHV BN9	65 E4
Avis Rd NEWHV BN9	64 D4
Avis Wy NEWHV BN9	65 E5
Avon Cl LAN/SOMP BN15	38 D4
Avondale Cl FERR BN12	54 B2
Avondale Rd HOVE BN3	45 F3
SEAF BN25	70 D5
Aymer Rd HOVE BN3	44 C4

B

Baden Rd BRIE/ROTT BN2	46 D2
Badger Cl PTSD BN41	25 F5
Badgers Cl NEWHV BN9	68 C2
Badgers Copse SEAF BN25	71 G5
Badgers Dene LEWES BN7	17 G4
Badgers Fld PEAHV BN10	63 E4
Badger Wy BRI BN1	29 E1
Bainbridge Cl SEAF BN25	72 D1
Baker St BRI BN1	3 H1

Bakery Ms BRIE/ROTT BN2	46 C1
Balcombe Av SALV BN13	37 G5
Balcombe Rd PEAHV BN10	62 D5
Balfour Rd BRI BN1	27 H5
Balmoral Cl SEAF BN25	71 E2
Balsdean Rd BRIE/ROTT BN2	48 B3
Bamford Cl BRIE/ROTT BN2	29 G5
Bampfield St PTSD BN41	43 F2
Bank Pas STEY/UB BN44	7 F3
Bankside BRI BN1	27 E2
Bankside Ct BRI BN1 *	27 E2
Bannings V BRIE/ROTT BN2	61 H5
Banstead Cl FERR BN12	54 A4
Baranscraig Av BRI BN1	14 A5
Barbary La FERR BN12	53 E4
Barcombe Av SEAF BN25	73 G1
Barcombe Cl SEAF BN25	71 G1
Barcombe Rd BRI BN1	29 F2
Barfield Pk LAN/SOMP BN15	39 H4
Barley Cl PEAHV BN10	62 D3
Barn Cl LEWES BN7	32 A2
SALV BN13	36 D3
SEAF BN25	71 E3
Barnes Rd PTSD BN41	43 F2
Barnett Rd BRI BN1	28 B5
Barnet Wy HOVE BN3	26 A4
Barn Field Gdns	
BRIE/ROTT BN2	46 C4
Barn Hatch Cl LEWES BN7	16 C4
Barn Ri BRI BN1	27 F2
SEAF BN25	71 E3
Barn Rd LEWES BN7	17 G1
Barons Cl SEAF BN25	70 A3
Barons Down Rd LEWES BN7	16 C4
Barons Wk LEWES BN7	16 C4
Barrhill Av BRI BN1	13 H5
Barrington Cl SEAF BN25	54 A3
Barrington Rd FERR BN12	54 B3
Barrow Cl BRI BN1	28 C5
Barrowfield Cl HOVE BN3	27 E5
Barrowfield Dr HOVE BN3	27 E5
Barrow Hl BRI BN1	28 C5
Barry Wk BRIE/ROTT BN2	46 C4
Bartholomews BRI BN1	3 G5
Bartholomew Sq BRI BN1 *	3 F5
Barton Cl SALV BN13	37 E5
Bashfords La SALV BN13	5 F1
Basin Rd North PTSD BN41	43 F4
Basin Rd South PTSD BN41	42 D4
Batemans Cl SALV BN13	35 H5
Batemans Rd BRIE/ROTT BN2	48 C3
Bates Rd BRI BN1	27 H5
Bath Pl WTHG BN11	5 F6
Bath Rd WTHG BN11	4 A7
Bath St BRI BN1	2 E1
Battle Cl SEAF BN25	71 G3
Bavant Rd BRI BN1	27 G5
Baxter Rd LEWES BN7	16 D2
Baxter St BRIE/ROTT BN2	46 C3
Bay Tree Cl SHOR BN43	42 A1
Bayview Rd PEAHV BN10	67 G3
Bay Vue Rd NEWHV BN9	68 B3
Baywood Gdns BRIE/ROTT BN2	48 A1
Bazehill Rd BRIE/ROTT BN2	61 E2
Beach Cl SEAF BN25	70 B5
Beachcroft Pl LAN/SOMP BN15	57 G1
Beach Gn SHOR BN43	40 D4
Beach Pde WTHG BN11	5 H5
Beach Rd NEWHV BN9	69 E2
SHOR BN43	41 E5
Beachside Cl FERR BN12	54 C4
Beacon Cl BRI BN1	28 A5
SEAF BN25	70 B3
Beacon Dr SEAF BN25	70 B3
Beacon Hl BRIE/ROTT BN2	60 C2
Beacon Rd SEAF BN25	70 B4
Beaconsfield Pde BRI BN1 *	46 A2
Beaconsfield Rd BRI BN1	46 A2
PTSD BN41	43 F2
Beaconsfield Vls BRI BN1	45 H1
Beal Crs BRI BN1	28 B5
Bear Rd BRIE/ROTT BN2	46 C2
Bear Yd LEWES BN7	17 F3
Beatty Av BRI BN1	14 D5
Beaufort Ter BRIE/ROTT BN2	46 C4

Beaumont Rd SALV BN13 ....37 H5
Beccles Rd WTHG BN11 ....4 B4
Becket Rd SALV BN13 ....55 E2
Beckett Wy LEWES BN7 ....17 E1
Beckley Cl BRIE/ROTT BN2 ....47 E5
Beckworth Cl SALV BN13 ....35 H5
Bedford Pl BRI BN1 ....2 C4
Bedford Rw WTHG BN11 ....5 C5
Bedford Sq WTHG BN11 ....2 C5
Bedford St BRIE/ROTT BN2 ....58 C1
Beech Cl PTSD BN41 ....24 D4
Beechers Rd PTSD BN41 ....24 D4
Beeches Av SALV BN13 ....37 H3
The Beeches BRI BN1 ....27 F4
Beech Gv BRIE/ROTT BN2 ....29 E4
  LAN/SOMP BN15 * 39 H5
Beechlands Cl ANG/EP BN16 .....52 A4
Beech Rd SALV BN13 ....18 C1
Beech Vw ANG/EP BN16 ....34 A3
Beech Wy ANG/EP BN16 ....52 A1
Beechwood Av BRI BN1 ....27 H3
  SALV BN13 ....36 D3
Beechwood Cl BRI BN1 ....27 H3
Beeding Av HOVE BN3 ....26 D4
Beeding Cl LAN/SOMP BN15 .....39 F2
Beehive Cl FERR BN12 ....53 F4
Beehive La FERR BN12 ....53 E4
Bee Rd PEAHV BN10 ....63 E5
Belfast St HOVE BN3 ....44 D3
Belgrave Crs SEAF BN25 ....70 D3
Belgrave Pl BRIE/ROTT BN2 ......58 D1
Belgrave Rd SEAF BN25 ....70 B4
Belgrave St BRIE/ROTT BN2 ....3 J2
Belle Vue WTHG BN11 * 4 B4
Bellevue Gdns BRIE/ROTT BN2 ..58 C1
Bellingham Crs HOVE BN3 ....43 H2
Bell La LEWES BN7 ....16 D4
Bell Md HOVE BN3 * 2 A1
Bellview Rd SALV BN13 ....37 E5
Belmont BRI BN1 ....45 G3
Belmont Ct BRI BN1 * 45 G3
Belmont St BRI BN1 ....3 H1
Belsize Cl WTHG BN11 ....4 A3
Belsize Rd WTHG BN11 ....4 A3
Belton Rd BRIE/ROTT BN2 ....46 B2
Belvedere Av LAN/SOMP BN15 ..39 F4
Belvedere Gdns SEAF BN25 ....71 E3
Belvedere Ter HOVE BN3 ....2 C3
Bembridge St BRIE/ROTT BN2 ...46 C2
Benbow Cl SHOR BN43 ....41 F4
Benedict Cl WTHG BN11 ....56 D2
Benedict Dr WTHG BN11 ....56 C2
Benenden Cl SEAF BN25 ....71 E4
Benett Av HOVE BN3 ....26 D5
Benett Dr HOVE BN3 ....26 D5
Benfield Cl PTSD BN41 ....43 G3
Benfield Crs PTSD BN41 ....43 G1
Benfield Wy PTSD BN41 ....43 G3
Bengairn Av BRI BN1 ....14 A5
Bennett Rd BRIE/ROTT BN2 ....59 E1
Bentham Rd BRIE/ROTT BN2 .....46 C3
Berberis Cl SHOR BN43 ....41 H1
Beresford Rd BRIE/ROTT BN2 ....46 D5
  NEWHV BN9 ....65 E4
Bergamot Crs SHOR BN43 ....42 A1
Berkeley Rd LEWES BN7 ....16 C4
Berkeley Sq WTHG BN11 ....55 E1
Berkshire Ct FERR BN12 * 53 H2
Bernard Pl BRIE/ROTT BN2 ....46 C3
Bernard Rd BRIE/ROTT BN2 ....46 C3
  WTHG BN11 ....54 D4
Berriedale Av HOVE BN3 ....44 A4
Berriedale Cl LAN/SOMP BN15 ...39 E3
Berriedale Dr LAN/SOMP BN15 ..39 E3
Berry Cl PEAHV BN10 ....62 C4
Berwick Cl SEAF BN25 ....70 B4
Berwick Rd BRIE/ROTT BN2 ....61 H2
Bessborough Ter
  LAN/SOMP BN15 ....57 F1
Bevendean Av BRIE/ROTT BN2 ..61 H4
Bevendean Crs BRIE/ROTT BN2 .29 E5
Bevendean Rd BRIE/ROTT BN2 ..46 D2
Bexhill Rd BRIE/ROTT BN2 ....48 B1
Bigwood Av HOVE BN3 ....45 F3
Billam Ter BRIE/ROTT BN2 * 3 J3
Birch Cl LAN/SOMP BN15 ....57 F1
Birches Cl SALV BN13 ....36 A5
Birch Grove Crs BRI BN1 ....28 A2
Birdham Pl BRIE/ROTT BN2 * 29 E4
Birdham Rd BRIE/ROTT BN2 ......29 E4
Birkdale Cl SALV BN13 ....36 B4
Birkdale Rd SALV BN13 ....36 B4
Birling Cl BRIE/ROTT BN2 ....46 D1
  SEAF BN25 ....70 B4
Bishops Cl SALV BN13 ....55 E1
  SEAF BN25 ....70 A4
Bishops Dr LEWES BN7 ....16 C4
Bishops Rd HOVE BN3 ....45 E1
Bishopstone Dr BRIE/ROTT BN2.61 F3

Bishopstone Rd SEAF BN25 ....70 A2
Blackdown Rd SALV BN13 ....36 D3
Black Lion St BRI BN1 ....3 G6
Blackman St BRI BN1 ....3 G2
Blacksmiths Crs
  LAN/SOMP BN15 ....38 D4
Blackthorn Cl BRI BN1 ....27 E4
  PTSD BN41 ....25 F5
Blakeney Av PEAHV BN10 ....68 A2
Blaker St BRIE/ROTT BN2 ....3 J5
Blatchington Cl SEAF BN25 ....70 D4
Blatchington Hl SEAF BN25 ....70 C4
Blatchington Rd HOVE BN3 ....44 D3
  SEAF BN25 ....70 C5
Blenheim Av SALV BN13 ....36 C4
Blenheim Pl BRI BN1 ....3 H3
Blenheim Rd LAN/SOMP BN15 ...57 F1
Blois Rd LEWES BN7 ....16 C1
Bloomsbury Pl BRIE/ROTT BN2 ..58 C1
Bloomsbury St BRIE/ROTT BN2 ..58 C1
Blue Haze Av SEAF BN25 ....71 F4
Bodiam Av BRIE/ROTT BN2 ....47 H1
  FERR BN12 ....53 G3
Bodiam Cl BRIE/ROTT BN2 ....29 H5
  SEAF BN25 ....71 G4
Bodmin Cl SALV BN13 ....36 B2
Bodmin Rd SALV BN13 ....36 B2
Bolney Av PEAHV BN10 ....67 E2
Bolney Rd BRIE/ROTT BN2 ....29 F3
Bolsover Rd HOVE BN3 ....44 A3
  SALV BN13 ....54 C2
Bonchurch Rd BRIE/ROTT BN2 ..46 C2
Bond St BRI BN1 ....3 G4
Borough St BRI BN1 ....2 C4
Borrow King Cl BRIE/ROTT BN2 .46 D2
Bostal Rd STEY/UB BN44 ....7 E5
Bost Hl SALV BN13 ....18 C5
Boston St BRI BN1 ....3 G2
Boughey Pl LEWES BN7 ....17 F1
The Boulevard SALV BN13 ....54 C1
Boundary Rd WTHG BN11 ....4 A6
Boundary Rd BRIE/ROTT BN2 ....59 E2
  HOVE BN3 ....43 G4
  LAN/SOMP BN15 ....40 B5
  WTHG BN11 ....55 E4
The Boundary SEAF BN25 ....72 C1
Boundary Wy ANG/EP BN16 ......52 B3
Boundstone Cl
  LAN/SOMP BN15 ....39 F3
Boundstone La
  LAN/SOMP BN15 ....39 E4
Bourne Cl SALV BN13 ....35 H4
Bowden Ri SEAF BN25 ....70 C2
Bowers Ct WTHG BN11 ....4 B6
Bowmans Rd STEY/UB BN44 ....7 F2
Bowness Av LAN/SOMP BN15 ....39 E5
Bowring Wy BRIE/ROTT BN2 .....58 D1
Boxgrove FERR BN12 ....53 H1
Boxgrove Cl LAN/SOMP BN15 ...39 H2
Boyce's St BRI BN1 ....3 F5
Brackenbury Cl PTSD BN41 ....25 F5
Bracken Rd SEAF BN25 ....73 E2
Bradford Rd LEWES BN7 ....16 D3
Brading Rd BRIE/ROTT BN2 ....46 C2
Braemore Rd HOVE BN3 ....44 A4
Braeside Av BRI BN1 ....13 H5
Bramber Av HOVE BN3 ....26 B4
  PEAHV BN10 ....67 G2
Bramber Av North PEAHV BN10.63 G5
Bramber Cl LAN/SOMP BN15 .....39 F2
  PEAHV BN10 ....67 G2
  SEAF BN25 ....72 D1
Bramber La SEAF BN25 ....72 D1
Bramber Rd SALV BN13 ....38 A3
  SEAF BN25 ....72 D1
  STEY/UB BN44 ....7 F4
Bramble Cl SALV BN13 ....36 B3
Bramble Crs SALV BN13 ....36 B3
Brambledean Rd PTSD BN41 ......43 F3
Bramble La SALV BN13 ....36 B3
Bramble Ri BRI BN1 ....27 E2
Brambletyne Av
  BRIE/ROTT BN2 ....61 H4
Brambletyne Cl ANG/EP BN16 ...34 A4
Bramble Wy BRI BN1 ....28 C1
Bramley Cl SALV BN13 ....37 H3
Bramley Rd SALV BN13 ....37 H4
Bramleys LEWES BN7 ....32 A2
Bramley Wy ANG/EP BN16 ....52 A1
Brands Cl NEWHV BN9 ....64 D3
Brangwyn Av BRI BN1 ....27 G1
Brangwyn Crs BRI BN1 ....27 G1
Brangwyn Dr BRI BN1 ....27 G1
Brangwyn Wy BRI BN1 ....27 G2
Brasslands Dr PTSD BN41 ....42 D1
Braybon Av BRI BN1 ....27 H3
Braypool La BRI BN1 ....13 F4
Brazen Cl NEWHV BN9 ....68 A1

Breach Cl STEY/UB BN44 ....7 F3
Bread St BRI BN1 ....3 G4
Brecon Cl SALV BN13 ....36 D3
Brede St BRIE/ROTT BN2 ....47 E5
Brendon Rd SALV BN13 ....36 D3
Brentwood Crs BRI BN1 ....28 B4
Brentwood Rd BRI BN1 ....28 B4
Bretts Fld PEAHV BN10 ....63 E3
Brewer St BRIE/ROTT BN2 ....46 B3
Briar Cl BRIE/ROTT BN2 ....48 B2
Briarcroft Rd BRIE/ROTT BN2 ....48 B3
The Bricky PEAHV BN10 ....63 F5
Bridge Cl FERR BN12 ....54 A2
  LAN/SOMP BN15 ....39 G5
Bridge Rd SALV BN13 ....4 C2
Bridge St NEWHV BN9 ....68 D1
Bridgewick Cl LEWES BN7 ....17 F1
Bridgnorth Cl SALV BN13 ....35 H5
Bridle Wy PEAHV BN10 ....62 C5
Brierley Gdns LAN/SOMP BN15 .39 H4
Brigden St BRI BN1 ....45 H3
Brighton Pl BRI BN1 ....3 C5
Brighton Rd LAN/SOMP BN15 ....57 H1
  LEWES BN7 ....16 A5
  NEWHV BN9 ....68 B2
  SHOR BN43 ....40 D4
  WTHG BN11 ....5 J5
Brighton Sq BRI BN1 * 3 G5
Brills La BRI BN1 ....3 G6
Brisbane Cl SALV BN13 ....35 H4
Bristol Av LAN/SOMP BN15 ....40 A5
Bristol Gdns BRIE/ROTT BN2 .....59 E1
Bristol Ga BRIE/ROTT BN2 ....58 D1
Bristol Ms BRIE/ROTT BN2 ....59 E1
Bristol Pl BRIE/ROTT BN2 ....59 E1
Bristol Rd BRIE/ROTT BN2 ....58 C1
Bristol St BRIE/ROTT BN2 ....59 E1
Brittania Cl BRIE/ROTT BN2 ....59 G2
Brittany Rd HOVE BN3 ....43 H4
  SALV BN13 ....55 G1
Broadfields BRIE/ROTT BN2 ....29 E4
Broadfields Rd BRIE/ROTT BN2 ..29 E4
Broad Gn BRIE/ROTT BN2 ....48 C4
Broad Rig Av HOVE BN3 ....25 H4
Broad St BRIE/ROTT BN2 ....3 H6
  SEAF BN25 ....70 D5
Broadview Gdns SALV BN13 ......36 C2
Broadwater Bvd SALV BN13 ......37 E3
Broadwater Hall SALV BN13 * 4 C1
Broadwater Ms SALV BN13 * 37 H5
Broadwater Rd SALV BN13 ....4 C1
Broadwater St East SALV BN13 ..37 H5
Broadwater St West SALV BN13 .37 G4
Broadwater Wy SALV BN13 ....37 H5
The Broadway LAN/SOMP BN15 .40 A5
Brock Ct SEAF BN25 * 71 G5
Brockley Cl SALV BN13 ....4 C1
Bromley Rd BRIE/ROTT BN2 ......46 B3
  SEAF BN25 ....71 F4
Brompton Cl BRI BN1 ....27 C1
Brook Barn Wy FERR BN12 ....54 C4
Brook Cl WTHG BN11 ....56 C1
Brookdean Rd WTHG BN11 ....56 D2
Brooker Pl HOVE BN3 ....44 C3
Brooker St HOVE BN3 ....44 D3
Brook La FERR BN12 ....53 E4
Brooklyn Av WTHG BN11 ....54 D3
Brooklyn Chambers
  WTHG BN11 * 54 D3
Brooklyn Rd SEAF BN25 ....70 C5
Brooks Cl LEWES BN7 ....17 E1
  NEWHV BN9 ....68 C2
Brookside NEWHV BN9 ....64 B3
Brookside Cl FERR BN12 ....53 E2
Brookside Rd ANG/EP BN16 ....52 D5
Brooks Rd LEWES BN7 ....17 F2
Brook St LEWES BN7 ....17 E2
Brook Wy LAN/SOMP BN15 ....39 G3
Broomfield Av PEAHV BN10 ....66 B1
  SALV BN13 ....37 F5
Broomfield Dr PTSD BN41 ....25 E4
Brou Cl ANG/EP BN16 ....52 B4
Brougham Rd WTHG BN11 ....56 C2
Browning Rd LAN/SOMP BN15 ..39 G2
  WTHG BN11 ....4 B3
Brownleaf Rd BRIE/ROTT BN2 ...48 C5
The Brow BRIE/ROTT BN2 ....48 B2
Bruce Av WTHG BN11 ....54 D3
Bruce Vls WTHG BN11 * 54 D2
Bruce Wy WTHG BN11 ....54 D3
Brunswick Ms HOVE BN3 ....2 A4
Brunswick Pl HOVE BN3 ....2 B3
Brunswick Rd HOVE BN3 ....2 B3
  SHOR BN43 ....41 F3
  WTHG BN11 ....4 C7
Brunswick Sq HOVE BN3 ....2 B4
Brunswick St East HOVE BN3 ....2 A4
Brunswick St West HOVE BN3 .....2 A4
Brunswick Ter HOVE BN3 ....2 A4

Buci Crs SHOR BN43 ...
Buckhurst Cl BN10
Buckhurst Rd PEAHV BN10
Buckingham Av SHOR BN43
Buckingham Cl BRI BN1 * ...
  SEAF BN25
  SHOR BN43
Buckingham Ms SHOR BN43
Buckingham Pl BRI BN1
Buckingham Rd BRI BN1
  SHOR BN43
  WTHG BN11
Buckingham St SHOR BN43
Buckland Rd SEAF BN25
Buckle By-Pass SEAF BN25
Buckle Cl SEAF BN25
Buckle Dr SEAF BN25
Buckle Ri SEAF BN25
Buckler St PTSD BN41
Buckley Cl HOVE BN3
Buckthorn Cl SEAF BN25
Buckwell Ct LEWES BN7
Bulkington Av SALV BN13
Buller Rd BRIE/ROTT BN2
The Burchens SALV BN13 * ...
Burford Cl SALV BN13
Burley Cl LAN/SOMP BN15 * ...
Burlington Gdns PTSD BN41
Burlington Rd FERR BN12
Burlington St BRIE/ROTT BN2
Burlow Cl BRIE/ROTT BN2
Burnes V BRIE/ROTT BN2
Burnham Cl BRIE/ROTT BN2
Burnham Rd SALV BN13
Burnside Crs LAN/SOMP BN15
Burrell Av LAN/SOMP BN15
Burrell Buildings
  LAN/SOMP BN15 * ...
The Burrells SHOR BN43
Burstead Cl BRI BN1
Burton Vls HOVE BN3
Burwash Cl ANG/EP BN16
Burwash Rd HOVE BN3
Bury Dr FERR BN12
Bushby Cl LAN/SOMP BN15
Bush Cl BRIE/ROTT BN2
  PEAHV BN10
Bush Cottage Cl PTSD BN41
Bush Farm Dr PTSD BN41
Bush Rd NEWHV BN9
Busticle La LAN/SOMP BN15
Butchers La NEWHV BN9
Bute St BRIE/ROTT BN2
Butler Ct SALV BN13
Buttercup Wk BRI BN1
Button Ct BRIE/ROTT BN2 * ...
Butts Rd STHW BN42
Buxted Ri BRI BN1
Buxton Rd BRI BN1
Bydown SEAF BN25
The Byeways SEAF BN25
Byron Rd WTHG BN11
Byron St HOVE BN3
The Byway BRI BN1
Byworth Cl BRIE/ROTT BN2

C

Caburn Crs LEWES BN7
Caburn Rd HOVE BN3
Cairo Av PEAHV BN10
Cairo Av South PEAHV BN10
Caister's Cl HOVE BN3
Caledonian Pl WTHG BN11 * ...
Caledonian Rd BRIE/ROTT BN2
Callon Cl SALV BN13 * ...
Cambridge Gv HOVE BN3
Cambridge Ms HOVE BN3
Cambridge Rd HOVE BN3
  WTHG BN11
Camden St PTSD BN41
Camelford St BRIE/ROTT BN2
Campbell Ct FERR BN12 * ...
Campbell Rd BRI BN1
Canada Cl PEAHV BN10
Canberra Rd SALV BN13
Canfield Cl BRIE/ROTT BN2
Canfield Rd BRIE/ROTT BN2
Canning St BRIE/ROTT BN2
Cannon Pl BRI BN1
Canons Wy STEY/UB BN44
Canterbury Ct SALV BN13
Canterbury Dr BRIE/ROTT BN2
Canterbury Rd SALV BN13
Cantercrow Hl NEWHV BN9
Capel Av PEAHV BN10
Carden Av BRI BN1

n Cl *BRI* BN1 .... 28 A1
n Crs *BRI* BN1 .... 28 A1
n HI *BRI* BN1 .... 28 B2
Down *PEAHV* BN10 .... 62 D4
rooke Cl *LAN/SOMP* BN15 ... 39 G2
rooke Dr *SALV* BN13 .... 35 H5
rooke Rd *BRIE/ROTT* BN2 .... 46 D3
e Rd *HOVE* BN3 .... 44 B4
n *BRI* BN25 .... 70 B4
n HI *BRIE/ROTT* BN2 .... 3 J4
n Ms *WTHG* BN11 .... 55 E3
n Rd *SEAF* BN25 .... 70 B4
e Av *BRIE/ROTT* BN2 .... 46 C3
e St *BRIE/ROTT* BN2 .... 46 C3
gie Cl *SALV* BN13 .... 37 G5
gie Gdns *SALV* BN13 .... 37 G5
gie Rd *SALV* BN13 .... 37 G5
orth Rd *LAN/SOMP* BN15 .... 38 D5
Cl *BRI* BN1 .... 27 H1
ne Cl *SEAF* BN25 .... 70 B3
Cl *LAN/SOMP* BN15 .... 39 G3
Banks *LEWES* BN7 .... 17 E3
Cl *SALV* BN13 .... 54 D1
Y/UB BN44 .... 7 G4
Ditch La *LEWES* BN7 * 17 E3
La *STEY/UB* BN44 .... 7 G4
Precincts *LEWES* BN7 * 17 E3
Rd *SALV* BN13 .... 54 D1
Sq *BRI* BN1 .... 3 G5
St *BRI* BN1 .... 2 D4
Ter *LEWES* BN7 * 17 E3
Wy *SALV* BN13 .... 54 D1
Y/UB BN44 .... 7 G3
rine V *BRIE/ROTT* BN2 .... 48 C2
auseway *BRIE/ROTT* BN2 .... 46 D4
R BN2 .... 54 B2
BN25 .... 72 C1
rs Gdns *BRI* BN1 .... 27 F4
edars *BRI* BN1 .... 27 G4
E/ROTT* BN2 * 46 B2
AHV BN10 * 63 E4
rwell Cl *NEWHV* BN9 * 64 B3
al Av *PEAHV* BN10 .... 66 C1
LV BN31 .... 18 D4
recourt Cl *SALV* BN13 .... 4 D1
recourt Rd *SALV* BN13 .... 4 D1
rion Rd *BRI* BN1 .... 2 E3
born Cl *BRIE/ROTT* BN2 ...... 58 D1
inch Cl *SALV* BN13 .... 36 A5
ey *BRIE/ROTT* BN2 .... 61 E4
ey Crs *BRIE/ROTT* BN2 .... 62 A4
ey Rd *BRI* BN1 .... 29 E3
t Cl *FERR* BN12 .... 53 E5
t Gdns *FERR* BN12 .... 53 F5
t Rd *FERR* BN12 .... 53 E4
ont Dr *HOVE* BN3 .... 27 G4
ont Wy *SALV* BN13 .... 36 B5
kland Rd *BRIE/ROTT* BN2 .... 48 C2
ey Rd *PTSD* BN41 .... 24 D4
ners Cl *BRIE/ROTT* BN2 ...... 60 D3
oners Ms *BRIE/ROTT* BN2 ... 60 D3
ington Cl *BRI* BN1 .... 29 E1
4F BN25 .... 70 D2
pions Rw *HOVE* BN3 * 45 F2
ctonbury Dr *SHOR* BN43 ..... 41 E1
ctonbury Rd *HOVE* BN3 .... 45 G3
cton Cl *WTHG* BN11 .... 54 D2
cton View Rd *WTHG* BN11 ... 54 D2
dlers Wy *STEY/UB* BN44 .... 7 E4
dos Rd *WTHG* BN11 .... 4 E3
nel Vw *STHW* BN42 * 42 C3
nel View Rd
E/ROTT* BN2 .... 47 H2
try Rd *SALV* BN13 .... 37 E4
el Cl *SEAF* BN25 .... 70 C4
el HI *LEWES* BN7 .... 17 G3
el Ms *HOVE* BN3 .... 2 E3
el PI *PTSD* BN41 .... 43 F3
el Rd *PTSD* BN41 .... 43 E3
HG BN11 * 4 E3
el St *BRIE/ROTT* BN2 .... 3 J5
WHV BN9 .... 68 D1
el *BRIE/ROTT* BN2 .... 58 D1

Chappell Cft *WTHG* BN11 * 4 B4
Charlecote Rd *WTHG* BN11 .... 5 C4
Charles St *HOVE* BN3 .... 26 C4
SEAF BN25 .... 70 B3
Charles St *BRIE/ROTT* BN2 .... 3 H6
Charlotte St *BRIE/ROTT* BN2 .... 3 K6
Charlston Av *NEWHV* BN9 .... 68 A3
The Charltons *BRI* BN1 .... 28 D1
Charlton St *STEY/UB* BN44 .... 7 E3
Charmandean La *SALV* BN13 ...... 37 H3
Charmandean Rd *SALV* BN13 ...... 37 H4
Chartfield *HOVE* BN3 .... 26 C5
Chartfield Wy *HOVE* BN3 * 26 D5
Chartwell Cl *SEAF* BN25 .... 70 C4
Chartwell Rd *LAN/SOMP* BN15 ... 39 F5
The Chase *SALV* BN13 .... 18 C2
Chatham PI *BRI* BN1 .... 2 E1
SEAF BN25 .... 72 C1
Chatham Rd *WTHG* BN11 .... 56 C2
Chatsmore Crs *FERR* BN12 .... 53 G2
Chatsworth Av *PEAHV* BN10 ...... 62 C4
Chatsworth Av *PEAHV* BN10 ...... 62 C5
Chatsworth Pk *PEAHV* BN10 ...... 62 D4
Chatsworth Rd *BRI* BN1 .... 45 G2
WTHG BN11 .... 5 F5
Chatsworth Sq *HOVE* BN3 .... 2 A1
Chaucer Rd *WTHG* BN11 .... 4 B3
Cheal Cl *SHOR* BN43 .... 41 G4
Cheapside *BRI* BN1 .... 3 H2
Chelston Av *HOVE* BN3 .... 43 H3
Cheltenham PI *BRI* BN1 .... 3 H3
Chelwood Av *FERR* BN12 .... 54 A4
Chelwood Cl *BRI* BN1 .... 28 C1
Chene Rd *PEAHV* BN10 .... 67 H2
Chepstow Ct *BRI* BN1 .... 29 F2
Cherry Gdns *SALV* BN13 .... 36 C1
Cherry Tree Cl *SALV* BN13 .... 36 B1
Cherry Wk *SALV* BN13 .... 36 C1
Cherwell Rd *SALV* BN13 .... 36 A2
Chesham Cl *FERR* BN12 .... 54 C3
Chesham PI *BRIE/ROTT* BN2 ...... 58 D1
Chesham Rd *BRIE/ROTT* BN2 ..... 58 D1
Chesham St *BRIE/ROTT* BN2 ...... 58 D1
Chesley Cl *SALV* BN13 .... 36 A4
Chesswood Cl *WTHG* BN11 .... 5 K1
Chesswood Rd *WTHG* BN11 .... 5 K1
Chester Av *LAN/SOMP* BN15 ...... 57 G1
WTHG BN11 .... 5 K2
Chesterfield Rd *FERR* BN12 .... 54 B2
Chester Ter *BRI* BN1 .... 46 A1
Chesterton Av *SEAF* BN25 .... 71 F5
Chesterton Dr *SEAF* BN25 .... 71 F5
Chestnut Ct *ANG/EP* BN16 .... 52 A4
The Chestnuts
BRIE/ROTT BN2 * 46 B2
Chestnut Wk *SALV* BN13 .... 53 H1
Chestnut Wy *NEWHV* BN9 .... 68 B1
Cheviot Cl *ANG/EP* BN16 .... 52 A3
SALV BN13 .... 36 C2
Cheviot Rd *SALV* BN13 .... 36 C2
Chichester Cl *BRIE/ROTT* BN2 * . 58 D1
BRIE/ROTT BN2 * 61 G4
HOVE BN3 .... 26 A3
PEAHV BN10 .... 67 H1
Chichester Ct *WTHG* BN11 * 55 E3
Chichester Dr East
BRIE/ROTT BN2 .... 61 G5
Chichester Dr West
BRIE/ROTT BN2 .... 61 G4
Chichester PI *BRIE/ROTT* BN2 ... 58 D1
Chichester Rd *SEAF* BN25 .... 70 C5
Chichester Ter *BRIE/ROTT* BN2 . 58 D1
Chiddingley Cl *BRIE/ROTT* BN2 . 47 F5
Chilgrove Cl *FERR* BN12 .... 53 H2
Chiltern Cl *ANG/EP* BN16 .... 52 A3
SHOR BN43 .... 42 A2
Chiltern Crs *SALV* BN13 .... 36 C2
Chiltington Cl *BRIE/ROTT* BN2 .. 61 G3
Chiltington Wy *BRIE/ROTT* BN2 . 61 G3
Chippers Cl *SALV* BN13 .... 54 D1
Chippers Rd *SALV* BN13 .... 54 D1
Chippers Wk *SALV* BN13 * 54 D1
Chorley Av *BRIE/ROTT* BN2 ...... 61 F3
Chrisdory Rd *PTSD* BN41 .... 24 C4
Christchurch Rd *WTHG* BN11 ...... 4 E3
Christie Rd *LEWES* BN7 .... 16 C3
Church Cl *BRI* BN1 .... 27 H2
LAN/SOMP BN15 .... 39 G2
SALV BN13 .... 35 F1
STEY/UB BN44 .... 8 A1
Church Farm Wk *STEY/UB* BN44 .. 8 A1
Church Gn *SHOR* BN43 .... 42 A3
Church HI *BRI* BN1 .... 27 H1
NEWHV BN9 .... 68 C1
Church House Rd *STHW* BN42 ... 42 D1
SEAF BN25 .... 70 B3
Churchill Rd *LEWES* BN7 .... 16 D1
SEAF BN25 .... 70 B3
Churchill Sq *BRI* BN1 * 2 E4
Church La *FERR* BN12 .... 53 E3

LAN/SOMP BN15 .... 38 C3
LEWES BN7 .... 17 E2
LEWES BN7 .... 31 H2
SEAF BN25 .... 72 C1
STEY/UB BN44 .... 7 F3
STHW BN42 .... 42 C3
Church Md *STEY/UB* BN44 .... 7 F3
Church Rd *HOVE* BN3 .... 44 D4
PTSD BN41 .... 43 F3
SALV BN13 .... 37 E5
Church Rw *LEWES* BN7 * 17 E3
Church St *BRI* BN1 .... 2 E3
PTSD BN41 .... 43 F3
SEAF BN25 .... 70 C5
SHOR BN43 .... 41 F3
STEY/UB BN44 .... 7 F3
Church Wk *WTHG* BN11 .... 5 K4
Church Wy *SALV* BN13 .... 37 E5
Church Way Cl *SALV* BN13 .... 37 E5
Chute Av *SALV* BN13 .... 36 C1
Chute Wy *SALV* BN13 .... 36 C1
Chyngton Av *SEAF* BN25 .... 71 F4
Chyngton Gdns *SEAF* BN25 ...... 71 F4
Chyngton La *SEAF* BN25 .... 71 G5
Chyngton La North *SEAF* BN25 . 71 G5
Chyngton PI *SEAF* BN25 .... 73 F1
Chyngton Rd *SEAF* BN25 .... 73 E1
Chyngton Wy *SEAF* BN25 .... 73 F5
Cinquefoil *PEAHV* BN10 .... 63 E5
Cinque Ports Wy *SEAF* BN25 .... 71 F4
The Circle *ANG/EP* BN16 .... 52 A5
Circus St *BRIE/ROTT* BN2 .... 3 H4
Cissbury Av *PEAHV* BN10 .... 67 G3
SALV BN13 .... 18 D5
Cissbury Crs *BRIE/ROTT* BN2 .... 62 A4
Cissbury Dr *SALV* BN13 .... 18 D4
Cissbury Gdns *SALV* BN13 .... 19 E4
Cissbury Rd *FERR* BN12 .... 53 E2
HOVE BN3 .... 45 G3
SALV BN13 .... 37 G4
Clapham Cl *SALV* BN13 .... 35 F1
Clapham Common *SALV* BN13 .. 35 E2
Claremont Rd *NEWHV* BN9 .... 65 F4
SEAF BN25 .... 70 B5
Clarence Ms *SEAF* BN25 * 70 C5
Clarence Sq *BRI* BN1 .... 2 E4
Clarendon Cl *BRIE/ROTT* BN2 ... 58 C1
PTSD BN41 .... 44 D3
Clarendon Rd *HOVE* BN3 .... 44 D3
SALV BN13 .... 38 A4
SHOR BN43 .... 42 A2
Clarendon Ter *BRIE/ROTT* BN2 . 58 D1
Clarendon Vis *HOVE* BN3 .... 44 D3
Clare Rd *LEWES* BN7 .... 16 C2
Clarke Av *HOVE* BN3 .... 26 B4
Clayfields *PEAHV* BN10 .... 66 D1
Clays HI *STEY/UB* BN44 .... 7 G4
Clayton Rd *BRIE/ROTT* BN2 ...... 46 D3
Clayton Wy *HOVE* BN3 .... 26 B4
Clementine Av *SEAF* BN25 .... 70 B3
Clermont Rd *BRI* BN1 .... 27 G5
Clermont Ter *BRI* BN1 .... 27 G5
Cleveland Cl *SALV* BN13 .... 36 D2
Cleveland Rd *BRI* BN1 .... 28 A5
SALV BN13 .... 36 D2
Cleve Ter *LEWES* BN7 .... 16 C4
Cliff Ap *BRIE/ROTT* BN2 .... 59 F1
Cliff Av *PEAHV* BN10 .... 67 G3
Cliff Cl *SEAF* BN25 .... 72 D2
Cliffe High St *LEWES* BN7 .... 17 F3
Cliff Gdns *PEAHV* BN10 .... 62 B5
SEAF BN25 .... 72 D2
Cliff Park Cl *PEAHV* BN10 .... 67 H1
Cliff Rd *BRIE/ROTT* BN2 .... 59 F2
SEAF BN25 .... 72 D2
The Cliff *BRIE/ROTT* BN2 .... 59 F1
Clifton Ct *WTHG* BN11 * 4 D3
Clifton Gdns *WTHG* BN11 * 4 D3
Clifton HI *BRI* BN1 .... 2 D2
Clifton Ms *BRI* BN1 * 2 E2
Clifton PI *BRI* BN1 .... 2 E2
Clifton Rd *BRI* BN1 .... 2 E2
NEWHV BN9 .... 68 D1
WTHG BN11 .... 4 D3
Clifton St *BRI* BN1 .... 3 F2
Clifton Ter *BRI* BN1 .... 2 E3
Clifton Wy *PEAHV* BN10 .... 62 C5
Clinton La *SEAF* BN25 .... 70 C5
Clinton PI *SEAF* BN25 .... 70 C5
Clive Av *FERR* BN12 .... 54 B3
Clivedale Gdns *STEY/UB* BN44 ... 7 F3
Cloisters *NEWHV* BN9 .... 68 C1
The Close *BRI* BN1 .... 27 F2
LAN/SOMP BN15 .... 57 H1
NEWHV BN9 .... 65 F3
SEAF BN25 .... 72 D1
SHOR BN43 .... 41 F2
Clover La *FERR* BN12 .... 53 E4

Clovers End *BRI* BN1 .... 14 B5
Clover Wy *PTSD* BN41 .... 25 F5
Club Wk *ANG/EP* BN16 .... 52 A5
Cluny St *LEWES* BN7 .... 17 E4
Clyde Cl *SALV* BN13 .... 36 A3
Clyde Rd *BRI* BN1 .... 46 A2
SALV BN13 .... 36 A3
Clyde Ter *STEY/UB* BN44 * 7 G3
Coach House Ms *WTHG* BN11 ..... 4 D5
Coastal Rd *ANG/EP* BN16 .... 52 B5
Cobden Rd *BRIE/ROTT* BN2 ...... 46 C3
WTHG BN11 .... 4 D4
Cobton Dr *HOVE* BN3 .... 26 C4
Cockshut Rd *LEWES* BN7 .... 17 E5
Cokeham Gdns
LAN/SOMP BN15 .... 39 E4
Cokeham La *LAN/SOMP* BN15 .. 39 E5
Cokeham Rd *LAN/SOMP* BN15 .. 39 E3
Colbourne Av *BRIE/ROTT* BN2 .. 28 D5
Colbourne Rd *HOVE* BN3 .... 2 C1
Coldean La *BRI* BN1 .... 14 C4
Coldharbour La *SALV* BN13 ...... 34 D1
Colebrook Cl *WTHG* BN11 .... 5 K2
Colebrook Rd *BRI* BN1 .... 27 F3
STHW BN42 .... 42 D3
Coleman Av *HOVE* BN3 .... 44 A3
Coleman St *BRIE/ROTT* BN2 .... 3 K1
Coleridge Cl *FERR* BN12 .... 53 H2
Coleridge Crs *FERR* BN12 .... 53 H2
Coleridge Rd *FERR* BN12 .... 53 H2
Coleridge St *HOVE* BN3 .... 44 C2
Colgate Cl *BRIE/ROTT* BN2 ...... 47 F4
Colindale Rd *FERR* BN12 .... 53 E3
Colindale Rd North *FERR* BN12 . 53 E3
College Cl *PTSD* BN41 .... 24 D4
College Gdns *BRIE/ROTT* BN2 .. 58 C1
WTHG BN11 .... 55 E3
College HI *STEY/UB* BN44 .... 7 F4
College PI *BRIE/ROTT* BN2 .... 58 C1
College Rd *BRIE/ROTT* BN2 ...... 58 C1
SEAF BN25 .... 72 C1
STEY/UB BN44 .... 8 C3
College St *BRIE/ROTT* BN2 .... 58 C1
STEY/UB BN44 .... 8 C3
College Ter *BRIE/ROTT* BN2 ..... 46 C5
Collingwood Cl *PEAHV* BN10 .... 63 E4
Collingwood Ct *SHOR* BN43 ...... 41 F4
Collingwood Rd *FERR* BN12 ...... 54 A1
Colne Cl *SALV* BN13 .... 36 A3
Columbia Dr *SALV* BN13 .... 36 A4
Colvill Av *SHOR* BN43 .... 40 D2
Combe Dr *STEY/UB* BN44 .... 7 F5
Commerce Wy
LAN/SOMP BN15 .... 39 E5
Compass Ct *PTSD* BN41 * 24 D1
Compton Av *BRI* BN1 .... 2 E2
FERR BN12 .... 53 H3
Compton Rd *BRI* BN1 .... 45 G1
The Compts *PEAHV* BN10 .... 62 B4
Coney Furlong *PEAHV* BN10 ..... 63 F4
Congreve Rd *SALV* BN13 .... 37 G5
Coniston Cl *LAN/SOMP* BN15 ... 39 G3
Coniston Rd *FERR* BN12 .... 54 A1
Connaught Av *SHOR* BN43 .... 41 E2
Connaught Rd *HOVE* BN3 .... 44 C4
SEAF BN25 .... 70 B5
Connaught Ter *HOVE* BN3 .... 44 D3
Connell Dr *BRIE/ROTT* BN2 ...... 48 C3
Convent Gdns *SALV* BN13 .... 18 C1
Conway PI *HOVE* BN3 .... 44 D1
Conway St *HOVE* BN3 .... 44 D1
Cooksbridge Rd
BRIE/ROTT BN2 .... 47 E4
Coolham Dr *BRIE/ROTT* BN2 .... 47 F4
Coombe Dro *STEY/UB* BN44 .... 7 E4
Coombe Lea *HOVE* BN3 * 45 E4
Coombe Ri *BRIE/ROTT* BN2 ...... 61 H2
SALV BN13 .... 19 E5
Coombe Rd *BRIE/ROTT* BN2 ..... 46 D1
LEWES BN7 * 17 F2
STEY/UB BN44 .... 7 E4
Coombes Rd *LAN/SOMP* BN15 .. 40 C1
Coombe Ter *BRIE/ROTT* BN2 .... 46 C1
Coombe V *BRIE/ROTT* BN2 ...... 61 H2
Copse HI *BRI* BN1 .... 27 F2
Copthorne Cl *SALV* BN13 .... 37 E3
Copthorne HI *SALV* BN13 .... 36 D3
Corbyn Crs *SHOR* BN43 .... 41 G3
Cordons *LEWES* BN7 .... 31 H2
Corfe Cl *SALV* BN13 .... 35 H5
Cornelius Av *NEWHV* BN9 .... 68 A3
Corner Garth *FERR* BN12 .... 53 F4
Cornfield Cl *SEAF* BN25 .... 70 D5
Cornfield Rd *SEAF* BN25 .... 70 D5
Cornford Ct *PTSD* BN41 .... 25 F5
Cornwall Av *PEAHV* BN10 .... 67 G3
Cornwall Gdns *BRI* BN1 .... 27 G4
Coronation St *BRIE/ROTT* BN2 .. 46 C3
Corsica Cl *SEAF* BN25 .... 72 D2
Corsica Rd *SEAF* BN25 .... 72 C1

Cortis Av *SALV* BN13 ....37 G5
Cote St *SALV* BN13 ....36 A1
Cotswold Cl *SALV* BN13 ....36 C2
Cotswold Pl *BRIE/ROTT* BN2 * 47 F5
Cotswold Rd *SALV* BN13 ....36 D3
The Cotswolds *STHW* BN42 ......42 C3
Cotswold Wy *ANG/EP* BN16 ......52 A3
Cottage Cl *NEWHV* BN9 ....64 D4
Cottenham Rd *WTHG* BN11 ....5 J2
Countryside Farm Pk
    STEY/UB BN44 * 8 A1
County Oak Av *BRI* BN1 ....28 B1
The Course *LEWES* BN7 ....16 D4
Court Cl *BRI* BN1 ....13 G5
Court Farm Cl *NEWHV* BN9 ....64 B3
Court Farm Rd *BRIE/ROTT* BN2 ...60 C2
    HOVE BN3 ....26 B5
    NEWHV BN9 ....68 C3
Courtfields *LAN/SOMP* BN15 * ...39 F5
Courtlands Cl *FERR* BN12 ....54 C4
Courtlands Wy *FERR* BN12 ....54 C4
Court Ord Rd *BRIE/ROTT* BN2 ....60 C2
Court Rd *LEWES* BN7 ....17 F4
The Courtyard *WTHG* BN11 * 4 A3
Coventry Ct *WTHG* BN11 * 55 E3
Coventry St *BRI* BN1 ....45 G2
The Covers *SEAF* BN25 ....72 D1
Cowden Rd *BRIE/ROTT* BN2 ....61 H5
Cowdens Cl *HOVE* BN3 ....25 H3
Cowdray Cl *FERR* BN12 ....54 B4
Cowdray Ct *FERR* BN12 ....53 G5
Cowdray Dr *FERR* BN12 ....54 B4
Cowfold Rd *BRIE/ROTT* BN2 ......47 E5
Cowley Dr *BRIE/ROTT* BN2 ....48 C3
    LAN/SOMP BN15 ....39 H5
Cowper Rd *WTHG* BN11 ....4 A3
Cowper St *HOVE* BN3 ....44 C3
Coxham La *STEY/UB* BN44 * 7 E2
Crabtree Ar *LAN/SOMP* BN15 * ...39 G4
Crabtree Av *BRI* BN1 ....28 A2
Crabtree La *LAN/SOMP* BN15 .....39 G4
Cradle Hill Rd *SEAF* BN25 ......71 E2
Cradock Pl *SALV* BN13 ....36 C2
Craignair Av *BRI* BN1 ....13 H5
Cranbourne St *BRI* BN1 ....3 F4
Cranedown *LEWES* BN7 ....16 C5
Cranleigh Av *BRIE/ROTT* BN2 ....61 F4
Cranleigh Rd *SALV* BN13 ....37 F5
Cranmer Av *HOVE* BN3 ....44 B1
Cranmer Cl *LEWES* BN7 ....17 F4
Cranmer Rd *SALV* BN13 ....55 E2
Cranworth Rd *WTHG* BN11 ....5 J2
Craven Pl *BRIE/ROTT* BN2 * 46 D5
Craven Rd *BRIE/ROTT* BN2 ....46 D4
Crawley Rd *BRI* BN1 ....28 D1
Crayford Rd *BRIE/ROTT* BN2 .....46 D1
Crescent Cl *BRIE/ROTT* BN2 .....48 C2
Crescent Dr North
    BRIE/ROTT BN2 ....48 D2
Crescent Dr South
    BRIE/ROTT BN2 ....48 D3
Crescent Pl *BRIE/ROTT* BN2 .....58 C1
Crescent Rd *BRIE/ROTT* BN2 .....46 B2
    WTHG BN11 ....5 J4
The Crescent *ANG/EP* BN16 * 52 A5
    BRIE/ROTT BN2 ....29 E5
    LAN/SOMP BN15 ....57 G1
    NEWHV BN9 ....65 F4
    STEY/UB BN44 ....7 F4
    STHW BN42 ....42 D2
Crespin Wy *BRI* BN1 ....46 C1
Cresta Rd *NEWHV* BN9 ....68 A2
Crest Rd *NEWHV* BN9 ....65 F4
Crest Wy *PTSD* BN41 ....25 H4
Crestway Pde *BRI* BN1 * 28 C5
The Crestway *BRI* BN1 ....46 C1
Cricketers Pde *SALV* BN13 * 37 H4
Cricketfield Rd *SEAF* BN25 .....72 C1
Cripps Av *PEAHV* BN10 ....63 F4
Cripps La *STEY/UB* BN44 ....7 G3
Crisp Rd *LEWES* BN7 ....16 C1
Crockhurst Hl *SALV* BN13 ....36 B3
Crocks Dean *PEAHV* BN10 ....63 F3
Croft Av *STHW* BN42 ....42 B3
Croft Cl *SEAF* BN25 ....70 C5
Croft Dr *PTSD* BN41 ....25 E4
Crofters Wd *STEY/UB* BN44 * 7 H4
Croft La *SEAF* BN25 ....70 C5
Croft Rd *BRI* BN1 ....27 F3
The Croft *ANG/EP* BN16 * 52 A4
    BRI BN1 * 45 G2
Cromleigh Wy *STHW* BN42 ....24 C5
Cromwell Rd *HOVE* BN3 ....45 E3
Cromwell St *BRIE/ROTT* BN2 .....46 C3
Crooked La *SEAF* BN25 ....72 D1
Crosby Cl *SALV* BN13 ....36 B4
Croshaw Cl *LAN/SOMP* BN15 .....39 F5
Crossbush Rd *BRIE/ROTT* BN2 ....47 E4
Cross La *SALV* BN13 ....18 C1

Cross Rd *STHW* BN42 ....42 B2
Crossroad Cl *STHW* BN42 ....42 B2
Cross St *BRI* BN1 ....46 A3
    HOVE BN3 ....2 B4
    WTHG BN11 ....4 D2
Cross Wy *LEWES* BN7 ....16 C3
Crossways *ANG/EP* BN16 ....52 B3
Crossways Av *FERR* BN12 ....53 G1
The Crossway *BRI* BN1 ....28 B5
    PTSD BN41 ....25 E3
Crouchfield Cl *SEAF* BN25 * 72 D1
Crouch La *SEAF* BN25 ....72 C1
Crowborough Dr *FERR* BN12 .....53 H3
Crowborough Rd
    BRIE/ROTT BN2 ....61 H5
Crowhurst Rd *BRI* BN1 ....14 B5
Crown Buildings
    LAN/SOMP BN15 * 57 E1
Crown Cl *HOVE* BN3 * 2 A2
Crown Gdns *BRI* BN1 * 3 F3
Crown Hl *SEAF* BN25 ....70 C2
Crown Pl *PTSD* BN41 ....43 E2
    SHOR BN43 ....41 H4
Crown St *BRI* BN1 ....2 E4
Cubitt Ter *BRIE/ROTT* BN2 * 58 D1
Cuckfield Crs *SALV* BN13 ....36 D4
Cuckmere Rd *NEWHV* BN9 ....68 A3
    SEAF BN25 ....73 F1
Cuckmere Wy *BRI* BN1 ....28 B2
Cuilfail *LEWES* BN7 ....17 G3
Culpepper Cl *BRIE/ROTT* BN2 ....28 D5
Culver Rd *LAN/SOMP* BN15 ....39 G4
Cumberland Av *FERR* BN12 ....36 B5
Cumberland Dr *BRI* BN1 ....27 G5
Cumberland Rd *ANG/EP* BN16 ....34 A5
    BRI BN1 ....27 G5
Cumbrian Cl *SALV* BN13 ....36 C3
The Curlews *SHOR* BN43 ....41 G2
Curvins Wy *LAN/SOMP* BN15 .....39 H3
Curwen Pl *BRI* BN1 ....27 G4
Curzon Cl *SALV* BN13 ....36 D4
Cuthbert Rd *BRIE/ROTT* BN2 ....46 C4
The Cygnets *SHOR* BN43 ....41 F2
Cypress Av *SALV* BN13 ....36 A5
Cypress Cl *SHOR* BN43 ....41 F1

D

Dacre Gdns *STEY/UB* BN44 ....8 B5
Dacre Rd *NEWHV* BN9 ....68 D2
Dagmar St *WTHG* BN11 ....5 F2
Dale Av *BRI* BN1 ....27 H2
Dale Crs *BRI* BN1 ....27 H1
Dale Dr *BRI* BN1 ....27 H1
Dale Rd *LEWES* BN7 ....16 C4
    WTHG BN11 ....56 D1
Dale Vw *HOVE* BN3 ....25 H5
Dale View Gdns *HOVE* BN3 ....25 H5
Dallington Rd *HOVE* BN3 ....44 B2
Damon Cl *PEAHV* BN10 ....67 E1
Dana Ldg *PEAHV* BN10 * 66 C1
Dane Cl *SEAF* BN25 ....72 B1
Danehill Rd *BRIE/ROTT* BN2 .....47 F5
Dane Rd *SEAF* BN25 ....72 B1
Daniel Cl *LAN/SOMP* BN15 ....39 H3
Dankton Gdns *LAN/SOMP* BN15 ...38 D3
Dankton La *LAN/SOMP* BN15 .....38 D3
Dapper's La *ANG/EP* BN16 ....34 A4
Darcey Dr *BRI* BN1 ....28 A1
Darlington Cl *ANG/EP* BN16 .....34 A5
Dart Cl *SALV* BN13 ....36 B2
Dartmouth Cl *BRIE/ROTT* BN2 ....47 F1
Dartmouth Crs *BRIE/ROTT* BN2 ...47 F1
Darwall Dr *SEAF* BN25 ....71 E5
D'Aubigny Rd *BRIE/ROTT* BN2 ....46 B1
Davey Dr *BRI* BN1 ....46 B2
Davey's La *LEWES* BN7 ....17 G2
Davigdor Rd *HOVE* BN3 ....2 B1
Dawes Av *WTHG* BN11 ....5 K2
Dawes Cl *WTHG* BN11 ....5 K2
Dawlish Cl *BRIE/ROTT* BN2 ......47 E1
Dawn Cl *STEY/UB* BN44 ....8 B3
Dawn Crs *STEY/UB* BN44 ....8 B3
Dawson Ter *BRIE/ROTT* BN2 .....46 B1
Deacons Dr *PTSD* BN41 ....25 F5
Deacons Wy *STEY/UB* BN44 ....8 B2
Deacon Wy *SALV* BN13 ....38 B5
Dean Av *SEAF* BN25 ....71 G3
Dean Cl *PTSD* BN41 ....25 G5
Dean Court Rd *BRIE/ROTT* BN2 ...60 C5
Deanery Cl *LEWES* BN7 ....17 F1
Dean Gdns *PTSD* BN41 ....25 G5
Dean Rd *SEAF* BN25 ....72 D1
Deans Cl *BRIE/ROTT* BN2 ....48 C2
Dean St *BRI* BN1 ....2 D4
Deanway *HOVE* BN3 ....26 D4
Deborah Ter *PEAHV* BN10 ....66 C1

De Braose Wy *STEY/UB* BN44 ......7 G4
De Courcel Rd *BRIE/ROTT* BN2 ...59 E2
Decoy Rd *SALV* BN13 ....38 B5
Deerswood Cl *SALV* BN13 ....35 H5
The Deeside *BRI* BN1 ....14 A5
De Grey Cl *LEWES* BN7 ....17 F2
Delaware Rd *LEWES* BN7 ....16 A5
De La Warr Gn *LEWES* BN7 * 16 D1
De Montfort Rd
    BRIE/ROTT BN2 ....46 C3
    LEWES BN7 ....16 D3
Dencher Rd *LEWES* BN7 ....32 A4
Deneside *BRI* BN1 ....27 F2
The Dene *HOVE* BN3 ....25 H4
Dene V *BRI* BN1 ....27 F2
The Deneway *BRI* BN1 ....27 F3
    LAN/SOMP BN15 ....39 E4
Denmark Rd *PTSD* BN41 ....43 G3
Denmark Ter *BRI* BN1 ....2 D2
Denmark Vls *HOVE* BN3 ....44 D3
Dennis Hobden Cl
    BRIE/ROTT BN2 ....47 E1
Denton Cl *FERR* BN12 ....53 H2
Denton Dr *BRI* BN1 ....28 A2
    NEWHV BN9 ....65 E4
Denton Island *NEWHV* BN9 ......64 C5
Denton Ri *NEWHV* BN9 ....65 E3
Denton Rd *NEWHV* BN9 ....65 F3
Derek Av *HOVE* BN3 ....43 H4
Derek Rd *LAN/SOMP* BN15 ....39 F2
Derwent Cl *LAN/SOMP* BN15 .....39 E3
Derwent Dr *FERR* BN12 ....36 B5
Desmond Wy *BRIE/ROTT* BN2 .....47 F4
Devils Dyke Rd *BRI* BN1 ....11 G3
    HOVE BN3 ....26 C2
Devonian Cl *BRIE/ROTT* BN2 * ...46 B3
Devonport Pl *WTHG* BN11 ....56 C2
Devonport Rd *WTHG* BN11 ....56 C2
Devonshire Cl *HOVE* BN3 * 45 E2
Devonshire Pl *BRIE/ROTT* BN2 ...3 J6
De Warrenne Rd *LEWES* BN7 .....16 D3
Dewe Rd *BRIE/ROTT* BN2 ....46 C1
The Dewpond *PEAHV* BN10 ....62 D4
The Dicklands *LEWES* BN7 ....51 F2
Ditchling Cl *FERR* BN12 ....53 H1
Ditchling Crs *BRI* BN1 ....28 C2
Ditchling Gdns *BRI* BN1 ....46 A1
Ditchling Ri *BRI* BN1 ....46 A2
Ditchling Rd *BRI* BN1 ....3 H1
    BRI BN1 ....14 C4
Dog La *STEY/UB* BN44 ....7 F3
Dolphin Ms *BRI* BN1 * 3 H6
    SHOR BN43 * 41 H3
Dolphin Rd *SHOR* BN43 ....41 H3
Dolphin Wy *SHOR* BN43 ....41 H3
Dominion Buildings
    SALV BN13 * 56 B1
Dominion Cl *SALV* BN13 ....56 A1
Dominion Rd *SALV* BN13 ....38 A5
Dominion Wy *SALV* BN13 ....38 B5
Dominion Wy West *SALV* BN13 ...38 B5
Donald Hall Rd *BRIE/ROTT* BN2 ..46 C5
Donkey Ms *HOVE* BN3 ....2 B4
Donnington Rd *BRIE/ROTT* BN2 ..48 C4
Doone End *FERR* BN12 ....53 F5
Dorchester Gdns *WTHG* BN11 ....55 E3
Dorothy Av *PEAHV* BN10 ....67 E2
Dorothy Av North *PEAHV* BN10 ..63 E2
Dorothy Rd *HOVE* BN3 ....43 H2
Dorset Gdns *BRIE/ROTT* BN2 .....3 J5
Dorset Ms *BRIE/ROTT* BN2 * 3 H5
Dorset Pl *BRIE/ROTT* BN2 ....3 J5
    SALV BN13 * 37 G5
Dorset Rd *LEWES* BN7 * 17 F4
Dorset St *BRIE/ROTT* BN2 ....3 H5
Douglas Av *WTHG* BN11 ....54 D3
Douglas Cl *WTHG* BN11 ....54 D3
Dovecote Ms *LAN/SOMP* BN15 ...39 F2
Dover Cl *SEAF* BN25 ....71 G3
Dover Rd *BRI* BN1 ....28 A5
    WTHG BN11 ....55 E4
Dower Cl *BRIE/ROTT* BN2 ....60 D2
Downash Cl *BRIE/ROTT* BN2 .....47 E4
Downhill Vw *BRIE/ROTT* BN2 ....48 C3
Downland Av *PEAHV* BN10 ....67 G2
    STHW BN42 ....42 B1
Downland Cl *BRIE/ROTT* BN2 ....47 F1
    SALV BN13 ....18 C1
    STEY/UB BN44 ....8 B1
    STHW BN42 ....42 B1
Downland Ct *PTSD* BN41 ....24 D5
Downland Crs *HOVE* BN3 ....26 B4
Downland Dr *HOVE* BN3 ....26 B4
Downland Rd *BRIE/ROTT* BN2 ....47 H2
    STEY/UB BN44 ....8 B2
Downlands Av *SALV* BN13 ....37 H3
Downlands Cl *LAN/SOMP* BN15 ..39 E3
Downlands Gdns *SALV* BN13 .....38 A3
Downlands Pde *SALV* BN13 ......38 A3

Downs Cl *LAN/SOMP* BN15 ....57 F1
    LEWES BN7 ....16 D3
Downscroft *STEY/UB* BN44 ....7 H4
Downside *BRI* BN1 ....14 A5
    HOVE BN3 ....26 D4
    LEWES BN7 ....16 D3
    SHOR BN43 ....41 G2
Downside Av *SALV* BN13 ....37 H3
Downside Cl *SALV* BN13 ....37 H3
    SHOR BN43 ....41 G2
Downs Link *STEY/UB* BN44 ....7 H4
Downs Md *LAN/SOMP* BN15 * 57 F1
Downs Rd *SEAF* BN25 ....71 E3
Downs Valley Rd
    BRIE/ROTT BN2 ....48 D4
Downsview *HOVE* BN3 ....26 A4
Downs Vw *PEAHV* BN10 ....67 G1
Downsview Av *BRIE/ROTT* BN2 ...48 D4
Downsview Rd *ANG/EP* BN16 ....52 A5
    PTSD BN41 ....43 E2
    SEAF BN25 ....72 D1
Downs Wk *PEAHV* BN10 ....67 G2
Downsway *BRIE/ROTT* BN2 ....48 D4
    SHOR BN43 ....41 G2
    STHW BN42 ....42 B1
Down Ter *BRIE/ROTT* BN2 ....46 C5
The Down *HOVE* BN3 ....26 A4
Downview Av *FERR* BN12 ....36 A5
Downview Rd *FERR* BN12 ....36 A5
Down View Rd *WTHG* BN11 ....55 E4
Drake Av *FERR* BN12 ....36 A5
Drakes Cl *LAN/SOMP* BN15 ......39 H3
Draxmont Wy *BRI* BN1 ....27 H3
Draycliff Cl *FERR* BN12 ....53 H3
The Driftway *STEY/UB* BN44 ......8 B2
The Drive *ANG/EP* BN16 ....52 A5
    HOVE BN3 ....2 A4
    LAN/SOMP BN15 ....57 F1
    NEWHV BN9 ....65 F4
    SHOR BN43 ....41 H2
    STHW BN42 ....42 B2
    WTHG BN11 ....5 F3
The Driveway *SHOR* BN43 ....41 H3
Drove Av *BRIE/ROTT* BN2 ....48 B3
Drove Crs *PTSD* BN41 ....25 E5
Drove Rd *BRIE/ROTT* BN2 ....48 B3
    NEWHV BN9 ....65 E3
    PTSD BN41 ....25 E5
Drovers Cl *PTSD* BN41 ....25 E5
The Drove *BRI* BN1 ....14 C4
    BRI BN1 ....28 C5
    NEWHV BN9 ....65 E3
The Droveway *HOVE* BN3 ....44 D2
Drummond Ct *FERR* BN12 * 36 A5
Drummond Rd *FERR* BN12 ....36 A5
Duchess Dr *SEAF* BN25 ....70 C3
Dudley Rd *BRI* BN1 ....46 B1
Dudwell Rd *BRIE/ROTT* BN2 .....48 C3
Dukes Cl *SEAF* BN25 ....71 E5
Dukes La *BRI* BN1 * 3 G5
    STEY/UB BN44 ....7 F4
Duke's Mound *BRIE/ROTT* BN2 ...3 K6
Duke St *BRI* BN1 ....3 G5
Dukes Yd *STEY/UB* BN44 ....7 F4
Dulwich Cl *SEAF* BN25 ....71 E5
Dunster Cl *BRI* BN1 ....46 B1
Dunvan Cl *LEWES* BN7 ....17 F2
Durham Cl *BRIE/ROTT* BN2 ......47 F1
Durrington Gdns *FERR* BN12 * ...36 A5
Durrington Hl *SALV* BN13 ....36 A4
Durrington La *SALV* BN13 ......36 A4
Dyke Cl *HOVE* BN3 ....26 C3
Dyke Rd *BRI* BN1 ....27 G3
    HOVE BN3 ....26 C2
Dyke Road Av *BRI* BN1 ....27 F1
Dyke Road Dr *BRI* BN1 ....45 G1
Dyke Road Pl *BRI* BN1 ....27 G3
Dymchurch Cl *SEAF* BN25 ....72 A1
Dymock Cl *SEAF* BN25 ....72 A1

E

Earls Cl *SEAF* BN25 ....71 G3
East Albany Rd *SEAF* BN25 .....73 E2
East Av *FERR* BN12 ....53 H1
Eastbank *STHW* BN42 ....42 C1
Eastbourne Rd *BRIE/ROTT* BN2 ...3 J5
    SEAF BN25 ....73 F1
Eastbourne Ter *SEAF* BN25 * 73 F1
Eastbridge Rd *NEWHV* BN9 ......69 E1
Eastbrook Rd *PTSD* BN41 ....43 F3
Eastbrook Wy *PTSD* BN41 ....43 E3
Eastcourt Rd *SALV* BN13 ....37 H4
East Dean Ri *SEAF* BN25 ....73 G1
East Dr *BRIE/ROTT* BN2 ....3 J6
Eastergate Cl *FERR* BN12 ......53 H2
Eastergate Rd *BRIE/ROTT* BN2 ..47 E1

n Av *SHOR* BN43 ....**41** G3
n Cl *ANG/EP* BN16 ....**52** B3
n Pl *BRIE/ROTT* BN2 ....**59** E1
n Rd *BRIE/ROTT* BN2 ....**3** K5
/ROTT* BN2 ....**58** C1
n Ter *BRIE/ROTT* BN2 ....**58** D1
te St *LEWES* BN7 ....**17** F3
te Whf *LEWES* BN7 * **17** F3
ghland Furlong
BN25 * **70** D4
l Dr *PTSD* BN41 ....**25** F5
l Wy *PTSD* BN41 ....**43** F1
g Cl *SALV* BN13 ....**38** B5
d *FERR* BN12 ....**53** F4
eadway *SHOR* BN43 ....**41** G4
nslow Cl *FERR* BN12 ....**53** E3
rt La *LEWES* BN7 ....**17** E4
BRI BN1 ....**3** B3
NM* **30** A1
OMP* BN15 ....**57** C1
ES BN7 ....**17** F3
BN41 ....**43** G4
BN25 ....**70** C5
BN43 ....**41** F3
ne *SALV* BN13 ....**36** B4
y *LEWES* BN7 ....**16** B2
ck Cl *BRI* BN1 ....**14** B5
Gdns *HOVE* BN3 ....**45** E3
Gv *HOVE* BN3 ....**45** E3
Mnr *HOVE* BN3 * **45** E3
Pl *BRIE/ROTT* BN2 ....**58** D1
Av *HOVE* BN3 ....**45** E4
Vls *HOVE* BN3 ....**44** D3
on Av *BRI* BN1 ....**46** A1
on Gdns *SHOR* BN43 ....**41** F1
ll Cl *SALV* BN13 ....**36** D3
ll Wy *PTSD* BN41 ....**24** D5
rgh Rd *BRIE/ROTT* BN2 ....**46** B2
BN25 ....**70** B5
m *PEAHV* BN10 ....**66** D2
v North *PEAHV* BN10 ....**63** E5
ton Rd *SALV* BN13 ....**36** A4
d Av *BRIE/ROTT* BN2 ....**61** H2
E BN3 ....**26** C4
d Cl *HOVE* BN3 ....**26** C4
BN25 ....**26** C4
ds Ter *LAN/SOMP* BN15 * **38** B3
d St *BRIE/ROTT* BN2 ....**3** J5
ES BN7 ....**17** F3
Cl *LAN/SOMP* BN15 ....**39** E4
am Cl *BRIE/ROTT* BN2 ....**61** G3
on Cl *BRIE/ROTT* BN2 ....**29** C2
on Rd *BRIE/ROTT* BN2 ....**29** F3
rt Rd *HOVE* BN3 ....**43** H1
ont Pl *BRIE/ROTT* BN2 ....**3** K5
Av *LAN/SOMP* BN15 ....**39** G3
Av *BRIE/ROTT* BN2 ....**61** F4
Av *FERR* BN12 ....**54** D4
Rd *FERR* BN12 ....**54** C2
PTSD BN41 ....**25** F5
BN1 ....**46** A3
d *WTHG* BN11 ....**5** J3
r Cl *BRI* BN1 ....**27** F2
Cl *SEAF* BN25 ....**70** D4
s *BRIE/ROTT* BN2 ....**60** C2
BRIE/ROTT BN2 ....**60** C1
dns *SEAF* BN25 ....**71** G4
d *FERR* BN12 ....**54** B3
th Av *HOVE* BN3 ....**26** C4
th Cl *HOVE* BN3 ....**26** C4
BN25 ....**69** G2
th Pl *LAN/SOMP* BN15 ....**39** E5
th Rd *SHOR* BN43 ....**42** A2
G BN10 ....**3** D4
HOVE BN3 ....**44** D3
BN41 ....**43** G3
SALV BN13 ....**36** C2
ANG/EP BN16 ....**52** B4
HOVE* BN3 ....**27** E5
BN25 ....**71** G5
BN43 ....**41** F1
NEWHV* BN9 ....**68** B1
HOVE BN3 ....**44** A1
BRIE/ROTT BN2 ....**46** C3
SOMP* BN15 ....**39** F5
G BN11 ....**54** D2
ove La *STEY/UB* BN44 ....**7** F3
st Cl *ANG/EP* BN16 ....**34** A4
Rd *BRIE/ROTT* BN2 ....**3** J3
FERR BN12 ....**53** F2
SALV BN13 ....**18** C1
PTSD BN41 ....**43** F2
G BN10 ....**5** G5
r *LAN/SOMP* BN15 ....**39** F4
a Av *BRI* BN1 ....**27** G5
ne Cl *LAN/SOMP* BN15 ....**39** F4
SEAF BN25 * **72** C1
NEWHV BN9 ....**64** C5

Elrington Rd *HOVE* BN3 ....**45** E1
Elsie Rd *WTHG* BN11 ....**4** B6
Elsted Crs *BRI* BN1 ....**28** C1
Elverlands Cl *FERR* BN12 ....**53** F5
Elvin Crs *BRIE/ROTT* BN2 ....**60** C1
Ely Cl *SALV* BN13 ....**54** D1
Ely Rd *SALV* BN13 ....**54** D1
Emerald Quay *SHOR* BN43 ....**41** G4
English Cl *HOVE* BN3 ....**44** A2
English Pas *LEWES* BN7 * **17** F3
Ennerdale Dr *LAN/SOMP* BN15 ....**38** D5
Enterprise Ct *FERR* BN12 * **54** A2
E Plan Est *NEWHV* BN9 * **64** D4
Eridge Gn *LEWES* BN7 ....**16** D2
Eridge Rd *HOVE* BN3 ....**26** C5
Eriskay Ct *SALV* BN13 ....**35** H5
Eriswell Rd *WTHG* BN11 ....**4** D5
Erringham Rd *SHOR* BN43 ....**41** E2
Erroll Rd *HOVE* BN3 ....**43** G4
Esher Cl *SEAF* BN25 ....**70** D4
Eskbank Av *BRI* BN1 ....**14** A5
Esplanade *SEAF* BN25 ....**72** D2
Esplanade Ct *WTHG* BN11 * **5** K5
Esplanade Ms *SEAF* BN25 ....**72** C1
The Esplanade *PEAHV* BN10 ....**66** C1
WTHG* BN11 ....**5** J5
Essennigh Dr *SALV* BN13 ....**35** H4
Essex Ms *NEWHV* BN9 * **68** C5
Essex Pl *BRIE/ROTT* BN2 ....**58** C1
NEWHV* BN9 * **68** C1
Essex St *BRIE/ROTT* BN2 ....**3** K5
BRIE/ROTT* BN2 ....**58** C1
Estate Rd *NEWHV* BN9 ....**68** D1
Ethelred Rd *SALV* BN13 ....**55** E1
Ethel St *HOVE* BN3 ....**44** D3
Ethelwulf Rd *SALV* BN13 ....**55** E1
Etherton Wy *SEAF* BN25 ....**71** E4
Eton Cl *SEAF* BN25 ....**71** E4
Eton Rd *WTHG* BN11 ....**55** E2
Evelyn Av *NEWHV* BN9 ....**68** C1
Evelyn Rd *LEWES* BN7 ....**16** D2
SALV* BN13 ....**55** H1
Evelyn Ter *BRIE/ROTT* BN2 ....**3** J3
Evershed Ct *PEAHV* BN10 * **66** B1
Evershed Wy *SHOR* BN43 ....**41** H3
Ewart St *BRIE/ROTT* BN2 ....**3** K2
Ewhurst Rd *BRIE/ROTT* BN2 ....**46** C2
Exceat Cl *BRIE/ROTT* BN2 ....**47** E4
The Excelsior *BRI* BN1 * **27** F3
Exeter Cl *WTHG* BN11 * **55** E4
Exeter St *BRI* BN1 ....**45** G2
Exmoor Cl *SALV* BN13 ....**36** B3
Exmoor Crs *SALV* BN13 ....**36** C1
Exmoor Dr *SALV* BN13 ....**36** C2

F

Fairdene *STHW* BN42 ....**42** D1
Fairfield *PEAHV* BN10 * **66** D1
Fairfield Cl *SHOR* BN43 ....**41** H1
Fairfield Gdns *PTSD* BN41 ....**43** F1
Fairfields *SALV* BN13 ....**37** E5
Fairholme Rd *NEWHV* BN9 ....**65** F4
Fairhurst *PEAHV* BN10 * **66** B1
Fairlawn Dr *SALV* BN13 ....**55** H1
Fairlawns *SHOR* BN43 ....**41** G2
Fairlie Gdns *BRI* BN1 ....**27** G4
Fairlight Av *PEAHV* BN10 ....**66** B1
Fairview Av *FERR* BN12 ....**54** A4
Fairview Ri *BRI* BN1 ....**27** F2
Fairview Rd *LAN/SOMP* BN15 ....**39** G3
Fairway Crs *PTSD* BN41 ....**25** G5
Fairways Cl *SEAF* BN25 ....**73** C1
Fairways Rd *SEAF* BN25 ....**73** F1
The Fairway *LAN/SOMP* BN15 ....**40** A5
NEWHV* BN9 ....**68** A2
Falaise Rd *NEWHV* BN9 ....**65** F4
Falcon Cl *SHOR* BN43 ....**41** H4
Fallowfield Cl *HOVE* BN3 ....**26** B5
Fallowfield Crs *HOVE* BN3 ....**26** A5
Falmer Av *BRIE/ROTT* BN2 ....**61** F3
FERR* BN12 ....**53** H4
Falmer Cl *FERR* BN12 ....**54** A4
Falmer Gdns *BRIE/ROTT* BN2 ....**48** B2
Falmer House Rd *BRI* BN1 ....**15** H1
Falmer Rd *BRIE/ROTT* BN2 ....**30** B5
Faraday Cl *SALV* BN13 ....**36** A1
Farman St *HOVE* BN3 ....**44** D4
Farm Cl *PTSD* BN41 ....**25** E5
SEAF* BN25 ....**71** F4
Farm Hl *BRIE/ROTT* BN2 ....**48** B2
Farm Ms *HOVE* BN3 ....**2** A3
Farm Rd *HOVE* BN3 ....**2** B3
Farm Wy *STHW* BN42 ....**43** E3
Farmway *HOVE* BN3 ....**25** H5
Farncombe Rd *LEWES* BN7 ....**17** G3
WTHG* BN11 ....**5** J4

Farnefold Rd *STEY/UB* BN44 ....**7** F2
Fereday Cl *LAN/SOMP* BN15 ....**39** G4
Ferndale Rd *HOVE* BN3 ....**45** F3
Ferndale Wk *ANG/EP* BN16 ....**34** A4
Fernhurst Cl *BRI* BN1 ....**28** C1
Fernhurst Crs *BRI* BN1 ....**28** B2
Fernhurst Dr *FERR* BN12 ....**53** G3
Fernwood Ri *BRI* BN1 ....**27** F2
Ferrers Rd *LEWES* BN7 ....**16** D2
Ferring Cl *FERR* BN12 ....**53** E5
Ferring Grange Gdns
FERR BN12 ....**53** E3
Ferringham La *FERR* BN12 ....**53** E4
Ferringham Wy *FERR* BN12 ....**53** E5
Ferring La *FERR* BN12 ....**53** F2
Ferring Marine *FERR* BN12 ....**53** F5
Ferring St *FERR* BN12 ....**53** E3
Ferry Rd *SHOR* BN43 ....**41** F4
Fetherston Rd *LAN/SOMP* BN15 ....**39** G3
Feversham Cl *SHOR* BN43 ....**41** H4
Field Cl *LAN/SOMP* BN15 ....**39** F4
SEAF* BN25 ....**73** F1
Field Place Pde *FERR* BN12 * **54** C2
Field Rw *WTHG* BN11 ....**4** D5
Fifth Av *LAN/SOMP* BN15 ....**39** G3
SALV* BN13 ....**37** G2
Finches Cl *LAN/SOMP* BN15 ....**39** F5
The Finches *SHOR* BN43 ....**41** G2
Findon Av *BRIE/ROTT* BN2 ....**62** A4
Findon By-Pass *SALV* BN13 ....**18** B1
Findon Cl *HOVE* BN3 ....**26** B4
SEAF* BN25 ....**71** G5
Findon Rd *BRIE/ROTT* BN2 ....**47** F5
SALV* BN13 ....**37** E1
Finsbury Rd *BRIE/ROTT* BN2 ....**3** K2
Fir Cl *BRIE/ROTT* BN2 ....**48** D3
Fircroft Av *LAN/SOMP* BN15 ....**39** F2
Fircroft Cl *BRI* BN1 ....**27** G4
Firle Cl *SEAF* BN25 ....**70** C3
Firle Crs *LEWES* BN7 ....**16** B3
Firle Dr *SEAF* BN25 ....**70** C3
Firle Gra *SEAF* BN25 ....**70** C3
Firle Rd *BRIE/ROTT* BN2 ....**46** C4
LAN/SOMP* BN15 ....**39** F1
PEAHV* BN10 ....**62** D4
SEAF* BN25 ....**70** C4
Firsdown Cl *SALV* BN13 ....**18** C5
Firsdown Rd *SALV* BN13 ....**36** C1
First Av *HOVE* BN3 ....**45** E5
LAN/SOMP* BN15 ....**39** G4
NEWHV* BN9 ....**68** C1
SALV* BN13 ....**37** G2
Fishermans Wk *SHOR* BN43 ....**40** D4
Fishersgate Cl *PTSD* BN41 ....**43** E3
Fishersgate Ter *PTSD* BN41 ....**43** E3
Fisher St *LEWES* BN7 ....**17** E3
Fitch Dr *BRIE/ROTT* BN2 ....**47** E1
Fittleworth Cl *FERR* BN12 ....**53** C1
Fitzgerald Av *SEAF* BN25 ....**72** C1
Fitzgerald Pk *SEAF* BN25 ....**72** D1
Fitzgerald Rd *LEWES* BN7 ....**17** F1
Fitzherbert Dr *BRIE/ROTT* BN2 ....**46** D2
Fitzjohns Rd *LEWES* BN7 ....**16** C2
Fitzroy Rd *LEWES* BN7 ....**16** D1
Flag Sq *SHOR* BN43 ....**41** F4
Fletcher Rd *SALV* BN13 ....**38** A5
Fletching Cl *BRIE/ROTT* BN2 ....**47** F4
Flimwell Cl *BRIE/ROTT* BN2 ....**47** E5
Flint Cl *PTSD* BN41 ....**25** F5
SEAF* BN25 ....**70** C2
The Flints *LEWES* BN7 ....**32** A2
Florence Av *HOVE* BN3 ....**43** H4
Florence Pl *BRI* BN1 ....**46** B1
Florence Rd *BRI* BN1 ....**46** A2
The Florets *STEY/UB* BN44 * **8** B3
Florida Cl *SALV* BN13 ....**53** F5
Florida Gdns *FERR* BN12 * **53** F5
Florida Rd *FERR* BN12 ....**53** F5
Florlandia Cl *LAN/SOMP* BN15 ....**38** D5
Foamcourt Waye *FERR* BN12 ....**53** H2
Folkestone Cl *SEAF* BN25 ....**71** G3
Fonthill Rd *HOVE* BN3 ....**44** D2
Fontwell Cl *SALV* BN13 ....**37** E2
Foredown Cl *PTSD* BN41 ....**25** F5
Foredown Dr *PTSD* BN41 ....**43** F1
Foredown Rd *PTSD* BN41 ....**25** F5
Forest Rd *BRI* BN1 ....**29** E2
SALV* BN13 ....**37** H4
Forge Cl *PTSD* BN41 ....**25** F5
Fort Hvn *SHOR* BN43 ....**42** A4
Fort Ri *NEWHV* BN9 ....**68** B3
Fort Rd *NEWHV* BN9 ....**68** B3
Forward Cl *NEWHV* BN9 ....**65** E3
The Fosse *LEWES* BN7 * **17** E3
Foster Cl *SEAF* BN25 ....**70** C4
Foundry La *LEWES* BN7 ....**17** G3
Foundry St *BRI* BN1 ....**3** G3
Foundry Ter *LEWES* BN7 * **17** G3
Fountains Cl *BRI* BN1 ....**28** B5

Founthill Av *BRIE/ROTT* BN2 ....**61** F4
Founthill Rd *BRIE/ROTT* BN2 ....**61** F4
Fourth Av *HOVE* BN3 ....**44** D5
LAN/SOMP* BN15 ....**39** G3
SALV* BN13 ....**37** H3
Fowey Cl *SHOR* BN43 ....**41** H4
Foxdown Rd *BRIE/ROTT* BN2 ....**48** B3
Foxglove Wk *SALV* BN13 ....**54** A1
Foxhill *PEAHV* BN10 ....**63** E4
Foxhunters Rd *PTSD* BN41 ....**24** D4
Fox Lea *SALV* BN13 ....**18** C2
Foxley La *SALV* BN13 ....**36** D2
Fox Wy *PTSD* BN41 ....**25** E4
Foxwood Av *ANG/EP* BN16 ....**52** A1
Framfield Cl *BRI* BN1 ....**29** E1
Frampton Ct *FERR* BN12 * **54** A3
Frampton Pl *SHOR* BN43 ....**40** D2
The Framptons *ANG/EP* BN16 ....**52** B4
France La *SALV* BN13 ....**34** D2
Francis St *BRI* BN1 ....**3** H1
Franklands Cl *SALV* BN13 ....**36** D3
Franklin Rd *BRIE/ROTT* BN2 ....**46** C3
PTSD* BN41 ....**43** G3
SALV* BN13 ....**36** C3
SHOR* BN43 ....**42** A2
Franklin St *BRIE/ROTT* BN2 ....**46** C3
Frant Rd *HOVE* BN3 ....**26** C5
Frederick Gdns *BRI* BN1 * **3** F3
Frederick Pl *BRI* BN1 ....**3** F3
Frederick St *BRI* BN1 ....**3** F3
Frederick Ter *BRI* BN1 * **3** F3
Freehold St *SHOR* BN43 ....**41** E3
Freehold Ter *BRIE/ROTT* BN2 ....**46** B1
Freeland Cl *SEAF* BN25 ....**69** G4
Freemans Rd *PTSD* BN41 ....**43** E2
Freshbrook Cl *LAN/SOMP* BN15 ....**39** G5
Freshbrook Rd
LAN/SOMP BN15 ....**39** H5
Freshfield Pl *BRIE/ROTT* BN2 ....**46** C5
Freshfield Rd *BRIE/ROTT* BN2 ....**46** C5
Freshfields Cl *LAN/SOMP* BN15 ....**39** F4
Freshfields Dr *LAN/SOMP* BN15 ....**39** F4
Freshfield St *BRIE/ROTT* BN2 ....**46** C4
Freshfield Wy *BRIE/ROTT* BN2 ....**46** C5
Friar Cl *BRI* BN1 ....**28** A3
Friar Crs *BRI* BN1 ....**27** H4
Friar Rd *BRI* BN1 ....**28** A3
Friars' Av *PEAHV* BN10 ....**67** G3
Friars' Wk *LEWES* BN7 ....**17** F3
Friar Wk *BRI* BN1 ....**27** H3
SALV* BN13 ....**54** D2
Frimley Cl *BRIE/ROTT* BN2 ....**48** C3
Friston Cl *BRIE/ROTT* BN2 ....**29** F3
SEAF* BN25 ....**70** B4
Frith Rd *HOVE* BN3 ....**44** C2
Frobisher Cl *FERR* BN12 ....**54** B1
Frobisher Wy *FERR* BN12 ....**54** B1
Fulbeck Av *SALV* BN13 ....**35** H4
Fuller Rd *LEWES* BN7 ....**16** C1
Fullwood Av *NEWHV* BN9 ....**68** B1
Fulmar Cl *HOVE* BN3 ....**45** F1
The Furlongs *STEY/UB* BN44 ....**7** F4
Furze Cl *SALV* BN13 ....**18** B5
Furze Hl *HOVE* BN3 ....**2** C2
Furzeholme *SALV* BN13 ....**18** C5
Furze Rd *SALV* BN13 ....**18** B5

G

Gableson Av *BRI* BN1 ....**26** D3
Gainsborough Av
SALV BN13 ....**38** A3
Gainsborough Ldg *SALV* BN13 * **55** G1
Gaisford Cl *SALV* BN13 ....**55** C1
Gaisford Rd *SALV* BN13 ....**55** F1
Galliers Cl *BRI* BN1 ....**28** B1
The Gallops *LEWES* BN7 ....**16** C3
Galsworthy Cl *FERR* BN12 ....**53** H2
Galsworthy Rd *FERR* BN12 ....**53** H2
Gannon Rd *WTHG* BN11 ....**5** K3
Garden Cl *ANG/EP* BN16 ....**34** A3
LAN/SOMP* BN15 ....**39** E4
PTSD* BN41 ....**43** G2
SHOR* BN43 ....**41** H1
Gardener St *PTSD* BN41 ....**43** E2
The Gardens *PTSD* BN41 ....**43** G2
STHW* BN42 ....**42** D3
Garden St *LEWES* BN7 ....**17** E4
Gardner Rd *PTSD* BN41 ....**43** E3
Gardner St *BRI* BN1 ....**3** G4
Garrick Rd *SALV* BN13 ....**55** F1
Gatcombe Cl *SALV* BN13 * **35** H5
Gatewycke Ter *STEY/UB* BN44 * **7** F3
Geneva Rd *NEWHV* BN9 ....**68** D2
George St *BRIE/ROTT* BN2 ....**3** J5
HOVE* BN3 ....**44** D4
PTSD* BN41 ....**43** E3

George V Av *LAN/SOMP* BN15......**40** B5
  WTHG BN11..................................**54** D3
Georgia Av *SALV* BN13...............**55** H1
Gerald Rd *SEAF* BN25................**72** D2
  WTHG BN11..................................**54** D4
Gerard St *BRI* BN1.......................**46** A2
Ghyllside Rd *BRIE/ROTT* BN2.....**47** E1
Gibbon Rd *NEWHV* BN9.............**68** B2
Gildredge Rd *SEAF* BN25............**70** D5
Gladstone Pl *BRIE/ROTT* BN2.....**46** C2
Gladstone Rd *PTSD* BN41...........**43** F3
Gladstone Ter *BRIE/ROTT* BN2...**46** B3
Gladys Av *PEAHV* BN10..............**67** F2
Gladys Rd *HOVE* BN3..................**43** H2
Glastonbury Rd *HOVE* BN3.........**43** H4
Glebe Cl *LAN/SOMP* BN15.........**39** G3
  LEWES BN7..................................**16** C4
  STHW BN42...................................**42** C3
Glebe Dr *SEAF* BN25...................**70** C5
Glebelands Cl *SHOR* BN43..........**41** H2
Glebe Rd *SALV* BN13..................**55** E1
Glebeside Av *SALV* BN13............**37** E5
Glebeside Cl *SALV* BN13.............**37** F5
Glebe Vls *HOVE* BN3...................**43** H3
Glebe Wy *LAN/SOMP* BN15.......**39** G3
Glenbarrie Wy *FERR* BN12..........**52** D2
Glendale Rd *HOVE* BN3..............**45** F3
Glendor Rd *HOVE* BN3................**44** A4
Gleneagles Cl *SEAF* BN25...........**69** G4
Glenfalls Av *BRI* BN1....................**14** A5
Glen Gdns *FERR* BN12................**53** F3
Glen Ri *BRI* BN1...........................**26** D2
Glen Rise Cl *BRI* BN1..................**26** D2
The Glen *SALV* BN13...................**37** E3
Gleton Av *HOVE* BN3..................**25** H5
Gloucester Ms *BRI* BN1 *............**3** H4
Gloucester Pas *BRI* BN1...............**3** H3
Gloucester Pl *BRI* BN1..................**3** H3
Gloucester Rd *BRI* BN1.................**3** G3
Gloucester St *BRI* BN1..................**3** H3
Glynde Av *BRIE/ROTT* BN2.........**61** G3
  FERR BN12..................................**53** F3
Glyndebourne Av
  BRIE/ROTT BN2.........................**61** G4
Glynde Cl *FERR* BN12.................**53** F3
  NEWHV BN9...............................**64** D3
Glynde Rd *BRIE/ROTT* BN2........**46** D4
Glynn Ri *PEAHV* BN10................**62** D4
Glynn Rd *PEAHV* BN10...............**63** E4
Glynn Rd West *PEAHV* BN10......**62** D4
Godfrey Cl *LEWES* BN7...............**17** E1
Godstalls La *STEY/UB* BN44.........**7** F3
Godwin Rd *HOVE* BN3................**43** H2
Golden Acre *ANG/EP* BN16.........**52** B5
Golden Av *ANG/EP* BN16............**52** B4
Golden Avenue Cl
  ANG/EP BN16.............................**52** B5
Golden La *HOVE* BN3 *.................**2** B4
Gold La *PEAHV* BN10..................**63** E3
Goldsmid Rd *BRI* BN1....................**2** D1
Goldsmith Rd *SALV* BN13...........**56** A1
Goldstone Cl *HOVE* BN3.............**26** D4
Goldstone Crs *HOVE* BN3............**26** C5
Goldstone La *HOVE* BN3.............**44** D2
Goldstone Rd *HOVE* BN3............**44** D3
Goldstone St *HOVE* BN3.............**44** D3
Goldstone Vls *HOVE* BN3............**44** D3
Goldstone Wy *HOVE* BN3............**26** C5
Golf Dr *BRI* BN1..........................**28** B4
Goodwood Rd *SALV* BN13..........**37** F3
Goodwood Wy *BRIE/ROTT* BN2..**29** E4
Gordon Av *SHOR* BN43...............**41** G4
Gordon Rd *BRI* BN1....................**27** H5
  LAN/SOMP BN15.......................**39** E4
  PTSD BN41...................................**43** E3
  SHOR BN43..................................**41** F3
  WTHG BN11....................................**5** F3
Gorham Av *BRIE/ROTT* BN2........**61** G3
Gorham Cl *BRIE/ROTT* BN2.........**61** G3
Gorham Wy *PEAHV* BN10...........**62** A5
Goring Cha *FERR* BN12...............**53** G1
Goring Rd *FERR* BN12.................**54** B3
  STEY/UB BN44..............................**7** F4
Goring St *FERR* BN12..................**53** G2
Goring Wy *FERR* BN12................**53** F3
Gorringe Cl *SHOR* BN43..............**42** B3
Gorse Av *SALV* BN13...................**37** F4
Gorse Cl *PTSD* BN41...................**24** D3
Gorse Dr *SEAF* BN25...................**70** D2
Gorse La *SALV* BN13...................**18** C5
Gorse Vw *ANG/EP* BN16 *..........**52** C5
Gows Cft *HOVE* BN3...................**32** A2
Gowscroft *LEWES* BN7 *..............**32** C3
Graffham Cl *BRIE/ROTT* BN2......**47** E4
Grafton Dr *LAN/SOMP* BN15......**39** E4
Grafton Gdns *LAN/SOMP* BN15..**39** E4
Grafton Pl *WTHG* BN11.................**4** E5
Grafton Rd *WTHG* BN11................**4** E5
Grafton St *BRIE/ROTT* BN2...........**3** K6

Graham Av *BRI* BN1.....................**27** G3
  PTSD BN41...................................**24** D3
Graham Crs *PTSD* BN41...............**24** D3
Graham Rd *WTHG* BN11................**4** E5
Grand Av *HOVE* BN3...................**45** E4
  LAN/SOMP BN15.......................**39** G3
  SEAF BN25..................................**70** A3
  WTHG BN11..................................**55** H3
Grand Crs *BRIE/ROTT* BN2..........**61** E4
Grand Junction Rd *BRI* BN1...........**3** G6
Grand Pde *BRIE/ROTT* BN2...........**3** H3
Grand Parade Ms
  BRIE/ROTT BN2............................**3** H4
  FERR BN12..................................**53** E4
Grange Cl *BRI* BN1......................**45** C1
  FERR BN12..................................**53** E4
Grange Ct *FERR* BN12 *...............**53** E3
Grange Park Rd *FERR* BN12.........**53** E4
Grange Rd *HOVE* BN3.................**44** A3
  LEWES BN7..................................**17** E4
  STHW BN42...................................**42** C3
Grangeways *BRI* BN1...................**27** G2
Grantham Rd *BRI* BN1.................**46** A1
Grantsmead *LAN/SOMP* BN15....**39** G3
Grant St *BRIE/ROTT* BN2...............**3** K1
Granville Rd *HOVE* BN3................**2** C1
The Graperies *BRIE/ROTT* BN2....**46** C5
Grasmere Av *LAN/SOMP* BN15...**38** D4
Grasmere Av *PEAHV* BN10..........**62** B5
Gratwicke Rd *WTHG* BN11............**4** D6
Gravelly Crs *LAN/SOMP* BN15....**39** H4
Great College St
  BRIE/ROTT BN2...........................**58** C1
Greatham Rd *SALV* BN13............**36** D1
Greenacres *BRI* BN1 *..................**45** H1
  PEAHV BN10...............................**63** E3
  SHOR BN43..................................**41** E2
  STEY/UB BN44...............................**8** A1
Greenacres Ring *ANG/EP* BN16...**34** A4
Greenbank Av *BRIE/ROTT* BN2...**61** H4
Green Cl *STHW* BN42...................**42** C3
Green Ct *STHW* BN42 *................**42** C3
Greenfield Cl *BRI* BN1.................**28** A2
Green Field Cl *STHW* BN42..........**42** C2
Greenfield Crs *BRI* BN1...............**27** H2
Green Ga *PEAHV* BN10................**63** E4
Greenhill Wy *PEAHV* BN10.........**63** E3
Greenland Cl *SALV* BN13............**36** C4
Greenland Rd *SALV* BN13...........**36** C4
Green La *BRIE/ROTT* BN2............**48** C4
  LEWES BN7..................................**16** C3
  SEAF BN25..................................**72** C1
Greenleas *HOVE* BN3..................**25** H5
Greenoaks *LAN/SOMP* BN15......**39** F2
Green Pk *FERR* BN12...................**53** F2
Green Rdg *BRI* BN1.....................**26** D2
The Green *BRIE/ROTT* BN2..........**60** D3
  HOVE BN3...................................**27** E5
Greentrees *LAN/SOMP* BN15......**39** E4
Greentrees Cl *LAN/SOMP* BN15..**39** E4
Greentrees Crs
  LAN/SOMP BN15.......................**39** E4
Green Wk *SEAF* BN25..................**73** F1
Greenways *BRIE/ROTT* BN2.........**60** B2
  PTSD BN41...................................**43** F1
  STHW BN42...................................**42** D1
Greenways Cnr
  BRIE/ROTT BN2 *.......................**60** B1
Greenways Crs *FERR* BN12..........**53** F4
  SHOR BN43..................................**41** H1
Greenwell Cl *SEAF* BN25.............**71** F4
Greenwich Wy *PEAHV* BN10.......**67** E1
Greet Rd *LAN/SOMP* BN15.........**39** F3
Grenville Av *FERR* BN12..............**54** B2
Grenville Cl *FERR* BN12...............**54** A2
Greyfiars *HOVE* BN3....................**45** F3
Greyfriars Cl *SALV* BN13.............**37** E4
Greystoke Ms *FERR* BN12............**53** E3
Greystoke Rd *FERR* BN12............**53** E3
Greystone Av *SALV* BN13............**36** D5
Griffith's Av *LAN/SOMP* BN15....**39** F2
Grinstead Av *LAN/SOMP* BN15...**39** G4
Grinstead La *LAN/SOMP* BN15...**39** G4
Grinstead Mt *BRIE/ROTT* BN2 *...**47** F5
Grooms Cl *ANG/EP* BN16............**34** A5
Grosvenor Rd *SEAF* BN25...........**70** C4
  WTHG BN11....................................**4** E4
Grosvenor St *BRIE/ROTT* BN2......**3** K5
Grove Bank *BRIE/ROTT* BN2 *.....**3** J3
Grove Hl *BRIE/ROTT* BN2.............**3** J3
The Grovelands
  LAN/SOMP BN15.......................**57** G1
Grover Av *LAN/SOMP* BN15........**39** F4
Grove Rd *SALV* BN13..................**37** E5
  SEAF BN25..................................**70** D5
Grove St *BRIE/ROTT* BN2..............**3** K2
The Grove *FERR* BN12.................**53** E3
  NEWHV BN9...............................**65** E3
Guardswell Pl *SEAF* BN25...........**70** C5

Guernsey Rd *FERR* BN12.............**53** F5
Guildford Cl *SALV* BN13..............**55** E1
Guildford Rd *BRI* BN1....................**3** F2
  SALV BN13..................................**55** E2
Guildford St *BRI* BN1.....................**3** F2
Guinness Trust Bungalows
  NEWHV BN9 *............................**65** G3
Gundreda Rd *LEWES* BN7............**16** D2

H

Haddington Cl *HOVE* BN3...........**44** D4
Haddington St *HOVE* BN3...........**44** D3
Hadley Av *SALV* BN13..................**37** H3
Hadlow Cl *BRIE/ROTT* BN2.........**46** D4
Hadlow Wy *LAN/SOMP* BN15.....**39** H4
Hadrian Av *STHW* BN42..............**42** D2
Haig Av *BRI* BN1..........................**28** D1
Hailsham Av *BRIE/ROTT* BN2......**61** H2
Hailsham Cl *ANG/EP* BN16..........**52** E3
Hailsham Rd *WTHG* BN11............**54** D4
Hairpin Cft *PEAHV* BN10.............**63** E4
Halewick Cl *LAN/SOMP* BN15....**39** E2
Halewick La *LAN/SOMP* BN15....**39** E2
Half Moon La *SALV* BN13...........**36** D3
Half Moon Pde *SALV* BN13 *.......**36** D3
Halifax Dr *SALV* BN13.................**36** A4
Halland Rd *BRIE/ROTT* BN2........**29** F3
Hall Av *SALV* BN13......................**37** E3
Hall Cl *SALV* BN13......................**37** E3
Hallett Rd *BRIE/ROTT* BN2..........**46** D3
Hallyburton Rd *HOVE* BN3..........**43** H2
Halsbury Cl *WTHG* BN11................**5** H1
Halsbury Rd *WTHG* BN11..............**5** J2
Hamble Gdns *SALV* BN13............**36** A3
Hamble La *LAN/SOMP* BN15......**38** D4
Hamble Wy *SALV* BN13...............**36** A3
Ham Cl *WTHG* BN11....................**56** C1
Hamilton Ct *PTSD* BN41.............**25** E4
  SALV BN13..................................**38** A5
Hamilton Ct *FERR* BN12..............**54** B2
Hamilton Ms *LAN/SOMP* BN15 *.**39** E3
Hamilton Rd *BRI* BN1..................**45** H2
  LAN/SOMP BN15.......................**39** F3
Ham La *LEWES* BN7.....................**17** F4
Hammond Dr *SALV* BN13............**36** B2
Hammy Cl *SHOR* BN43................**41** H2
Hammy La *SHOR* BN43................**41** H2
Hammy Wy *SHOR* BN43..............**41** H2
Hampden Rd *BRIE/ROTT* BN2.....**46** C3
Hampshire Ct *BRIE/ROTT* BN2 *...**3** K6
Hampstead Rd *BRI* BN1...............**45** F1
Hampton Pl *BRI* BN1.....................**2** D4
Hampton St *BRI* BN1.....................**2** D4
Hampton Ter *BRI* BN1....................**2** D3
Ham Rd *SHOR* BN43....................**41** F3
  WTHG BN11..................................**56** C2
Hamsey Cl *BRIE/ROTT* BN2.........**47** F5
Hamsey Cl *LEWES* BN7...............**16** C2
Hamsey La *SEAF* BN25................**73** H1
Hamsey Rd *BRIE/ROTT* BN2........**61** H5
Ham Wy *WTHG* BN11..................**56** C1
Hancock Wy *SHOR* BN43............**41** H4
Hangleton Cl *HOVE* BN3..............**25** H5
Hangleton Gdns *HOVE* BN3.........**43** H4
Hangleton Gra *FERR* BN12..........**52** E2
Hangleton La *FERR* BN12............**52** D1
  HOVE BN3...................................**25** G5
Hangleton Manor Cl *HOVE* BN3..**25** H4
Hangleton Rd *HOVE* BN3............**26** A5
Hangleton Valley Dr *HOVE* BN3...**25** H4
Hangleton Wy *HOVE* BN3............**25** H5
Hanover Cl *SEAF* BN25................**69** G2
Hanover Crs *BRIE/ROTT* BN2........**3** K1
Hanover Ms *BRIE/ROTT* BN2........**3** K1
Hanover Pl *BRIE/ROTT* BN2........**46** B3
Hanover St *BRIE/ROTT* BN2..........**3** K1
Hanover Ter *BRIE/ROTT* BN2........**3** K1
Hanson Rd *NEWHV* BN9..............**68** B2
Harbour View Cl *SEAF* BN25 *.....**69** H2
Harbour View Rd *NEWHV* BN9....**68** B2
Harbour Wy *SHOR* BN43.............**41** G4
Hardwick Rd *HOVE* BN3..............**26** A4
Hardwick Wy *HOVE* BN3.............**26** A3
Hardy Cl *SHOR* BN43..................**41** F4
Harebell Dr *PTSD* BN41..............**24** D3
Harefield Av *SALV* BN13..............**54** D1
Harfield Cl *NEWHV* BN9..............**65** F3
Harison Rd *SEAF* BN25................**71** E4
Harlech Cl *SALV* BN13.................**35** H5
Harmsworth Crs *HOVE* BN3.........**26** A4
Harpers Rd *NEWHV* BN9.............**68** C1
Harrington Pl *BRI* BN1.................**28** B5
Harrington Rd *BRI* BN1................**27** G5
Harrington Vls *BRI* BN1...............**27** H5
Harrison Ct *SALV* BN13...............**38** B5

Harrison Rd *SALV* BN13..............
Harrow Cl *SEAF* BN25.................
Harrow Rd *WTHG* BN11..............
Hartfield Av *BRI* BN1...................
Hartfield Rd *BRIE/ROTT* BN2......
  SEAF BN25
Harting Cl *FERR* BN12.................
Hartington Pl *BRIE/ROTT* BN2....
Hartington Rd *BRIE/ROTT* BN2...
Hartington Ter *BRIE/ROTT* BN2...
Hartington Vls *BRIE/ROTT* BN2...
Harvard Cl *LEWES* BN7...............
Harvest Cl *PEAHV* BN10.............
Harvey Rd *FERR* BN12................
Harveys Wy *LEWES* BN7.............
Harwood Av *FERR* BN12.............
Hastings Av *SEAF* BN25..............
Hastings Rd *BRIE/ROTT* BN2......
  WTHG BN11
Havelock Rd *BRI* BN1..................
Haven Brow *SEAF* BN25..............
Havenside *SHOR* BN43...............
The Haven *LAN/SOMP* BN15 *....
Haven Wy *NEWHV* BN9..............
Hawkenbury Wy *LEWES* BN7......
Hawkhurst Pl *BRI* BN1 *..............
Hawkhurst Rd *BRI* BN1...............
Hawkins Cl *SHOR* BN43..............
Hawkins Crs *SHOR* BN43............
Hawkins Rd *SHOR* BN43.............
Hawth Cl *SEAF* BN25..................
Hawth Crs *SEAF* BN25.................
Hawth Gv *SEAF* BN25..................
Hawth Hl *SEAF* BN25...................
Hawthorn Bank
  BRIE/ROTT BN2 *.......................
Hawthorn Cl *BRIE/ROTT* BN2......
Hawthorn Crs *SALV* BN13............
Hawthorn Gdns *SALV* BN13.........
Hawthorn Ri *NEWHV* BN9...........
Hawthorn Rd *SALV* BN13............
Hawthorn Wy *PTSD* BN41...........
Hawth Park Rd *SEAF* BN25..........
Hawth Ri *SEAF* BN25...................
Hawth Wy *SEAF* BN25.................
Haybourne Cl *BRIE/ROTT* BN2....
Haybourne Rd *BRIE/ROTT* BN2...
Hayes Cl *PTSD* BN41...................
Hayley Rd *LAN/SOMP* BN15.......
Hayling Gdns *SALV* BN13............
Hayling Ri *SALV* BN13.................
Haynes Rd *SALV* BN13................
Haynes Wy *SALV* BN13...............
Hayward Rd *LEWES* BN7.............
Haywards Rd *BRI* BN1.................
Hazel Cl *NEWHV* BN9..................
  PTSD BN41
Hazeldene *SALV* BN13.................
Hazeldene Meads *BRI* BN1..........
Hazelhurst Crs *SALV* BN13..........
Hazelmead Dr *ANG/EP* BN16......
Hazel Rd *ANG/EP* BN16...............
Hazelwood Cl *SALV* BN13...........
Headland Av *SEAF* BN25.............
Headland Cnr *SEAF* BN25 *.........
Headlands Cl *PEAHV* BN10..........
Heathdown Cl *PEAHV* BN10........
Heather La *SALV* BN13................
Heatherstone Rd *WTHG* BN11.....
Heathfield Av *BRIE/ROTT* BN2....
Heathfield Crs *PTSD* BN41...........
Heathfield Dr *PTSD* BN41............
Heathfield Rd *SEAF* BN25............
Heath Hill Av *BRIE/ROTT* BN2.....
Heathy Brow *PEAHV* BN10..........
Hebe Rd *SHOR* BN43..................
Heene Pl *WTHG* BN11.................
Heene Rd *WTHG* BN11.................
Heene Ter *WTHG* BN11................
Heene Wy *WTHG* BN11................
Heighton Crs *NEWHV* BN9...........
Heighton Rd *NEWHV* BN9............
The Heights *BRI* BN1....................
  SALV BN13
Helena Cl *PTSD* BN41.................
Helena Rd *PEAHV* BN10..............
Hellingly Cl *BRIE/ROTT* BN2.......
Hempstead Rd *BRIE/ROTT* BN2...
Henderson Wk *STEY/UB* BN44....
Hendon St *BRIE/ROTT* BN2.........
Henfield Cl *BRIE/ROTT* BN2........
  FERR BN12
Henfield Rd *STEY/UB* BN44.........
Henfield Wy *HOVE* BN3...............
Henge Wy *PTSD* BN41.................
Henley Rd *BRIE/ROTT* BN2.........
Henry Fletcher Cl *ANG/EP* BN16..
Henty Rd *FERR* BN12..................

/ BN13 ....4 C1
rt Rd *BRI* BN1.....................27 H5
/SOMP BN15.....................38 D1
ord St *BRIE/ROTT* BN2...........3 K5
ard Wy *LEWES* BN7 ....17 F2
one CI *FERR* BN12................52 D2
t Ter *SALV* BN13 *................18 C1
Rd *FERR* BN12.....................53 F5
sdale Rd *BRIE/ROTT* BN2.....48 D2
erons *LAN/SOMP* BN15 *.....57 H1
rd *BRI* BN1.........................28 B5
HG BN11...............................4 E3
n Av *BRI* BN1......................13 H5
ott CI *LAN/SOMP* BN15.......39 D2
orth CI *BRIE/ROTT* BN2........48 D2
ank *BRI* BN1.......................27 E2
rook CI *BRIE/ROTT* BN2........28 D5
ere Wy *SALV* BN13..............35 H5
CI *PTSD* BN41.....................43 E1
oft Vis *BRI* BN1...................45 C1
own STHW BN42...................42 D1
own Av *SALV* BN13..............37 E5
own CI *ANG/EP* BN16...........34 A5
N12.......................................53 E2
W BN42.................................42 D1
ead Rd *HOVE* BN3...............45 C3
ES BN7...............................16 C2
own Wy *FERR* BN12............53 E2
eld CI *ANG/EP* BN16.............34 A5
eld Crs *BRI* BN1..................28 A2
eld Rd *SALV* BN13...............37 E4
elds *BRI* BN1.......................29 E2
rove Gdns *WTHG* BN11.........4 B5
ands CI *SALV* BN13.............36 C1
ands Rd *PTSD* BN41............43 F1
BN25.....................................70 D5
Park Av *HOVE* BN3.............26 A4
ted Pk *PEAHV* BN10.............63 F3
BRIE/ROTT BN2.....................3 J5
/ROTT BN2............................60 D4
ES* BN7................................17 F3
VHV BN9................................68 C1
D BN41...................................43 E1
/ BN13...................................37 E5
BN25....................................72 C1
R BN43.................................41 E3
V/UB BN44...............................7 F3
HG BN11................................5 G4
ew *LAN/SOMP* BN15...........39 F1
w *SALV* BN13......................36 D1
ew Av North *BRI* BN1...........27 G1
ew Av South *BRI* BN1..........27 G1
ew Rd *BRI* BN1....................27 G1
HV BN10...............................66 A1
ew Wy *BRI* BN1...................27 G1
e Rd *BRIE/ROTT* BN2...........28 D5
ays *PTSD* BN41...................25 F5
ghway *BRIE/ROTT* BN2........28 D5
HV BN10................................67 H2
CI *SALV* BN13.....................36 B5
e Pk *FERR* BN12.................36 B5
ve Rd *BRIE/ROTT* BN2..........61 H2
nk CI *PTSD* BN41................24 D4
n Av *LAN/SOMP* BN15.........39 F2
rn La *SALV* BN13................37 G3
rn Pde *LAN/SOMP* BN15 *...39 C2
ow *HOVE* BN3......................26 D3
w Rd *BRI* BN1.....................27 E3
t Rd *BRI* BN1.......................27 E2
est Rd *NEWHV* BN9..............68 C2
st Rd *NEWHV* BN9................68 C2
ift *PTSD* BN41.....................24 D5
HOVE BN3.............................26 D4
rm Wy STHW BN42................24 A5
n CI *LEWES* BN7..................17 C3
NEWHV BN9.........................65 F4
BN25.....................................70 A3
e Av *LAN/SOMP* BN15.........39 F2
BRIE/ROTT BN2...................61 F4
ES BN7...............................16 C2
VHV BN9................................65 F4
le *NEWHV* BN9....................68 D1
e *BRIE/ROTT* BN2................28 D5
D BN41.................................43 G1
W BN42.................................42 D1
e Av *SALV* BN13.................37 F3
* BN25..................................71 G4
le Crs *ANG/EP* BN16............34 A5
e Rd *LAN/SOMP* BN15.........39 C2
e Wy *BRI* BN1.....................27 E3
d *STEY/UB* BN44.....................7 E4
o *BRI* BN1..........................26 D2
o CI *PTSD* BN41.................24 D5
o Wy *NEWHV* BN9..............68 B3
w Crs *ANG/EP* BN16............52 A3
w Ri *SALV* BN13.................36 D1
w Rd *BRIE/ROTT* BN2..........47 G2
/ BN13...................................18 D5
eld *LEWES* BN7...................16 D4

Hindover Crs *SEAF* BN25.........71 E4
Hindover Rd *SEAF* BN25...........71 E4
Hinton CI *BRI* BN1....................28 C5
Hobart CI *SALV* BN13................36 A4
Hobs Acre *STEY/UB* BN44..........8 B3
Hoddern Av *PEAHV* BN10..........66 D2
Hodshrove PI *BRIE/ROTT* BN2 *...29 E4
Hodshrove Rd *BRIE/ROTT* BN2...29 E4
Hoe Ct *LAN/SOMP* BN15............40 A1
Hogarth Rd *HOVE* BN3..............44 B3
Hogs Edge *BRIE/ROTT* BN2.......29 C5
The Holdings *LEWES* BN7...........32 B2
Holland Ms *HOVE* BN3................2 A4
Holland Rd *HOVE* BN3.................2 A4
   STEY/UB BN44.............................7 F3
Holland St *BRIE/ROTT* BN2.........3 K3
Hollingbury Copse *BRI* BN1......28 A3
Hollingbury Crs *BRI* BN1...........46 B1
Hollingbury Gdns *SALV* BN13....19 E4
Hollingbury Park Av *BRI* BN1....28 A5
Hollingbury PI *BRI* BN1.............28 B5
Hollingbury Ri *BRI* BN1.............28 B4
Hollingbury Ri West *BRI* BN1....28 B4
Hollingbury Rd *BRI* BN1............46 B1
Hollingbury Ter *BRI* BN1...........46 B1
Hollingdean La *BRI* BN1............46 B2
Hollingdean Rd *BRIE/ROTT* BN2..46 C2
Hollingdean St *BRI* BN1............46 B1
Hollingdean Ter *BRI* BN1...........46 B1
Hollyacres *SALV* BN13...............36 A2
Holly CI *BRI* BN1.......................27 G4
   SALV BN13..................................36 A5
Holmbush CI *SHOR* BN43...........24 B5
Holmbush Wy STHW BN42............42 B1
Holmcroft Gdns *SALV* BN13.......18 C2
Holmdale Rd *NEWHV* BN9..........65 H4
Holmes Av *HOVE* BN3.................44 B1
Holmes CI *SEAF* BN25................69 C2
Holters Wy *SEAF* BN25..............70 D3
Holton HI *BRIE/ROTT* BN2..........48 C3
The Holt *SEAF* BN25..................70 D3
Holtview Rd *BRIE/ROTT* BN2.......47 H2
Homebush Av *BRIE/ROTT* BN2....61 H4
   LEWES BN7................................62 B2
Home Farm Rd *BRI* BN1.............28 D4
Homefield CI *SEAF* BN25............70 D4
Homefield Rd *SEAF* BN25............70 D4
   WTHG BN11.................................5 H2
Homelands Av *ANG/EP* BN16......52 A5
Home Rd *BRI* BN1......................27 G5
Honey Cft *HOVE* BN3.................25 H3
Honey La *ANG/EP* BN16.............34 A5
Honeysuckle CI
   LAN/SOMP BN15..........................39 F1
Honeysuckle La *SALV* BN13........18 B5
Hoopers CI *LEWES* BN7..............17 E1
Horley PI *BRIE/ROTT* BN2...........47 G1
Hornby PI *BRIE/ROTT* BN2 *........47 G1
Hornby Rd *BRIE/ROTT* BN2.........47 F1
Horsfield Rd *LEWES* BN7............16 D1
Horsham Av *PEAHV* BN10............66 D2
Horsham Av North
   PEAHV BN10...............................63 E5
Horsham CI *BRIE/ROTT* BN2.......47 F4
Horsham Rd *STEY/UB* BN44.........7 F1
Horton PI *ANG/EP* BN16.............52 A1
Horton Rd *BRI* BN1....................46 B1
Houndean CI *LEWES* BN7...........16 C4
Houndean Ri *LEWES* BN7...........16 C4
Hova Vis *HOVE* BN3...................44 D4
Hove Gdns *HOVE* BN3.................44 D2
Hove Park Rd *HOVE* BN3.............45 E1
Hove Park Vis *HOVE* BN3............44 D2
Hove Park Wy *HOVE* BN3............45 E1
Hove PI *HOVE* BN3.....................44 D5
Hove St *HOVE* BN3.....................44 C5
Howard Ct *HOVE* BN3 *...............26 B5
Howard PI *BRI* BN1.....................2 A1
Howard Rd *BRIE/ROTT* BN2.........46 C3
   LAN/SOMP BN15..........................39 C1
Howard St *WTHG* BN11................4 C3
Howard Ter *BRI* BN1....................2 A1
Howey CI *NEWHV* BN9................65 H4
Hoyle Rd *PEAHV* BN10................67 E1
Hudson CI *SALV* BN13.................36 B3
Hughes Rd *BRIE/ROTT* BN2.........46 B2
Humber Av *SALV* BN13...............36 A3
Humber CI *SALV* BN13................36 A3
Humphrey's Gap *SHOR* BN43......41 G4
Humphrys Rd *WTHG* BN11...........4 E5
Hunston CI *BRIE/ROTT* BN2........48 D3
Hurdis Rd *SEAF* BN25.................69 G2
Hurley Rd *SALV* BN13.................36 C1
Hurst Av *WTHG* BN11..................54 D3
Hurst Crs *PTSD* BN41..................43 F2
Hurstfield *LAN/SOMP* BN15.........39 F5
Hurst HI *BRI* BN1........................28 C2
Hurston CI *SALV* BN13................37 E2
Hutton Rd *BRI* BN1......................28 B4

Hyde CI *LEWES* BN7....................32 A2
Hyde La *STEY/UB* BN44.................8 B3
Hyde Sq *STEY/UB* BN44 *..............8 B2
Hyde St *STEY/UB* BN44.................8 B2
The Hyde *BRIE/ROTT* BN2............47 F1
Hylden CI *BRIE/ROTT* BN2............47 H1
Hythe CI *SEAF* BN25...................71 G3
   WTHG BN11...............................55 E4
Hythe Crs *SEAF* BN25.................71 G4
Hythe Rd *BRI* BN1......................28 A5
   WTHG BN11...............................55 E4
Hythe Vw *SEAF* BN25..................71 G4

Iden CI *BRIE/ROTT* BN2...............47 E5
Ifield CI *BRIE/ROTT* BN2..............62 B3
Iford CI *NEWHV* BN9....................64 D3
Ilex Ct *FERR* BN12 *....................53 H3
Ilex Wy *FERR* BN12.....................53 H3
Imperial Ar *BRI* BN1 *...................2 E4
Ingham Dr *BRI* BN1.....................45 F1
Inglecroft Ct *LAN/SOMP* BN15 *...39 E3
Ingle Green *LEWES* BN7..............16 D4
Ingleside Crs *LAN/SOMP* BN15....39 G5
Ingleside St *BRI* BN1...................46 B1
Ingram Crs East *HOVE* BN3.........44 A2
Ingram Crs West *HOVE* BN3........44 A3
Ingram Rd *STEY/UB* BN44 *...........7 E4
Inverness Rd *BRIE/ROTT* BN2......46 C2
Inwood Crs *BRI* BN1...................45 F1
Irelands La *LEWES* BN7...............16 D3
Irene Av *LAN/SOMP* BN15............39 F3
Isabel CI *SEAF* BN25...................70 C3
Isabel Crs *HOVE* BN3..................44 A2
Isfield Rd *BRI* BN1......................28 C5
Islingword PI *BRIE/ROTT* BN2......46 C4
Islingword Rd *BRIE/ROTT* BN2 *.....3 K1
Islingword St *BRIE/ROTT* BN2........3 K2
Iveagh Crs *NEWHV* BN9...............64 D4
Ivor CI *BRIE/ROTT* BN2................48 A1
Ivory PI *BRIE/ROTT* BN2 *.............3 J3
Ivy Arch CI *SALV* BN13...............18 D1
Ivy Arch Rd *SALV* BN13...............55 F2
Ivydore Av *SALV* BN13................36 A5
Ivydore CI *SALV* BN13.................36 B3
Ivy Ms *HOVE* BN3 *......................2 B4
Ivy PI *HOVE* BN3..........................2 B4
   WTHG BN11..................................4 B6

Jackson Ms *NEWHV* BN9..............68 C1
Jackson St *BRIE/ROTT* BN2..........3 K2
James CI *SALV* BN13...................36 D4
Japonica CI *SHOR* BN43..............41 H1
Jarvis La *STEY/UB* BN44................7 F3
Jason CI *PEAHV* BN10.................67 E1
Jay Rd *PEAHV* BN10....................67 G2
Jefferies La *FERR* BN12..............54 A4
Jersey Rd *FERR* BN12.................53 F2
Jersey St *BRIE/ROTT* BN2.............3 J2
Jesmond Rd *HOVE* BN3...............44 A3
Jevington CI *SALV* BN13.............35 H5
Jevington Dr *BRIE/ROTT* BN2......46 D1
   SEAF BN25................................70 A4
Jew St *BRI* BN1............................3 G4
John Howard Cotts
   BRIE/ROTT BN2 *.........................59 F1
Johns CI *PEAHV* BN10.................63 E3
Johnson Bank
   BRIE/ROTT BN2 *.........................46 C3
John St *BRIE/ROTT* BN2................3 J4
   SHOR BN43...............................41 E3
Jubilee Ct *BRIE/ROTT* BN2 *........29 E5
Jubilee Gdns *SEAF* BN25............71 E5
Jubilee Homes *NEWHV* BN9 *......68 C1
Jubilee Rd STHW BN42..................43 E2
Jubilee St *BRI* BN1.......................3 G4
Juggs CI *LEWES* BN7...................16 D4
Jugg's Rd *LEWES* BN7................16 D4
Julian Rd *HOVE* BN3.....................2 D1
Junction Rd *BRI* BN1....................3 F2
Juniper CI *PTSD* BN41.................25 F4
   SALV BN13................................36 A5
   SEAF BN25................................71 G5
Juno CI *FERR* BN12.....................54 A3
Jupp's La *FERR* BN12..................53 H2

Kammond Av *SEAF* BN25..............71 F3

Katherine Wy *SEAF* BN25............70 B3
Kearsley Dr *SALV* BN13...............37 E1
Kedale Rd *SEAF* BN25.................70 C4
Keere St *LEWES* BN7...................17 E4
Kelly Rd *HOVE* BN3......................45 F1
Kelso CI *SALV* BN13.....................54 C1
Kemp St *BRI* BN1..........................3 G3
Kemptown Ms
   BRIE/ROTT BN2 *.........................59 F1
Kemp Town PI *BRIE/ROTT* BN2....58 D1
Kendal Rd *HOVE* BN3..................44 B2
   LAN/SOMP BN15..........................39 E4
Kenilworth CI *BRIE/ROTT* BN2.....29 C5
Kenmure Av *BRI* BN1...................14 A5
Kennedy Wy *NEWHV* BN9............68 B3
Kennet CI *SALV* BN13..................36 B3
Kensington Gdns *BRI* BN1............3 G3
Kensington PI *BRI* BN1.................3 G3
Kensington St *BRI* BN1.................3 G3
Kent CI *SHOR* BN43.....................42 A3
Kent Flds *LEWES* BN7.................32 A2
Kenton Rd *HOVE* BN3...................43 H3
Kenwards *BRI* BN1.......................14 D5
Kenwood Quay
   LAN/SOMP BN15 *........................39 H5
Kerry Gdns *ANG/EP* BN16...........52 A3
Kestrel CI *HOVE* BN3...................45 F2
Keswick CI *FERR* BN12................36 B5
Kevin Gdns *BRIE/ROTT* BN2........48 C2
Kew St *BRI* BN1............................3 F3
Keymer Av *PEAHV* BN10..............67 F2
Keymer Crs *FERR* BN12...............54 A4
Keymer Rd *BRI* BN1....................28 B2
Keymer Wy *FERR* BN12...............54 A4
Keystone CI *FERR* BN12..............54 A4
Kilmore CI *SALV* BN13.................18 C1
Kimber CI *LAN/SOMP* BN15.........39 F5
Kimberley Rd *BRIE/ROTT* BN2......46 D2
   SEAF BN25................................70 A4
Kinfauns Dr *SALV* BN13...............18 B5
King Alfred CI *STEY/UB* BN44........7 F3
King Edward Av *HOVE* BN3............5 F1
King Edward CI *SALV* BN13...........5 G1
Kingfisher CI *SALV* BN13............36 A5
King George Rd *SHOR* BN43........42 A2
King George VI Av *HOVE* BN3.......26 C4
King George VI Dr *HOVE* BN3.......26 C4
King George VI Man
   HOVE BN3 *................................26 B5
King Henry's Rd *LEWES* BN7........16 D2
King PI *BRI* BN1............................3 F4
King's Av *NEWHV* BN9..................68 B3
Kings Barn End *STEY/UB* BN44 *....7 H3
King's Barn La *STEY/UB* BN44.......7 H2
King's Barn Vis *STEY/UB* BN44.....7 G3
Kingsbridge Ms *SALV* BN13.........36 B3
Kingsbury Rd *BRI* BN1.................46 A3
Kingsbury St *BRI* BN1..................46 A3
Kings CI *LAN/SOMP* BN15............39 H5
   PEAHV BN10...............................62 D4
Kings Crs *SHOR* BN43.................40 D5
Kings Dr *SHOR* BN43....................40 D4
King's Esp *HOVE* BN3..................44 C5
Kings Gap *SHOR* BN43................40 D5
King's Gdns *HOVE* BN3................44 D5
Kingsland CI *SHOR* BN43.............42 A3
Kingsland Rd *SALV* BN13.............37 H4
Kingsley CI *SALV* BN13...............56 B1
Kingsley Rd *BRI* BN1...................45 F1
   LEWES BN7...............................16 D2
Kingsmead *SEAF* BN25................70 C4
Kingsmead CI *SEAF* BN25............70 C4
   STEY/UB BN44.............................7 F5
King's Mead La *SEAF* BN25..........70 B4
Kingsmead Wk *SEAF* BN25..........70 C4
Kingsmead Wy *SEAF* BN25..........70 C4
Kingsmere *BRI* BN1 *...................27 G5
Kings Ms *HOVE* BN3....................44 D4
Kings Pde *BRI* BN1 *....................28 A5
King's Ride *SEAF* BN25................70 B4
King's Rd *BRI* BN1........................2 D5
   LAN/SOMP BN15..........................39 C5
   STHW BN42..................................42 B1
Kings Rd Arches *BRI* BN1.............3 F6
King's Stone Av *STEY/UB* BN44 *...7 H4
Kingsthorpe Rd *HOVE* BN3...........44 A2
Kingston Av *SEAF* BN25...............71 F5
Kingston Bay Rd *SHOR* BN43.......42 A4
Kingston Broadway
   SHOR BN43...............................42 A1
Kingston CI *BRI* BN1....................29 E3
   HOVE BN3..................................26 A5
   SEAF BN25................................71 F5
   SHOR BN43...............................42 A2
Kingston Gn *SEAF* BN25..............71 F5
Kingston La *ANG/EP* BN16............52 B4
   STHW BN42..................................42 B3
Kingston Rdg *LEWES* BN7............31 H1
Kingston Rd *LEWES* BN7..............32 C1

Kingston Wy *SEAF* BN25..............73 G1
   SHOR BN43..............42 A1
King St *BRI* BN1..............3 C4
   SALV BN13..............55 H1
Kings Wk *SHOR* BN43..............40 D5
Kingsway *HOVE* BN3..............44 B4
   SEAF BN25..............70 B4
   WTHG BN11 *..............54 D3
Kingswood St *BRIE/ROTT* BN2 ...3 H5
Kinleside Wy *ANG/EP* BN16..............34 A5
Kipling Av *BRIE/ROTT* BN2..............48 C2
   FERR BN12..............53 H2
Kirby Dr *PEAHV* BN10..............62 C4
Kithurst Cl *FERR* BN12..............53 H1
Kithurst Crs *FERR* BN12..............53 H1
Knepp Cl *BRIE/ROTT* BN2..............29 F5
Knole Rd *BRIE/ROTT* BN2..............61 E4
Knoll Cl *HOVE* BN3..............43 H1
Knoyle Rd *BRI* BN1..............27 G5

L

Laburnum Av *HOVE* BN3..............44 A1
Laburnum Cl *FERR* BN12..............53 F4
   LAN/SOMP BN15..............57 F1
Laburnum Gv *BRI* BN1 *..............28 B4
Ladies Mile Cl *BRI* BN1..............27 H1
Ladies' Mile Rd *BRI* BN1..............27 G1
Ladycross Cl *SEAF* BN25..............71 F5
Ladydell Rd *WTHG* BN11 *..............5 J2
Ladysmith Rd *BRIE/ROTT* BN2 ...46 D2
Laine Cl *BRI* BN1..............27 G4
Laines Rd *STEY/UB* BN44..............7 E4
Lake Dr *PEAHV* BN10..............62 D5
Lambert Pl *LEWES* BN7..............17 F1
Lambleys La *SALV* BN13..............38 B3
Lambourne Cl *BRI* BN1..............28 C5
Lambourne Rd *BRI* BN1..............28 C5
Lamorna Gdns *FERR* BN12..............53 F5
Lamorna Gv *SALV* BN13..............37 G4
Lancaster Rd *BRI* BN1..............45 H3
   FERR BN12..............54 C3
Lancaster St *LEWES* BN7..............17 E3
Lancing Cl *LAN/SOMP* BN15..............39 F4
Lancing Pk *LAN/SOMP* BN15..............57 F1
Landport Rd *LEWES* BN7..............16 D1
Landsdown Rd *SEAF* BN25..............71 G3
Landseer Rd *HOVE* BN3..............44 C2
Lanfranc Rd *SALV* BN13..............4 A1
Langbury Cl *FERR* BN12..............52 D2
Langbury La *FERR* BN12..............53 E2
Langdale Cl *LAN/SOMP* BN15..............39 F5
Langdale Gdns *HOVE* BN3..............44 B4
Langdale Rd *HOVE* BN3..............44 B4
Langham Gdns *WTHG* BN11..............55 E4
Langley Crs *BRIE/ROTT* BN2..............48 B1
Langridge Dr *PTSD* BN41..............25 E5
Langton Rd *SALV* BN13..............4 E1
Lansdowne Ct *WTHG* BN11..............55 E5
Lansdowne Ms *HOVE* BN3..............2 A4
   WTHG BN11..............55 E5
Lansdowne Pl *HOVE* BN3..............2 A4
   WTHG BN11..............55 E5
Lansdowne Rd *HOVE* BN3..............2 B3
   WTHG BN11..............55 E5
Lansdowne Sq *HOVE* BN3..............2 A4
Lansdowne St *HOVE* BN3..............2 A3
Lansdown Pl *LEWES* BN7..............17 F4
Lapierre Rd *NEWHV* BN9..............68 B1
Larch Cl *BRIE/ROTT* BN2..............48 D3
Larke Cl *SHOR* BN43..............42 A3
Larkfield Cl *LAN/SOMP* BN15..............39 H5
Larkfield Wy *BRI* BN1..............28 A3
Lark Hl *HOVE* BN3..............26 A4
Lashmar Rd *ANG/EP* BN16..............52 A4
Latimer Rd *WTHG* BN11..............54 D4
Laughton Rd *BRIE/ROTT* BN2..............48 D2
Laurel Cl *SALV* BN13..............36 A5
Lauriston Rd *BRI* BN1..............27 G5
The Laurels *BRIE/ROTT* BN2 *..............46 B2
Lavant Cl *FERR* BN12..............53 E2
Lavender Hl *SHOR* BN43..............41 H1
Lavender St *BRIE/ROTT* BN2..............3 K6
Lavington Rd *SALV* BN13..............37 F4
Lavinia Ct *FERR* BN12..............54 A2
Lavinia Wy *ANG/EP* BN16..............52 A4
Lawes Av *NEWHV* BN9..............68 C1
The Lawns *LAN/SOMP* BN15..............39 E3
Lawrence Rd *HOVE* BN3..............44 B3
Laylands Rd *PTSD* BN41..............43 E3
Leahurst Ct *BRI* BN1..............27 G4
Leahurst Court Rd *BRI* BN1..............27 G4
Lea Rd *PEAHV* BN10..............62 D5
The Leas *PEAHV* BN10..............67 H3
Leconfield Rd *LAN/SOMP* BN15..............39 F5
Leeds Cl *SALV* BN13..............35 H5
Lee Rd *LEWES* BN7..............16 D2
Leeward Cl *SALV* BN13..............36 D5

Leeward Rd *SALV* BN13..............36 D5
Lee Wy *NEWHV* BN9..............64 B5
Leicester Rd *LEWES* BN7..............16 D3
Leicester St *BRIE/ROTT* BN2..............3 K5
Leicester Vls *HOVE* BN3..............43 H3
Leigh Rd *SALV* BN13..............37 H4
Leighton Av *SALV* BN13..............38 A4
Leighton Rd *HOVE* BN3..............44 C2
Lenham Av *BRIE/ROTT* BN2..............61 F4
Lenham Rd East
   BRIE/ROTT BN2..............61 F4
Lenham Rd West
   BRIE/ROTT BN2..............61 E4
Lenhurst Wy *SALV* BN13..............36 D5
Lennox Rd *HOVE* BN3..............44 B2
   SHOR BN43..............41 H2
   WTHG BN11..............5 F3
Lennox St *BRIE/ROTT* BN2..............3 K4
Leopold Rd *BRI* BN1..............2 E3
Lesser Foxholes *SHOR* BN43..............40 D1
Letchworth Cl *FERR* BN12..............53 E4
Lewes Cl *BRIE/ROTT* BN2..............62 A4
Lewes Crs *BRIE/ROTT* BN2..............59 E2
Lewes Ms *BRIE/ROTT* BN2 *..............59 E1
Lewes Rd *BRI* BN1..............29 C1
   BRIE/ROTT BN2..............3 J2
   NEWHV BN9..............68 C1
Lewes St *BRIE/ROTT* BN2..............3 J2
Lewin Cl *LAN/SOMP* BN15..............39 H3
Lewis Cl *NEWHV* BN9..............65 F3
Lewis Ct *SALV* BN13..............35 H5
Lewis Rd *LAN/SOMP* BN15..............39 F2
Lewry Cl *NEWHV* BN9..............68 B1
Lexden Ct *SEAF* BN25 *..............71 E4
Lexden Dr *SEAF* BN25..............70 D3
Lexden Rd *SEAF* BN25..............70 D3
Leybourne Cl *BRIE/ROTT* BN2..............47 G1
Leybourne Rd *BRIE/ROTT* BN2 ...29 C5
Library Pl *WTHG* BN11..............5 C5
Lichfield Ct *WTHG* BN11 *..............55 H4
Lilac Cl *SALV* BN13..............35 H5
Limbrick Cl *FERR* BN12..............54 A2
Limbrick Cnr *FERR* BN12..............54 A1
Limbrick La *FERR* BN12..............54 A2
Limbrick Wy *FERR* BN12..............53 H1
Lime Rd *SALV* BN13..............18 C1
The Limes *BRIE/ROTT* BN2 *..............46 B2
Lime Tree Av *SALV* BN13..............36 D1
Limney Rd *BRIE/ROTT* BN2..............47 E3
Lincett Av *SALV* BN13..............54 D2
Lincett Dr *SALV* BN13..............54 D2
Linchmere Av *BRIE/ROTT* BN2 ...61 C4
Lincoln Av *PEAHV* BN10..............66 C1
Lincoln Av South *PEAHV* BN10...66 C1
Lincoln Cots *PTSD* BN41..............3 K2
   SALV BN13..............54 D1
Lincoln St *BRIE/ROTT* BN2..............3 K2
The Lindens *BRIE/ROTT* BN2 *..............46 B3
Lindfield *PTSD* BN41 *..............43 E1
Lindfield Av *SEAF* BN25..............73 C1
Lindfield Cl *BRIE/ROTT* BN2..............61 F3
Lindum Rd *SALV* BN13..............36 D5
Lindum Wy *SALV* BN13..............36 D5
Lingfield Cl *SALV* BN13..............36 D4
Links Av *NEWHV* BN9..............68 A1
Links Cl *PTSD* BN41..............43 C2
   SEAF BN25..............71 E5
Links Rd *LAN/SOMP* BN15..............39 H4
   PTSD BN41..............43 C2
   SALV BN13..............37 E2
   SEAF BN25..............73 E1
The Linkway *BRI* BN1..............28 B5
   WTHG BN11 *..............4 C3
Linthouse Cl *PEAHV* BN10..............63 F3
Linton Rd *HOVE* BN3..............44 B2
Lions Ct *BRIE/ROTT* BN2 *..............47 E5
Lions Pl *SEAF* BN25..............72 D1
Liphook Cl *BRI* BN1..............46 C1
Lisher Rd *LAN/SOMP* BN15..............39 H3
Little Crs *BRIE/ROTT* BN2..............61 F4
Little Dr *FERR* BN12..............53 E4
Little Dro *STEY/UB* BN44..............7 F5
Little East St *BRI* BN1 *..............3 G6
   LEWES BN7..............17 F3
Little Gables *SALV* BN13..............36 D4
Littlehampton Rd *FERR* BN12..............52 C2
   SALV BN13..............36 D4
Little High St *SHOR* BN43..............41 E3
Littleworth Cl *BRIE/ROTT* BN2..............47 E1
Liverpool Gdns *WTHG* BN11..............5 F5
Liverpool Rd *WTHG* BN11..............5 F5

Liverpool Ter *WTHG* BN11..............5 F5
Livesay Crs *SALV* BN13..............55 H1
Livingstone Rd *HOVE* BN3..............44 D3
Livingstone St *BRIE/ROTT* BN2...46 D5
Lloyd Cl *HOVE* BN3..............45 E2
Lloyd Rd *HOVE* BN3..............45 F2
Lloyds Bank Chambers
   SEAF BN25 *..............70 C5
Lockitt Wy *LEWES* BN7..............32 A2
Locks Crs *PTSD* BN41..............43 F2
Locks Hl *PTSD* BN41..............43 F1
Lockwood Cl *BRIE/ROTT* BN2..............48 C3
Lockwood Crs *BRIE/ROTT* BN2 ...48 C3
Loddon Cl *SALV* BN13..............36 A2
Loder Gdns *SALV* BN13..............37 G5
Loder Pl *BRI* BN1..............27 H5
Loder Rd *BRI* BN1..............27 H5
Lodge Cl *LEWES* BN7..............16 C4
   PTSD BN41..............24 D5
Lodge Ct *SHOR* BN43..............41 E1
Lodsworth Cl *BRIE/ROTT* BN2...47 E3
Lomond Av *BRI* BN1..............14 A5
London Rd *BRI* BN1..............46 A3
London St *WTHG* BN11..............4 C3
London Ter *BRI* BN1..............46 A3
Longfellow Rd *WTHG* BN11..............4 B3
Long Furlong *SALV* BN13..............35 E1
Longhill Cl *BRIE/ROTT* BN2..............60 C2
Longhill Rd *BRIE/ROTT* BN2..............60 B1
Longlands *SALV* BN13..............37 H2
Longlands Gld *SALV* BN13..............37 H2
Longlands Spinney *SALV* BN13...37 H3
Long Meadow *SALV* BN13..............18 D3
Longridge Av *BRIE/ROTT* BN2...61 C5
The Lookout *PEAHV* BN10..............63 E2
Loose La *LAN/SOMP* BN15..............38 D4
The Lords *SEAF* BN25..............70 C2
Lorna Rd *HOVE* BN3..............45 E3
Lorne Rd *BRI* BN1..............46 A2
Lorraine Rd *NEWHV* BN9..............68 D1
Lotts La *LAN/SOMP* BN15..............39 E4
Lover's Wk *BRI* BN1..............45 H2
Lovers Walk Cots *BRI* BN1 *..............45 G2
Lovett Ct *FERR* BN12 *..............54 A1
Lower Beach Rd *SHOR* BN43..............41 F4
Lower Bevendean Av
   BRIE/ROTT BN2..............47 E1
Lower Chalvington Pl
   BRIE/ROTT BN2..............47 E5
Lower Dr *SEAF* BN25..............70 D3
   STHW BN42..............42 C1
Lower Market St *HOVE* BN3..............2 B4
Lower Pl *NEWHV* BN9..............68 C1
Lower Rock Gdns
   BRIE/ROTT BN2..............3 K6
Lowther Rd *BRI* BN1..............28 A5
   SALV BN13..............36 D5
Loxley Gdns *SALV* BN13 *..............4 C1
Loxwood *ANG/EP* BN16..............52 B2
Loxwood Av *SALV* BN13..............37 F5
Lucerne Cl *PTSD* BN41..............43 F1
Lucerne Rd *BRI* BN1..............45 H1
Lucinda Wy *SEAF* BN25..............70 D3
Lucksfield Wy *ANG/EP* BN16..............34 A5
Lucraft Rd *BRIE/ROTT* BN2..............29 F2
Ludlow Ri *BRIE/ROTT* BN2..............47 G1
Lulham Cl *PEAHV* BN10..............62 D3
Lullington Av *HOVE* BN3..............44 B2
Lullington Cl *SEAF* BN25..............73 F1
Lustrells Cl *BRIE/ROTT* BN2..............61 E3
Lustrells Crs *BRIE/ROTT* BN2..............61 E3
Lustrells Rd *BRIE/ROTT* BN2..............61 E3
Lustrells V *BRIE/ROTT* BN2..............61 F3
Luther St *BRIE/ROTT* BN2..............46 C3
Lyminster Av *BRI* BN1..............28 A2
Lynchet Cl *BRI* BN1..............28 C5
Lynchet Down *BRI* BN1..............28 C5
Lynchets Crs *HOVE* BN3..............25 H4
The Lynchets *LEWES* BN7..............17 G1
The Lynchette *SHOR* BN43..............41 F1
Lynchet Wk *BRI* BN1..............28 C5
Lynchmere Av *LAN/SOMP* BN15...39 F2
Lyndhurst Cnr *HOVE* BN3 *..............45 F3
Lyndhurst Rd *HOVE* BN3..............45 F3
   WTHG BN11..............5 G4
Lyn Rd *SALV* BN13..............36 A4
Lynton St *BRIE/ROTT* BN2..............46 C3
Lynwood Rd *BRIE/ROTT* BN2..............61 G5
Lyon Cl *HOVE* BN3..............2 B1
Lyons Wy *SALV* BN13..............38 A2

M

Mackie Av *BRI* BN1..............27 H1
Madehurst Cl *BRIE/ROTT* BN2...46 D3
Madeira Av *WTHG* BN11..............5 H4
Madeira Dr *BRIE/ROTT* BN2..............3 H6

Madeira Pl *BRIE/ROTT* BN2..............
Mafeking Rd *BRIE/ROTT* BN2..............
Magnolia Cl *SALV* BN13..............
Mainstone Rd *HOVE* BN3..............
Major Cl *BRI* BN1..............
Malcolm Cl *FERR* BN12..............
Maldon Rd *BRI* BN1..............
Malines Av *PEAHV* BN10..............
Malines Av South *PEAHV* BN10...
Mallett Cl *SEAF* BN25..............
Malling Cl *LEWES* BN7..............
Malling Down *LEWES* BN7..............
Malling Hl *LEWES* BN7..............
The Mallings *LEWES* BN7 *..............
Malling St *LEWES* BN7..............
Mallory Rd *HOVE* BN3..............
Malthouse Cl *LAN/SOMP* BN15..............
Malthouse La *BRIE/ROTT* BN2..............
The Malthouse *LEWES* BN7 *..............
Malvern Cl *WTHG* BN11..............
Malvern St *HOVE* BN3..............
Manchester St *BRIE/ROTT* BN2..............
Manitoba Wy *SALV* BN13..............
Manor Cl *BRIE/ROTT* BN2..............
   LAN/SOMP BN15..............
   SEAF BN25..............
   STHW BN42..............
   WTHG BN11..............
Manor Ct *LAN/SOMP* BN15 *..............
   SEAF BN25 *..............
   STHW BN42 *..............
Manor Crs *BRIE/ROTT* BN2..............
Manor Dr *PEAHV* BN10..............
Manor Field Ct *SALV* BN13 *..............
Manor Gdns *BRIE/ROTT* BN2..............
Manor Gn *BRIE/ROTT* BN2..............
Manor Hall Rd *STHW* BN42..............
Manor Hl *BRIE/ROTT* BN2..............
Manor Lea *WTHG* BN11 *..............
Manor Paddock *BRIE/ROTT* BN2...
Manor Pde *SALV* BN13 *..............
Manor Pl *BRIE/ROTT* BN2..............
Manor Rd *ANG/EP* BN16..............
   BRIE/ROTT BN2..............
   LAN/SOMP BN15..............
   PTSD BN41..............
   STEY/UB BN44..............
   WTHG BN11..............
Manor Rd North *SEAF* BN25..............
Manor Ter *LEWES* BN7 *..............
The Manor *WTHG* BN11 *..............
Manor View Ct *SALV* BN13..............
Manor Wy *BRIE/ROTT* BN2..............
   LAN/SOMP BN15..............
Mansell Rd *SHOR* BN43..............
Mansfield Cl *WTHG* BN11..............
Mansfield Rd *HOVE* BN3..............
   WTHG BN11..............
Manton Rd *BRIE/ROTT* BN2..............
Maple Cl *BRIE/ROTT* BN2..............
   SALV BN13..............
Maple Gdns *HOVE* BN3..............
Maplehurst Rd *PTSD* BN41..............
Maple Leaf Cl *NEWHV* BN9..............
The Maples *FERR* BN12..............
Maple Wk *LAN/SOMP* BN15..............
Mardale Rd *SALV* BN13..............
Mardyke *SHOR* BN43..............
Maresfield Rd *BRIE/ROTT* BN2..............
Margaret St *BRIE/ROTT* BN2..............
Margery Rd *HOVE* BN3..............
Marina Wy *BRIE/ROTT* BN2..............
Marine Av *HOVE* BN3..............
Marine Cl *BRIE/ROTT* BN2..............
   WTHG BN11..............
Marine Ct *PEAHV* BN10 *..............
Marine Crs *FERR* BN12..............
   SEAF BN25..............
Marine Dr *BRIE/ROTT* BN2..............
   FERR BN12..............
   SEAF BN25..............
Marine Gdns *BRIE/ROTT* BN2..............
Marine Pde *BRIE/ROTT* BN2..............
   SEAF BN25..............
   WTHG BN11..............
Marine Pl *WTHG* BN11..............
Mariners Cl *SHOR* BN43..............
The Mariners *LAN/SOMP* BN15 *..............
Marine Sq *BRIE/ROTT* BN2..............
Marine Vw *BRIE/ROTT* BN2..............
   NEWHV BN9..............
Marjoram Pl *SHOR* BN43..............
Mark Cl *SEAF* BN25..............
Market Fld *STEY/UB* BN44..............
Market La *LEWES* BN7..............
Market St *BRI* BN1..............
   LEWES BN7..............
   WTHG BN11..............
Markwick Ms *WTHG* BN11..............

rough Ms *BRI* BN1 .... 2 E4
rough Pl *BRI* BN1 .... 3 H4
rough Rd *FERR* BN12 .... 54 B3
SOMP BN15 .... 57 E1
rough St *BRI* BN1 .... 2 E3
rlinspike *SHOR* BN43 .... 41 G4
rle Rd *SALV* BN13 .... 38 A5
n Rd *BRIE/ROTT* BN2 .... 59 F1
on Rd *HOVE* BN3 .... 44 B3
all Av *SALV* BN13 .... 18 D4
alls Rw *BRI* BN1 .... 3 H1
/ROTT BN2 .... 46 B3
all Wy *HOVE* BN3 .... 44 B1
n Rd *SALV* BN13 .... 56 A1
o Ms *SEAF* BN25 * 72 C1
o Rd *SEAF* BN25 * 72 C1
a Gunn Rd
/ROTT BN2 .... 46 D1
n Rd *HOVE* BN3 .... 43 H4
artins *PEAHV* BN10 .... 62 D4
artlets *LAN/SOMP* BN15 ....39 E4
EN7 .... 17 F1
t Wy *FERR* BN12 .... 54 A3
artlet *HOVE* BN3 .... 45 F2
ts Cl *BRIE/ROTT* BN2 .... 60 C1
e Rd *SEAF* BN25 .... 70 D4
ck Rd *BRI* BN1 .... 45 F1
in La *STEY/UB* BN44 .... 7 H1
yn Cl *STEY/UB* BN44 .... 7 G5
yn Pk *STEY/UB* BN44 .... 7 F5
yn Pkwy *STEY/UB* BN44 * 7 F5
ce Rd *SEAF* BN25 .... 72 D2
w *SEAF* BN25 .... 71 F5
ridge Crs *FERR* BN12 .... 54 A2
ridge Sq *FERR* BN12 .... 54 A1
l *FERR* BN12 .... 54 A1
ots *BRIE/ROTT* BN2 * 46 C2
eld *ANG/EP* BN16 .... 52 A2
eld Av *PEAHV* BN10 .... 67 F2
eld Cl *BRI* BN1 .... 27 H2
v BN15 .... 57 E2
eld Crs *BRI* BN1 .... 27 H2
ower Sq *BRI* BN1 .... 3 G1
ower Wy *ANG/EP* BN16 ....52 A2
ew Wy *LEWES* BN7 .... 17 F1
t Rd *BRIE/ROTT* BN2 .... 46 B2
e Rd *BRIE/ROTT* BN2 .... 46 D3
ee Av *SALV* BN13 .... 18 D4
ee Cl *LAN/SOMP* BN15 ....38 D4
ee Wk *HOVE* BN3 .... 44 A1
rchar Cl *LAN/SOMP* BN15 ...39 H3
liam Rd *BRIE/ROTT* BN2 ...48 A1
ow Rd *BRIE/ROTT* BN2 ....60 C2
VE BN3 .... 26 D4
W BN42 .... 25 F5
HG BN11 .... 56 D2
ow Crs *WTHG* BN11 .... 56 D2
ow La *LAN/SOMP* BN15 ....39 G5
ow Pde *BRIE/ROTT* BN2 ....60 D2
ow Pk *ANG/EP* BN16 .... 52 B4
ow Rd *HOVE* BN3 .... 44 A1
owside *ANG/EP* BN16 .... 34 A4
owside Ct *FERR* BN12 * 53 G3
eadows *HOVE* BN3 .... 25 G4
VES BN7 .... 17 C1
ow Sweet Cl *SALV* BN13 * ...35 C5
owview *BRIE/ROTT* BN2 * ...47 E1
owview Rd
/SOMP BN15 .... 39 F2
ow Wy *FERR* BN12 .... 53 E3
F BN25 .... 71 F5
s Av *HOVE* BN3 .... 25 C4
s Cl *HOVE* BN3 .... 25 C4
s Rd *SEAF* BN25 .... 70 D5
leads *BRI* BN1 .... 28 D2
way Ct *SALV* BN13 * 35 C5
W BN42 .... 42 B2
way Crs *HOVE* BN3 .... 26 B5
eadway *BRIE/ROTT* BN2 ...47 E1
OR BN43 .... 41 F4
a Cl *LEWES* BN7 .... 17 E1
ham Cl *FERR* BN12 .... 53 F4
na Pl *HOVE* BN3 .... 44 D5
na Ter *HOVE* BN3 .... 44 D5
na Vls *HOVE* BN3 .... 44 D5
nerry Hl *BRIE/ROTT* BN2 ...29 E5
way Cl *SALV* BN13 .... 36 B3
hing Pl *NEWHV* BN9 * 68 D1
hing Ri *NEWHV* BN9 .... 68 D1
hing Rd *NEWHV* BN9 .... 68 D1
hing House La *BRI* BN1 ....3 G5
ourne Av *FERR* BN12 .... 54 A3
ourne Rd *FERR* BN12 .... 54 A3
ourne St *BRIE/ROTT* BN2 ...46 C2
ose Av *PTSD* BN41 .... 43 E1
C1

Melrose Cl *BRI* BN1 .... 28 C5
SALV BN13 .... 54 C1
Melville Rd *HOVE* BN3 .... 2 D1
Melville Wy *FERR* BN12 .... 54 A1
Mendip Cl *ANG/EP* BN16 ....52 A3
Mendip Crs *SALV* BN13 .... 36 C3
Mendip Rd *SALV* BN13 .... 36 C3
Mercread Rd *SEAF* BN25 ....70 D5
Meredith Rd *SALV* BN13 .... 5 J1
Merevale *BRI* BN1 .... 29 E1
Meridian Rd *LEWES* BN7 ....16 D2
Meridian Wy *PEAHV* BN10 ...66 D1
Merlin Cl *HOVE* BN3 .... 45 F2
Merryfield Crs *ANG/EP* BN16 ...34 A4
Mersey Cl *SALV* BN13 .... 36 A3
Mersey Rd *SALV* BN13 .... 36 A3
Mersham Gdns *FERR* BN12 ...54 A3
Merston Rd *BRIE/ROTT* BN2 ...48 C4
Merton Rd *HOVE* BN3 .... 5 D5
Metcalfe Av *NEWHV* BN9 ....64 B5
The Mews *WTHG* BN11 * 4 C4
Meyners Cl *BRI* BN1 .... 25 G4
Mickleton Av *HOVE* BN3 .... 43 H4
Middle Furlong *SEAF* BN25 ...70 D5
Middle Md *STEY/UB* BN44 ....7 F2
Middle Onslow Cl *FERR* BN12 * ...53 E2
Middle Rd *BRI* BN1 .... 45 G1
LAN/SOMP BN15 .... 39 F5
SHOR BN43 .... 41 H3
Middle St *BRI* BN1 .... 3 F6
BRI BN1 .... 30 A1
PTSD BN41 .... 43 G4
SHOR BN43 .... 41 H3
Middleton Av *HOVE* BN3 .... 43 H4
Middleton Ri *BRI* BN1 .... 29 E2
Middle Tyne *SALV* BN13 ....36 B5
Middle Wy *ANG/EP* BN16 ....52 D5
LEWES BN7 .... 16 C3
Midhurst Cl *FERR* BN12 .... 53 F3
Midhurst Dr *FERR* BN12 .... 53 F3
Midhurst Ri *BRI* BN1 .... 28 B1
Midhurst Wk *HOVE* BN3 ....26 B4
Midway Rd *BRIE/ROTT* BN2 ...48 A2
Mighell St *BRIE/ROTT* BN2 ....3 J4
Milbury Cl *FERR* BN12 .... 53 F5
Milcote Av *HOVE* BN3 .... 44 B2
Mildmay Rd *LEWES* BN7 ....16 C3
Mile Oak Crs *STHW* BN42 ....42 D1
Mile Oak Gdns *PTSD* BN41 ...43 E1
Mile Oak Rd *PTSD* BN41 ....24 D4
STHW BN42 .... 42 D1
Mill Av *SHOR* BN43 * 41 F1
Millberg Rd *SEAF* BN25 ....71 F4
Mill Cl *PTSD* BN41 .... 43 C1
Mill Ct *WTHG* BN11 * 27 E2
Millcroft *BRI* BN1 .... 4 B4
Millcroft Av *STHW* BN42 ....42 C1
Millcroft Gdns *STHW* BN42 ...42 C1
Millcross Rd *PTSD* BN41 ....43 F1
Milldown Rd *SEAF* BN25 ....70 D4
Mill Dr *HOVE* BN3 .... 26 C4
SEAF BN25 .... 71 E5
Mill Dro *SEAF* BN25 .... 69 F5
Millennium Cl *LAN/SOMP* BN15 ...40 B4
Miller Rd *BRI* BN1 .... 45 G1
Miller's Rd *BRI* BN1 .... 45 G1
Millfield *LAN/SOMP* BN15 ....39 E3
STEY/UB BN44 * 8 A2
Millfield Cl *SEAF* BN25 .... 71 E4
Millfield Cots *BRIE/ROTT* BN2 ...58 D1
Mill Hl *SHOR* BN43 .... 23 E5
Mill Hill Cl *SHOR* BN43 ....41 E1
Mill Hill Dr *SHOR* BN43 ....41 E1
Mill Hill Gdns *SHOR* BN43 ...41 E1
Mill House Gdns *WTHG* BN11 ...55 E3
Mill La *LEWES* BN7 .... 51 E3
PTSD BN41 .... 43 C1
SALV BN13 .... 36 D2
SHOR BN43 .... 41 E2
Mill Ri *BRI* BN1 .... 27 E2
Mill Rd *BRI* BN1 .... 27 E1
LAN/SOMP BN15 .... 39 G2
LEWES BN7 .... 17 C1
PTSD BN41 .... 43 F3
STEY/UB BN44 .... 7 E3
WTHG BN11 .... 4 B4
Mill Rw *BRI* BN1 * 2 B2
Millyard Crs *BRIE/ROTT* BN2 ...48 B3
Milner Rd *BRIE/ROTT* BN2 ...46 C1
Milnthorpe Rd *HOVE* BN3 ....44 B2
Milton Cl *LAN/SOMP* BN15 ...39 G5
Milton Dr *STHW* BN42 .... 42 D2
Milton Rd *BRI* BN1 .... 3 K1
WTHG BN11 .... 4 C4
Milton St *WTHG* BN11 .... 4 C4
Mimmack Cl *STEY/UB* BN44 ...7 F2
Mitchelldean *PEAHV* BN10 ...62 D4
Moat Wy *FERR* BN12 .... 54 C4
Modena Rd *HOVE* BN3 .... 44 B3

Molesworth St *HOVE* BN3 ....44 B2
Monarch Gdns *SEAF* BN25 * ...71 E3
Monarchs Wy *BRI* BN1 .... 25 H1
HOVE BN3 .... 2 C5
HOVE BN3 .... 44 D1
PTSD BN41 .... 24 C4
SHOR BN43 .... 9 H5
STEY/UB BN44 .... 7 C5
Monckton Wy *LEWES* BN7 ...32 A2
Monk Cl *BRI* BN1 .... 29 E1
Monks Av *LAN/SOMP* BN15 ...39 H4
Monks Cl *LAN/SOMP* BN15 ...39 G4
Monks La *LEWES* BN7 * 17 E4
Monks Wk *STEY/UB* BN44 ....8 B2
Monks Wy *LEWES* BN7 .... 17 E1
Monmouth St *HOVE* BN3 ....44 D3
Monmacute Rd *LEWES* BN7 ...16 C4
Montague Centre *WTHG* BN11 * ...5 F5
Montague Cl *SHOR* BN43 ....42 B3
Montague Pl *BRIE/ROTT* BN2 ...58 C1
WTHG BN11 .... 5 F6
Montague St *BRIE/ROTT* BN2 ...58 C1
WTHG BN11 .... 4 E6
Montefiore Rd *HOVE* BN3 .... 2 C1
Montford Cl *SHOR* BN43 ....42 B2
Montgomery St *HOVE* BN3 ...44 C3
Montpelier Crs *BRI* BN1 .... 2 D2
BRI BN1 .... 2 C3
Montpelier Rd *ANG/EP* BN16 ...52 A4
BRI BN1 .... 2 C5
Montpelier St *BRI* BN1 .... 2 D3
Montpelier Ter *BRI* BN1 .... 2 D3
Montpelier Vls *BRI* BN1 .... 2 D3
Montreal Rd *BRIE/ROTT* BN2 ...3 K3
Montreal Wy *SALV* BN13 ....36 A4
Montrose Cl *FERR* BN12 .... 54 A2
Monument Vw *BRIE/ROTT* BN2 ...46 D4
Moore Cl *SALV* BN13 .... 35 H4
Moorfoot Rd *SALV* BN13 ....36 C3
The Moorings *LAN/SOMP* BN15 ...39 H2
LEWES BN7 * 17 C3
SHOR BN43 .... 42 A4
Morecambe Rd *BRI* BN1 ....28 A1
Morestead *PEAHV* BN10 ....63 F4
Morland Av *SALV* BN13 .... 38 A3
Morley Cl *LEWES* BN7 .... 16 D5
Morley St *BRIE/ROTT* BN2 ....3 H3
Morningside Cl *SEAF* BN25 ...70 D4
Mornington Crs *HOVE* BN3 ...43 H3
Mornington Man *HOVE* BN3 * ...43 H3
Morris Rd *LEWES* BN7 .... 17 C3
Mortimer Rd *HOVE* BN3 ....44 B2
Moulsecoomb Pl
BRIE/ROTT BN2 * 28 D5
Moulsecoomb Wy
BRIE/ROTT BN2 .... 29 E4
Mount Caburn Crs *PEAHV* BN10 ...63 E3
Mount Cl *NEWHV* BN9 ....65 F5
Mount Dr *BRIE/ROTT* BN2 ....61 H3
Mountfield Rd *LEWES* BN7 ...17 F4
Mountfields *BRI* BN1 .... 28 C5
Mount Harry Rd *LEWES* BN7 ...16 C2
Mount Pl *LEWES* BN7 .... 17 E3
Mount Pleasant *BRIE/ROTT* BN2 ...3 K5
Mount Rd *NEWHV* BN9 ....65 F5
Mountview Rd *LAN/SOMP* BN15 ...39 F2
Mountway *LAN/SOMP* BN15 ...39 G1
Mount Zion Pl *BRI* BN1 ....3 F3
Mouse La *STEY/UB* BN44 ....6 D2
Moyne Cl *HOVE* BN3 .... 44 A1
Muirfield Cl *SALV* BN13 ....36 B4
Muirfield Rd *SALV* BN13 ....36 B4
Mulberry Cl *BRI* BN1 .... 27 H4
FERR BN12 .... 53 E3
LAN/SOMP BN15 .... 39 E3
SHOR BN43 .... 42 B1
Mulberry Ct *FERR* BN12 * 54 A3
Mulberry Gdns *FERR* BN12 ...54 A3
Mulberry La *FERR* BN12 ....54 A3
Murray Av *NEWHV* BN9 ....68 C1
Mushroom Fld *LEWES* BN7 ...32 A2
Myrtle Crs *LAN/SOMP* BN15 ...39 E5
Myrtle Rd *LAN/SOMP* BN15 ...39 F5

N

Namrik Ms *HOVE* BN3 .... 44 C4
Nanson Rd *BRI* BN1 .... 28 D1
Natal Rd *BRIE/ROTT* BN2 ....46 D1
Navarino Rd *WTHG* BN11 ....56 C2
Neill's Cl *NEWHV* BN9 .... 68 C1
Nelson Cl *LAN/SOMP* BN15 ...39 F2
Nelson Rd *FERR* BN12 .... 54 B1
Nelson Rw *BRIE/ROTT* BN2 ....3 J6
Nepcote *SALV* BN13 .... 18 C2
Nepfield Cl *SALV* BN13 .... 18 C2

Nesbitt Rd *BRIE/ROTT* BN2 ...46 D1
Netherfield Gn *BRIE/ROTT* BN2 ...48 D2
Nevill Av *HOVE* BN3 .... 44 B1
Nevill Cl *HOVE* BN3 .... 26 C5
Nevill Crs *LEWES* BN7 .... 16 C3
Neville Rd *PEAHV* BN10 ....67 F2
Nevill Gdns *HOVE* BN3 ....26 C5
Nevill Pl *HOVE* BN3 .... 26 C5
Nevill Rd *BRIE/ROTT* BN2 ....60 D4
HOVE BN3 .... 26 C5
LEWES BN7 .... 16 C2
Nevill Ter *LEWES* BN7 ....16 C3
Nevill Wy *HOVE* BN3 .... 26 C5
Newark Pl *BRIE/ROTT* BN2 ....3 J2
New Barn Cl *PTSD* BN41 ....25 F5
SHOR BN43 * 41 H1
New Barn Rd *BRIE/ROTT* BN2 ...60 C2
SHOR BN43 .... 41 H1
New Broadway *WTHG* BN11 * ...55 E2
New Church Rd *HOVE* BN3 ...43 H3
New Coastguard Cots
SEAF BN25 * 70 A4
New Dorset St *BRI* BN1 ....3 F5
Newells Cl *BRIE/ROTT* BN2 ...48 C1
New England Ri *PTSD* BN41 ...25 E3
New England Rd *BRI* BN1 ....2 E1
New England St *BRI* BN1 ....3 G1
Newfield La *NEWHV* BN9 ....68 C3
Newfield Rd *NEWHV* BN9 ....68 C1
New Gdns *LAN/SOMP* BN15 * ...38 B3
Newham Cl *STEY/UB* BN44 ....7 E3
Newham La *STEY/UB* BN44 ....6 D4
Newhaven Fort *NEWHV* BN9 * ...68 D5
Newhaven Hts *NEWHV* BN9 * ...68 C3
Newhaven Rd *SEAF* BN25 ....69 G3
Newhaven Sq *NEWHV* BN9 ...68 D3
Newhaven St *BRIE/ROTT* BN2 ...3 J2
Newick Cl *SEAF* BN25 .... 73 C1
Newick Rd *BRI* BN1 .... 29 E3
Newland Rd *STEY/UB* BN44 ....8 B2
WTHG BN11 .... 5 F2
Newlands Rd *BRIE/ROTT* BN2 ...61 E4
Newland St *WTHG* BN11 ....5 F2
Newling Wy *SALV* BN13 ....36 C1
Newman's Gdns
LAN/SOMP BN15 .... 38 D3
Newmarket Rd *BRIE/ROTT* BN2 ...46 C2
Newmarket Ter *BRIE/ROTT* BN2 ...46 C2
New Pde *WTHG* BN11 .... 5 J5
Newport Ms *WTHG* BN11 ....56 D2
Newport St *BRIE/ROTT* BN2 ...46 B3
New Rd *BRI* BN1 .... 3 G4
LEWES BN7 .... 17 E3
NEWHV BN9 .... 64 D5
SALV BN13 .... 36 A3
SHOR BN43 .... 41 F3
STEY/UB BN44 .... 8 B3
New Salts Farm Rd *SHOR* BN43 ...40 C4
New Steine *BRIE/ROTT* BN2 ....3 J6
New Steine Ms *BRIE/ROTT* BN2 ...3 J6
New St *WTHG* BN11 .... 4 E6
Newtimber Av *FERR* BN12 ...53 H2
Newtimber Dr *PTSD* BN41 ...43 E1
Newtimber Gdns *SHOR* BN43 ...41 F1
Newton Rd *LEWES* BN7 ....16 D2
PEAHV BN10 .... 67 E1
Newtown Rd *HOVE* BN3 ....44 D2
Nicolson Dr *SHOR* BN43 ....41 F2
Nile St *BRI* BN1 .... 3 G5
Ninfield Pl *BRIE/ROTT* BN2 ...47 E3
Nizells Av *HOVE* BN3 .... 2 B1
Nolan Rd *BRIE/ROTT* BN2 ...48 C3
The Nookery *ANG/EP* BN16 ...52 A4
Norbury Cl *LAN/SOMP* BN15 ...39 H2
Norbury Dr *LAN/SOMP* BN15 ...39 G2
Nore Rd *NEWHV* BN9 .... 68 B2
Norfolk Buildings *BRI* BN1 ....2 C4
Norfolk Cl *WTHG* BN11 * 4 C3
Norfolk Ms *BRI* BN1 .... 2 C4
Norfolk Rd *BRI* BN1 .... 2 C4
Norfolk Sq *BRI* BN1 .... 2 C4
Norfolk St *BRI* BN1 .... 2 C5
WTHG BN11 .... 4 C3
Norfolk Ter *BRI* BN1 .... 2 C5
Norman Cl *SEAF* BN25 .... 69 H2
Norman Crs *SHOR* BN43 ....41 F4
Normandy Dr *ANG/EP* BN16 ...52 A5
Normandy La *ANG/EP* BN16 ...52 A5
Normandy Rd *SALV* BN13 ....55 C1
Norman Rd *HOVE* BN3 .... 44 B4
NEWHV BN9 .... 68 C1
Normansal Cl *SEAF* BN25 ....71 E2
Normansal Park Av *SEAF* BN25 ...70 D3
Normans Ct *SHOR* BN43 * 41 F1
Normanton St *BRIE/ROTT* BN2 ...46 C3
Norman Wy *STEY/UB* BN44 ....7 F2
North Av *FERR* BN12 .... 54 C4
Northbourne Cl *SHOR* BN43 ...41 F2
Northbrook Cl *SALV* BN13 ....38 A4

Northbrook Rd SALV BN13........38 A4
North Camp La SEAF BN25........70 D4
Northcliffe Cl SEAF BN25........70 D4
North Cl PTSD BN41........43 E1
Northcote La PEAHV BN10........62 C4
North Ct LEWES BN7........17 G3
Northcourt Rd SALV BN13........4 D1
Northdown Cl NEWHV BN9........68 C2
Northdown Rd NEWHV BN9........68 B2
North Dr BRIE/ROTT BN2........46 C4
Northease Cl HOVE BN3........25 H5
Northease Dr HOVE BN3........25 H5
Northease Gdns HOVE BN3........26 A4
North Farm Rd
    LAN/SOMP BN15........39 H4
Northfield Cl SEAF BN25........70 D3
Northfield Ri BRIE/ROTT BN2........61 E3
    HOVE BN3........25 H3
Northfield Rd SALV BN13........37 E4
Northfield Wy BRI BN1........28 A3
North Gdns BRI BN1........3 F3
Northgate Cl BRIE/ROTT BN2........60 D3
    LAN/SOMP BN15........38 D4
North La ANG/EP BN16........52 B3
    NEWHV BN9 *........68 C1
    PTSD BN41........25 E5
North Pl BRI BN1........3 H4
North Quay Rd NEWHV BN9........64 C3
North Rd BRI BN1........3 G3
    LAN/SOMP BN15........39 G4
    PTSD BN41........25 E5
North St BRI BN1........3 F4
    LEWES BN7........17 F3
    SHOR BN43........41 E3
    WTHG BN11........5 F3
North Street Qd BRI BN1 *........3 F4
Northview Ter SALV BN13 *........18 C1
North Wy LEWES BN7........16 C2
    NEWHV BN9........68 D1
    SEAF BN25........70 D3
Northwood Av BRIE/ROTT BN2........62 A4
Norton Cl HOVE BN3........44 D4
Norton Dr BRIE/ROTT BN2........48 D2
Norton Rd HOVE BN3........44 D4
    LAN/SOMP BN15........39 F5
    NEWHV BN9........69 E1
Norton Ter NEWHV BN9........69 E1
Norway St PTSD BN41........43 G3
Norwich Cl BRIE/ROTT BN2........29 G5
Norwich Ct WTHG BN11 *........5 E4
Norwich Dr BRIE/ROTT BN2........29 G5
Nunnery Stable LEWES BN7........16 D3
Nursery Cl ANG/EP BN16........52 A5
    LAN/SOMP BN15........39 F2
    PTSD BN41........24 C3
    SHOR BN43........41 H2
Nursery La WTHG BN11........4 C6
Nursery Rd ANG/EP BN16........52 A1
Nutbourne Rd SALV BN13........55 F1
Nuthurst Cl BRIE/ROTT BN2........47 F5
Nuthurst Pl BRIE/ROTT BN2........47 F5
Nutley Av BRIE/ROTT BN2........61 H5
    FERR BN12........54 A4
Nutley Cl FERR BN12........54 A4
    HOVE BN3........26 B4
Nutley Crs FERR BN12........54 A4
Nutley Dr FERR BN12........54 A4
Nyetimber Hl BRIE/ROTT BN2........29 E5

O

Oakapple Rd STHW BN42........42 B1
Oak Cl BRI BN1........27 G4
    SALV BN13........36 C1
Oakdene Av PTSD BN41........24 C4
Oakdene Cl PTSD BN41........24 C4
Oakdene Crs PTSD BN41........24 C4
Oakdene Gdns PTSD BN41........24 C4
Oakdene Ri PTSD BN41........24 C3
Oakdene Wy PTSD BN41........24 C4
Oaklands Av BRIE/ROTT BN2........61 G4
Oakleigh Cl WTHG BN11........56 C1
Oakleigh Rd WTHG BN11........56 C1
Oakley Gdns ANG/EP BN16........52 A5
Oakwood Dr ANG/EP BN16........52 A1
Ocean Cl FERR BN12........53 E5
Ocean Dr FERR BN12........53 E5
Ocean Pde FERR BN12........53 E4
Offham Cl SEAF BN25........70 D3
Offham Rd LEWES BN7........16 C2
Offham Ter LEWES BN7 *........17 E3
Offington Av SALV BN13........37 F3
Offington Ct SALV BN13........37 G4
Offington Dr SALV BN13........37 F3
Offington Gdns SALV BN13........37 F3
Offington La SALV BN13........37 E4
Old Barn Wy STHW BN42........43 E3

Old Boat Wk BRI BN1........14 B5
Old Court Cl BRI BN1........27 H3
Olde Place Ms BRIE/ROTT BN2........60 D4
Old Farm Rd BRI BN1........27 H2
Oldfield Crs STHW BN42........42 B3
Old Fort Rd SHOR BN43........41 G4
Old London Rd BRI BN1........27 G2
Old Malling Wy LEWES BN7........17 E1
Old Market Sq STEY/UB BN44 *........7 G3
Old Mill Cl BRI BN1........27 G2
Old Nursery Cl SEAF BN25........71 F3
Old Parish La BRIE/ROTT BN2........48 B2
Old Rectory Gdns STHW BN42........42 B3
Old Salts Farm Rd
    LAN/SOMP BN15........39 H5
Old Shoreham Rd HOVE BN3........45 G3
    LAN/SOMP BN15........40 C1
    STHW BN42........42 D2
Old Steine BRI BN1........3 H5
Old Stocks SALV BN13 *........18 C1
Old Tree Pde SEAF BN25 *........72 C1
Old Worthing Rd ANG/EP BN16........52 B3
Oliver Cl BRIE/ROTT BN2........46 C5
Olive Rd HOVE BN3........44 A4
Onslow Dr FERR BN12........53 E3
Onslow Rd HOVE BN3........45 E1
Ontario Cl SALV BN13........36 A4
Ontario Gdns SALV BN13........36 A4
Ophir Rd WTHG BN11........56 C2
Orchard Av HOVE BN3........44 D1
    LAN/SOMP BN15........39 G3
    SALV BN13........37 E5
Orchard Cl FERR BN12........53 E2
    SALV BN13........37 F5
    SHOR BN43........41 E2
    STHW BN42........42 D2
Orchard Gdns HOVE BN3........44 D1
Orchard Ms NEWHV BN9........65 E3
Orchard Rd ANG/EP BN16........52 A3
    HOVE BN3........44 C1
    LEWES BN7........17 G2
Orchard Wy LAN/SOMP BN15........39 G3
Orchid Vw BRI BN1........28 C1
Oriental Pl BRI BN1........2 C5
Orient Rd LAN/SOMP BN15........40 C5
Orkney Ct SALV BN13........35 H5
Orme Rd WTHG BN11........4 C2
Ormonde Wy SHOR BN43........40 D4
Orpen Rd HOVE BN3........45 F1
Osborne Cl LAN/SOMP BN15........39 E4
Osborne Dr LAN/SOMP BN15........39 E4
Osborne Rd BRI BN1........27 H5
Osborne Vls HOVE BN3........44 D5
Osmonde Cl SALV BN13........4 D1
Osmond Rd HOVE BN3........2 C1
Ousedale Cl LEWES BN7........16 D3
Outlook Av PEAHV BN10........67 H2
Oval Cl PEAHV BN10........63 E3
The Oval SALV BN13........36 D5
Oval Waye FERR BN12........53 E5
Overdown Ri PTSD BN41........24 D3
Overhill STHW BN42........42 C1
Overhill Dr BRI BN1........27 G2
Overhill Gdns BRI BN1........27 G2
Overhill Wy BRI BN1........27 G1
Overmead SHOR BN43........41 E2
Over St BRI BN1........3 G2
Ovingdean Cl BRIE/ROTT BN2........48 B5
Ovingdean Rd BRIE/ROTT BN2........60 B1
Oxen Av SHOR BN43........41 F2
Oxford Ct BRI BN1........3 H1
Oxford Ms HOVE BN3........45 E3
Oxford Pl BRI BN1........3 H1
Oxford Rd WTHG BN11........4 E3
Oxford St BRI BN1........3 H1
Oxford Ter STEY/UB BN44 *........7 F3

P

Paddock Cl SALV BN13 *........55 F1
Paddock La LEWES BN7........17 E3
Paddock Rd LEWES BN7........17 E3
The Paddocks LAN/SOMP BN15........39 H5
    LEWES BN7........51 F2
    STEY/UB BN44........8 B1
The Paddock HOVE BN3........45 E1
    SHOR BN43........40 D1
Paddock Wy SALV BN13........18 C1
Pages La WTHG BN11........56 C2
Palace Pl BRI BN1........3 H5
Palatine Rd FERR BN12........54 A1
The Pallant FERR BN12........53 H1
Palma Ct WTHG BN11 *........4 A5
Palm Ct SALV BN13........36 C3
Palmeira Av HOVE BN3........45 E4
Palmeira Sq HOVE BN3........45 E5
Palmerston Av FERR BN12........54 A3

Palmerston Rd NEWHV BN9........65 G4
Palmers Wy SALV BN13........36 B1
Pankhurst Av BRIE/ROTT BN2........46 C4
The Pantiles FERR BN12 *........53 E2
Parade Man ANG/EP BN16........52 A5
The Parade ANG/EP BN16 *........52 A5
    BRI BN1 *........26 D3
    HOVE BN3 *........26 A5
Parham Cl BRIE/ROTT BN2........46 D5
    SALV BN13........36 D1
Parham Rd SALV BN13........36 D1
Park Av HOVE BN3........44 A3
    PEAHV BN10........62 C5
    SHOR BN43........41 G2
    WTHG BN11........5 H2
Park Cl BRI BN1........29 E2
    HOVE BN3........26 A4
    PTSD BN41........43 F1
    SALV BN13........37 E3
Park Crs BRIE/ROTT BN2........60 D4
    BRIE/ROTT BN2........60 D4
    PTSD BN41........43 E2
    WTHG BN11........4 D4
Park Crescent Pl
    BRIE/ROTT BN2........46 B3
Park Crescent Rd
    BRIE/ROTT BN2........46 B3
Park Crescent Ter
    BRIE/ROTT BN2........46 B3
Park Dr FERR BN12........53 F3
Park Drive Cl NEWHV BN9........65 F3
Parker Ct PTSD BN41........25 F5
Parkfield Ct SALV BN13........55 E1
Parkfield Rd SALV BN13........55 E1
Park Hl BRIE/ROTT BN2........3 K4
Parklands SHOR BN43........42 A2
Parklands Av FERR BN12........54 B4
Park La STHW BN42........42 B3
Park Mnr BRI BN1 *........27 F4
Parkmore Ter BRI BN1........45 H2
Park Ri HOVE BN3........26 A4
Park Rd BRI BN1........29 E2
    BRIE/ROTT BN2........60 D4
    LEWES BN7........17 E3
    PEAHV BN10........67 H3
    SEAF BN25........70 B5
    SHOR BN43........41 G2
    WTHG BN11........5 G2
Park Road Ter BRIE/ROTT BN2........3 K4
Parkside SHOR BN43........41 G1
    WTHG BN11........5 G1
Parkside Rd SEAF BN25........70 D4
Park Sq BRIE/ROTT BN2........59 F2
The Parks PTSD BN41........25 F4
Park St BRI BN1........30 A1
    BRIE/ROTT BN2........3 K5
The Park BRIE/ROTT BN2........61 E4
Park View Cl PEAHV BN10........62 C4
Park View Ri PEAHV BN10........62 C5
Park View Rd HOVE BN3........44 D1
Park View Ter BRI BN1........45 G2
Park Wy STHW BN42........42 D2
Park Way Cl STHW BN42........42 D2
Parochial Ms BRIE/ROTT BN2 *........3 H5
Parochial Ter BRIE/ROTT BN2 *........3 H5
Parsons Cl ANG/EP BN16........52 A1
Paston Pl BRIE/ROTT BN2........58 D1
Patcham By-Pass BRI BN1........27 G1
Patcham Gra BRI BN1........27 G2
Patchdean BRI BN1........27 H2
Patching Cl FERR BN12........53 H1
Patricia Av FERR BN12........54 B4
Patricia Cl FERR BN12........54 B4
Pavilion Buildings BRI BN1........3 G5
Pavilion Pde BRIE/ROTT BN2........3 H5
    WTHG BN11........5 F6
Pavilion Rd SALV BN13........4 B2
Pavilion St BRIE/ROTT BN2........3 H5
Paxmead Crs SALV BN13........38 B4
Payne Av HOVE BN3........44 B2
Paythorne Cl STHW BN42........42 B1
Peace Cl BRI BN1........46 C1
Peacock La BRI BN1........27 G3
Peak La ANG/EP BN16........52 C5
Pearsons Retreat WTHG BN11 *........56 D2
Peckham Cl LEWES BN7........17 E1
Peel Rd BRIE/ROTT BN2........59 F1
Pelham Cl PEAHV BN10........63 F4
Pelham Pl SEAF BN25 *........72 C1
Pelham Ri PEAHV BN10........63 F4
Pelham Rd SALV BN13........36 D5
    SEAF BN25........72 C1
Pelham Sq BRI BN1........3 H3
Pelham St BRI BN1........3 H2
Pelham Ter LEWES BN7........17 E3
Pelham Yd SEAF BN25 *........72 C1
Pellbrook Rd LEWES BN7........16 C1
Pemberton Cl LAN/SOMP BN15........39 G3
Pembroke Av FERR BN12........54 D3

HOVE BN3........
Pembroke Crs HOVE BN3........
Pembroke Gdns HOVE BN3........
Pembury Cl SALV BN13........
Pembury Rd SALV BN13........
Pende Cl LAN/SOMP BN15........
Pendine Av WTHG BN11........
Pendragon Ct HOVE BN3 *........
Penfold Rd SALV BN13........
Penfold Wy STEY/UB BN44........
Penhill Rd LAN/SOMP BN15........
Penhurst Pl CI STEY/UB BN44........
Penland's Cl STEY/UB BN44........
Penlands Ri STEY/UB BN44........
Penlands V STEY/UB BN44........
Penlands Wy STEY/UB BN44........
Penleigh Cl LAN/SOMP BN15........
Penns Ct STEY/UB BN44........
Pennycress Av SALV BN13........
Penstone Pk LAN/SOMP BN15........
Pentland Rd SALV BN13........
Pepperscoombe La
    STEY/UB BN44........
Percival Ter BRIE/ROTT BN2........
Perrots La STEY/UB BN44........
Perry Hl BRIE/ROTT BN2........
Perth Cl SEAF BN25........
Peter Rd LAN/SOMP BN15........
Pett Cl BRIE/ROTT BN2........
Petworth Av FERR BN12........
Petworth Rd BRI BN1........
Pevensey Cl SEAF BN25........
Pevensey Gdn WTHG BN11........
Pevensey Rd BRIE/ROTT BN2........
    NEWHV BN9........
    WTHG BN11........
The Peverells SEAF BN25........
Peverel Rd SALV BN13........
The Peverels SEAF BN25 *........
Peveril Cl LAN/SOMP BN15........
Peveril Dr LAN/SOMP BN15........
Phoenix Cswy LEWES BN7........
Phoenix Crs STHW BN42........
Phoenix Pl BRIE/ROTT BN2........
    LEWES BN7........
Phoenix Ri BRIE/ROTT BN2........
Phoenix Wy STHW BN42........
Phrosso Rd WTHG BN11........
Phyllis Av PEAHV BN10........
Picton St BRIE/ROTT BN2........
Piddinghoe Av PEAHV BN10........
Piddinghoe Cl PEAHV BN10........
Piddinghoe Md NEWHV BN9........
Polgrims Cl SALV BN13........
Pilgrims Ter SALV BN13 *........
Pilgrims Wk SALV BN13........
Piltdown Rd BRIE/ROTT BN2........
Pines Av SALV BN13........
The Pines BRIE/ROTT BN2 *........
Pinewood Cl ANG/EP BN16........
    SEAF BN25........
Pinfold Cl BRIE/ROTT BN2........
Pinwell Rd LEWES BN7........
Pipe Pas LEWES BN7 *........
Pipers Cl HOVE BN3........
Pitt Dr SEAF BN25........
Pitt Gdns BRIE/ROTT BN2........
Place La SEAF BN25........
Plainfields Av BRI BN1........
Plaistow Cl BRIE/ROTT BN2........
Plantation Cl SALV BN13........
Plantation Ri SALV BN13........
The Plantation ANG/EP BN16........
    SALV BN13........
Plantation Wy SALV BN13........
Playden Cl BRIE/ROTT BN2........
Plaza Pde WTHG BN11 *........
Plumpton Rd BRIE/ROTT BN2........
Plymouth Av BRIE/ROTT BN2........
Poling Cl FERR BN12........
Polperro Cl FERR BN12........
Pond La SALV BN13........
Pond Ms SALV BN13 *........
Pond Rd SHOR BN43........
Pony Farm SALV BN13........
Pool Va BRI BN1........
Poplar Av HOVE BN3........
Poplar Cl BRI BN1........
    HOVE BN3........
Poplar Rd SALV BN13........
The Poplars BRIE/ROTT BN2 *........
Portfield Av BRI BN1........
Port Hall Av BRI BN1........
Port Hall Ms BRI BN1........
Port Hall Pl BRI BN1........
Port Hall Rd BRI BN1........
Port Hall St BRI BN1........
Portland Av HOVE BN3........
Portland Ms BRIE/ROTT BN2 *........

...and Pl BRIE/ROTT BN2 ....58 C1
...and Rd HOVE BN3 ....43 H3
...HG BN1
...and Sq WTHG BN11 * 4 E5
...and St BRI BN1 ....3 F4
...and Vls HOVE BN3 ....43 H3
...Offices NEWHV BN9 * 69 E2
...w NEWHV BN9 ....65 E3
...way STEY/UB BN44.........7 E4
...r's La LEWES BN7 ....17 E4
...er's La LEWES BN7
...ere's La BRI BN13 ....37 F4
...d La STEY/UB BN44 ....8 B2
...d Wy ANG/EP BN16 ....34 A5
...ll Gdns NEWHV BN9 ....64 D4
...s Gv BRI BN1 ....2 E3
...s Rd BRI BN1 ....2 D3
...s Sq BRI BN1 ....2 D2
...s Vls BRI BN1 ....2 E3
...ings Cl SEAF BN25 ....73 G1
...ings Dr HOVE BN3 ....26 B4
...er Rd HOVE BN3 ....44 C2
...on Av LAN/SOMP BN15 ....39 F3
...on Circ BRI BN1 * 46 A3
...on Dro BRI BN1 ....27 H5
...on Gra BRI BN1 ....45 G1
...on Park Av BRI BN1 ....45 H1
...on Rd BRI BN1 ....27 G5
...on St BRI BN1
...on Village Ms BRI BN1 * 45 G1
...onville Rd BRI BN1 ....2 E1
...e Albert St BRI BN1 ....3 F5
...e Av LAN/SOMP BN15.........40 B5
...e Charles Cl STHW BN42 ....42 D1
...e Charles Rd LEWES BN7 ....17 G1
...e Edward's Rd
...VES BN7 ....16 C3
...e Regent's Cl
.../ROTT BN2 ....59 E1
...es Av HOVE BN3 ....44 C4
...es Cl SEAF BN25 ....70 C4
...e's Crs BRI BN1 ....46 B2
...VE BN3 ....44 C4
...e's Pl BRI BN1 ....3 G5
...e's Rd BRI BN1 ....46 B2
...ess Av SALV BN13 ....54 D2
...ess Dr SEAF BN25 ....70 B3
...ess Sq HOVE BN3 ....44 C4
...e's Ter BRIE/ROTT BN2 ....59 E1
...e William Cl SALV BN13 ....37 E2
...ep Rd HOVE BN3 ....44 C2
... Cl LAN/SOMP BN15 ....38 D3
...V BN13 ....55 E1
...' Crs LEWES BN7 ....17 E4
...c St BRIE/ROTT BN2 ....3 K3
...Fld STEY/UB BN44 ....8 A2
...' St LEWES BN7 ....17 F4
...' Ter LEWES BN7 ....17 F4
...riory BRI BN1 ....27 G2
...enade PEAHV BN10 ....66 C2
...HV BN10 ....67 E2
...ect Pl WTHG BN11 ....4 E6
...dence Pl BRI BN1 ....3 G1
...dence Ter WTHG BN11.........5 C4
...rough Cl BRIE/ROTT BN2.....47 F3

Q

...uadrangle SALV BN13 ....18 C2
...uadrant FERR BN12 ....54 A2
...cock Cl SALV BN13 ....36 D2
...cock Rd SALV BN13 ....36 D2
...y Bank Rd BRI BN1 ....28 B5
...y La SEAF BN25 ....71 E3
...y Rd NEWHV BN9 ....68 C3
...uashetts SALV BN13 * 37 H5
...ec St BRIE/ROTT BN2 ....3 K3
...n Alexandra Av HOVE BN3...26 C4
...n Anne's Cl LEWES BN7 * 17 E3
...n Caroline Cl HOVE BN3.........26 C4
...n Mary Av HOVE BN3 ....26 C4
...nsbury Ms BRI BN1 ....2 D5
...nsdown School Rd
...BN1 ....28 C4
...n's Gdns BRI BN1 ....3 G3
...VE BN3 ....45 G5
...ns Pde LAN/SOMP BN15 * ...39 G4
...n's Park Gdns SEAF BN25...70 A4
...n's Park Ri
.../ROTT BN2 ....46 C4
...n's Park Rd BRIE/ROTT BN2...3 K4
...n's Park Ter
...E/ROTT BN2.
...n's Pl BRI BN1 ....3 H2
...VE BN3 ....45 E4
...OR BN43 ....41 F3
...n Sq BRI BN1 ....3 F4
...n's Rd BRI BN1 ....3 F3

...LAN/SOMP BN15 ....57 H1
LEWES BN7 ....17 F1
STHW BN42 ....42 C1
WTHG BN11 ....4 C6
Queen St SALV BN13 ....55 C1
Queensway BRIE/ROTT BN2 ...46 D4
LAN/SOMP BN15 ....39 G4
SEAF BN25 ....71 E3
Queen Victoria Av HOVE BN3 ..26 C4
Querneby Cl SHOR BN43 ....42 B3

R

Rackham Cl SALV BN13 ....36 D5
Rackham Rd SALV BN13 ....36 D5
Radbone Cl SALV BN13 ....38 A4
Radinden Dr HOVE BN3 ....45 F1
Radinden Manor Rd HOVE BN3...45 G2
Radnor Cl SALV BN13 ....54 D1
Radnor Rd SALV BN13 ....54 D1
Raglan Av SALV BN13 ....36 C5
Railway Ap NEWHV BN9 ....68 D1
WTHG BN11 ....4 D2
Railway La LEWES BN7 ....17 F3
Railway Rd NEWHV BN9 ....68 D1
Railway St BRI BN1 ....3 F2
Raleigh Cl SHOR BN43 ....41 E4
Raleigh Crs FERR BN12 ....54 B2
Raleigh Wy FERR BN12 ....54 A1
Ranelagh Vls HOVE BN3 ....44 D2
Raphael Rd HOVE BN3 ....44 B3
Ravensbourne Av SHOR BN43...41 F1
Ravensbourne Cl SHOR BN43...41 F1
Raven's Rd SHOR BN43 ....41 F3
Ravenswood Dr
BRIE/ROTT BN2 ....48 D4
Rayford Cl PEAHV BN10 ....67 E1
Raymond Cl SEAF BN25 ....71 E3
Reading Rd BRIE/ROTT BN2 ...59 F1
Rectory Cl HOVE BN3 * 43 H3
NEWHV BN9 ....68 C2
SHOR BN43 ....42 B3
Rectory Farm Rd
LAN/SOMP BN15 ....38 D3
Rectory Gdns SALV BN13 ....37 G5
Rectory Rd NEWHV BN9 ....65 E3
SALV BN13 ....55 E1
SHOR BN43 ....42 A3
Rectory Wk LAN/SOMP BN15...38 D3
Redcross St BRI BN1 ....3 H2
Redhill Cl BRI BN1 ....27 E3
Redhill Dr BRI BN1 ....27 E3
Redvers Rd BRIE/ROTT BN2 ...46 D1
Redwood Cl SALV BN13 ....36 A5
Reeves Hl BRI BN1 ....28 D2
Regency Ms BRI BN1 ....2 D4
Regency Rd SALV BN13 ....2 E5
Regency Sq BRI BN1 ....2 D5
Regent Ar BRI BN1 ....3 G3
Regent Cl LAN/SOMP BN15 ...40 B4
Regent Hl BRI BN1 ....2 E4
Regent Rw BRI BN1 ....2 E4
Regents Cl SEAF BN25 ....70 C3
Regent St BRI BN1 ....3 G4
Reigate Rd BRI BN1 ....45 F1
WTHG BN11 ....54 D3
Reynolds Rd HOVE BN3 ....44 B3
Richardson Rd HOVE BN3 ....44 B4
Richington Wy SEAF BN25 ....71 F3
Richmond Ct WTHG BN11.........4 C4
Richmond Pde BRIE/ROTT BN2...3 H3
Richmond Pl BRIE/ROTT BN2 ...3 H3
Richmond Rd BRIE/ROTT BN2 ..46 B2
SEAF BN25 ....70 B5
WTHG BN11 ....4 B5
Richmond St BRIE/ROTT BN2...3 H3
Richmond Ter BRI BN1 ....3 J1
SEAF BN25 ....70 C5
Ridge Cl PTSD BN41 ....25 E3
Ridge Rd BRI BN1 ....15 H3
Ridgeside Av BRI BN1 ....27 G2
Ridge Vw BRI BN1 ....29 E2
Ridgeway STHW BN42 ....42 D1
Ridgeway Cl STHW BN42 ....42 D1
Ridgeway Gdns BRIE/ROTT BN2...48 B3
The Ridgeway SEAF BN25 ....70 D4
Ridgewood Av BRIE/ROTT BN2...61 G2
Ridgway Cl BRIE/ROTT BN2 ...48 B2
Ridgway Paddock LEWES BN7...31 H3
The Ridgway BRIE/ROTT BN2 ..48 B2
The Ridings BRIE/ROTT BN2 ...60 B1
PEAHV BN10 ....62 D4
SEAF BN25 ....70 D3
STEY/UB BN44 ....7 F5
Rifeside Gdns FERR BN12 ....53 G2
Rife Wy FERR BN12 ....53 G3
Rigden Rd HOVE BN3 ....45 E2

Riley Rd BRIE/ROTT BN2 ....46 C1
Ringmer Cl BRI BN1 ....29 E3
Ringmer Rd BRI BN1 ....29 F3
NEWHV BN9 ....68 B2
SALV BN13 ....54 C1
SEAF BN25 ....72 C1
Ring Rd LAN/SOMP BN15 ....39 G1
Ripley Rd WTHG BN11 ....54 D2
Ripon Ct WTHG BN11 * 4 C4
The Rise PTSD BN41 ....24 D5
River Cl SHOR BN43 ....41 E4
Riverdale LEWES BN7 ....17 E2
Riverside SHOR BN43 ....41 F4
STEY/UB BN44 ....8 A2
STHW BN42 ....42 C4
Riverside North NEWHV BN9 ...68 C1
Riverside Rd SHOR BN43 ....41 F4
Riverside South NEWHV BN9...68 C2
Roadean Cl SEAF BN25 ....71 E4
Robertson Rd BRI BN1 ....27 F5
Roberts Rd LAN/SOMP BN15...57 C1
Robert St BRI BN1 ....3 G3
Robin Davis Cl BRIE/ROTT BN2...47 E2
Robin Dene BRIE/ROTT BN2 ...59 E1
Robinson Cl LAN/SOMP BN15...39 G4
Robinson Rd NEWHV BN9 ....64 C5
Robson Ct FERR BN12 ....54 C3
Robson Rd FERR BN12 ....54 C3
Rochester Cl HOVE BN3 * 2 A2
SALV BN13 ....35 H5
Rochester Ct WTHG BN11 * 2 A3
Rochester Gdns HOVE BN3 ....2 A3
Rochester St BRIE/ROTT BN2...46 D5
Rochford Wy SEAF BN25 ....69 H2
Rock Gv BRIE/ROTT BN2 ....58 D1
Rockingham Cl SALV BN13 ....36 C4
Rockingham Ct SALV BN13 * ...36 C4
Rock Pl BRIE/ROTT BN2 ....3 K6
Rock St BRIE/ROTT BN2 ....59 E1
Roderick Av PEAHV BN10 ....66 D2
Roderick Av North PEAHV BN10...63 E3
Rodmell Av BRIE/ROTT BN2 ...61 H4
Rodmell Pl BRI BN1 * 28 A1
Rodmell Rd SALV BN13 ....36 C5
SEAF BN25 ....73 F1
Roedale Rd BRI BN1 ....46 B3
Roedean Crs BRIE/ROTT BN2...59 G1
Roedean Hts BRIE/ROTT BN2...59 G1
Roedean Pth BRIE/ROTT BN2...59 H2
Roedean Rd BRIE/ROTT BN2...59 G2
SALV BN13 ....36 C4
Roedean V BRIE/ROTT BN2 ...59 G2
Rogate Cl LAN/SOMP BN15 ...38 D3
SALV BN13 ....37 E4
Rogate Rd SALV BN13 ....37 E4
Roger's La SALV BN13 ....18 C3
Roman Av ANG/EP BN16 ....52 A1
Roman Cl SEAF BN25 ....69 H2
Roman Crs STHW BN42 ....42 C2
Roman Rd HOVE BN3 ....43 H4
STEY/UB BN44 ....7 G4
STHW BN42 ....42 C2
Roman Wk LAN/SOMP BN15...38 D3
Roman Wy STHW BN42 ....42 C2
Romany Cl PTSD BN41 ....43 F2
Romany Rd SALV BN13 ....35 H5
Romney Cl SEAF BN25 ....71 G4
Romney Rd BRIE/ROTT BN2...61 G4
WTHG BN11 ....54 D4
Romsey Cl BRI BN1 ....28 B5
Rookery Cl BRI BN1 ....45 G1
NEWHV BN9 ....65 E3
Rookery Wy NEWHV BN9 ....65 F3
SEAF BN25 ....69 H3
Ropetackle SHOR BN43 ....41 F3
Rope Wk SHOR BN43 ....41 E3
Rosebery Av BRIE/ROTT BN2...47 H2
FERR BN12 ....54 C5
Rosecroft Cl LAN/SOMP BN15...39 G5
Rosedene Cl BRIE/ROTT BN2...48 C4
Rose Hill Cl BRI BN1 ....46 A3
Rose Hill Ter BRI BN1 ....46 A3
Rosemary Av STEY/UB BN44 ....7 G3
Rosemary Cl PEAHV BN10 ....63 E3
STEY/UB BN44 ....7 G3
Rosemary Dr SHOR BN43 ....41 H1
Rosemount Cl SEAF BN25 ....69 G2
Rose Wk FERR BN12 ....54 C3
SEAF BN25 ....70 D4
Rose Walk Cl NEWHV BN9 ....68 D3
The Rose Wk NEWHV BN9 ....68 D3
Rossiter Rd LAN/SOMP BN15...39 G2
Rosslyn Av SHOR BN43 ....41 G3
Rosslyn Ct SHOR BN43 ....41 F3
Rosslyn Rd SHOR BN43 ....41 F3
Rothbury Rd HOVE BN3 ....43 H3
Rotherfield Cl BRI BN1 ....28 B1
Rotherfield Crs BRI BN1 ....28 B2

Rother Rd SEAF BN25 ....73 E1
Rothesay Cl SALV BN13 ....54 C1
Rothwell Ct NEWHV BN9 ....68 B1
Rotten Rw LEWES BN7 ....16 D4
Rottingdean Pl
BRIE/ROTT BN2 * 60 D1
The Rotyngs BRIE/ROTT BN2...60 D3
Rough Brow SEAF BN25 ....71 E4
Roundhay Av PEAHV BN10 * ...67 G2
Roundhill Crs BRIE/ROTT BN2...46 B2
Round Hill Rd BRI BN1 ....46 B2
Round Robin Ldg
STEY/UB BN44 * 6 C1
Roundstone Crs ANG/EP BN16...52 A3
Roundstone Dr ANG/EP BN16 ...52 A2
Roundstone La ANG/EP BN16...52 A2
Roundway BRI BN1 ....29 E2
Rowan Av HOVE BN3 ....44 A1
Rowan Cl PTSD BN41 ....42 D1
SEAF BN25 ....71 G5
Rowans Ct LEWES BN7 ....17 E3
The Rowans WTHG BN11 ....55 E3
Rowan Wy ANG/EP BN16 ....52 A1
BRIE/ROTT BN2 ....60 C2
Rowe Av PEAHV BN10 ....66 D2
Rowlands Rd WTHG BN11 ....4 B6
Roxburgh Cl SALV BN13 ....36 D3
Royal Buildings
LAN/SOMP BN15 * 57 F1
Royal Crs BRIE/ROTT BN2 ....58 C1
Royal Crescent Ms
BRIE/ROTT BN2 ....58 C1
Royal Dr SEAF BN25 ....70 C2
Royal George Pde SHOR BN43...41 H1
Royles Cl BRIE/ROTT BN2 ....61 E3
Rudgwick Av FERR BN12 ....53 G3
Rudyard Cl BRIE/ROTT BN2 ...48 C2
Rudyard Rd BRIE/ROTT BN2 ...48 C2
Rufus Cl LEWES BN7 ....17 E3
Rugby Cl SEAF BN25 ....71 F4
Rugby Pl BRIE/ROTT BN2 ....59 E1
Rugby Rd BRI BN1 ....46 A1
WTHG BN11 ....55 E2
Rusbridge La LEWES BN7 ....17 G3
Rushlake Cl BRI BN1 ....29 E2
Rushlake Rd BRI BN1 ....29 E1
Ruskin Rd HOVE BN3 ....44 B2
SALV BN13 ....56 B1
Rusper Rd BRI BN1 ....28 D1
SALV BN13 ....36 D5
Rusper Rd South SALV BN13 ...36 C5
Russell Cl SALV BN13 ....38 A5
Russell Crs BRI BN1 ....45 H3
Russell Ms BRI BN1 ....2 D4
Russell Pl BRI BN1 ....2 E5
Russell Rd BRI BN1 ....2 E5
Russell Rw LEWES BN7 ....17 E1
Russell's Cl ANG/EP BN16 ....52 B3
Russells Dr LAN/SOMP BN15...39 G5
Russell Sq BRI BN1 ....2 D4
Rustic Cl PEAHV BN10 ....62 D4
Rustic Rd PEAHV BN10 ....62 D3
Rustington Rd BRI BN1 ....28 A2
Rutland Gdns HOVE BN3 ....44 B3
Rutland Rd HOVE BN3 ....44 C3
Rycroft Cl FERR BN12 ....54 B4
Ryde Rd BRIE/ROTT BN2 ....46 D3
Rye Cl BRIE/ROTT BN2 ....62 A3
SEAF BN25 ....71 G4
WTHG BN11 ....55 E4
Ryecroft Gdns FERR BN12 ....54 A4
Ryelands Dr BRIE/ROTT BN2 ...28 D4

S

Sackville Cl LEWES BN7 ....17 E3
Sackville Crs SALV BN13 ....56 A1
Sackville Gdns HOVE BN3 ....44 B4
Sackville Rd HOVE BN3 ....44 C4
SALV BN13 ....5 H1
Sackville Wy SALV BN13 ....5 H1
Sadler Wy BRIE/ROTT BN2 ....47 F4
Saffron Cl SHOR BN43 ....42 A1
St Andrew's Cl FERR BN12 ....53 E3
St Andrew's Dr SEAF BN25 ....69 G2
St Andrews Gdns SALV BN13 ...55 E1
St Andrew's La LEWES BN7 ....17 F3
St Andrew's Rd BRI BN1 ....46 A1
PTSD BN41 ....43 F3
SALV BN13 ....54 D1
St Anne's Crs LEWES BN7 ....16 D3
St Annes Ter LEWES BN7 * 16 D3
St Anselm's Rd SALV BN13 ....4 A1
St Aubins Rd FERR BN12 ....53 F5
St Aubyns HOVE BN3 ....44 C4
St Aubyn's Crs PTSD BN41 ....43 F3
St Aubyn's Md BRIE/ROTT BN2...61 E4

St Aubyns Rd PTSD BN41 ....43 E3
St Aubyns South HOVE BN3.........44 C5
St Bernards Ct LAN/SOMP BN15...39 G5
St Botolph's Rd WTHG BN11 ....4 A2
St Crispians SEAF BN25 ....70 B5
St Cuthmans Cl BRIE/ROTT BN2...47 E4
St Cuthman's Rd LAN/SOMP BN44 ....7 F1
St Dunstan's Rd SALV BN13..........55 E2
St Elmo Rd SALV BN13...................4 H2
St Georges Gdns WTHG BN11 * 5 J4
St George's Ms BRI BN1 ....3 H3
St George's Pl BRI BN1 ....3 H3
St George's Rd BRIE/ROTT BN2...58 D1
  WTHG BN11 ....5 J3
St George's Ter BRIE/ROTT BN2...58 C1
St Giles Cl SHOR BN43..................41 H2
St Helen's Crs HOVE BN3.............25 H4
St Helen's Dr HOVE BN3...............25 H4
St Helens Rd BRIE/ROTT BN2.......46 D3
St Helier Rd FERR BN12 ....53 F5
St Heliers Av HOVE BN3................44 A3
St James Av LAN/SOMP BN3........39 G2
St James's Av BRIE/ROTT BN2........3 K6
St James's St BRI BN1 ....3 H5
St James's Street Ms
  BRIE/ROTT BN2...............................3 J5
St James St LEWES BN7...............17 E4
St John's Av FERR BN12...............54 A4
St John's Cl FERR BN12...............54 A4
St John's Hl LEWES BN7...............17 E3
St Johns Ms BRIE/ROTT BN2 *....58 C1
St John's Pl BRIE/ROTT BN2 ....3 J4
  HOVE BN3..45 E4
St John's Rd HOVE BN3...............45 E5
  SEAF BN25......................................72 C1
St John Ter LEWES BN7...............17 E3
St John St LEWES BN7.................17 E3
St Joseph's Cl HOVE BN3.............44 C2
St Julians Cl SHOR BN43..............42 A3
St Julian's La SHOR BN43............42 A3
St Keyna Av HOVE BN3.................43 H4
St Laurence Cl PEAHV BN10 * 62 C4
St Lawrence Av SALV BN13.........55 F1
St Leonard's Av HOVE BN3..........43 G4
St Leonards Cl NEWHV BN9.........65 F3
St Leonard's Gdns HOVE BN3......43 H4
St Leonard's Rd BRIE/ROTT BN2...46 D2
  HOVE BN3..43 G4
  NEWHV BN9.....................................65 F3
St Louie Cl STHW BN42................43 E2
St Luke's Cl LAN/SOMP BN15......56 D1
St Luke's Rd BRIE/ROTT BN2.......46 C4
St Luke's Ter BRIE/ROTT BN2......46 C4
St Malo Cl FERR BN12...................53 F5
St Margarets BRIE/ROTT BN2 *....61 E4
St Margaret's Pl BRI BN1 ....2 D5
St Margaret's Ri SEAF BN25.........69 G2
St Mark's Crs LAN/SOMP BN15....56 D1
St Mark's St BRIE/ROTT BN2.......59 E1
St Martins Crs NEWHV BN9.........64 D4
St Martin's Pl BRIE/ROTT BN2......46 C3
St Martin's St BRIE/ROTT BN2......46 B3
St Mary Magdalene St
  BRIE/ROTT BN2.............................46 B2
St Marys Cl LAN/SOMP BN15......38 C3
  SEAF BN25......................................70 C4
  SHOR BN43.....................................41 F3
St Mary's Pl BRIE/ROTT BN2.........3 K3
St Mary's Rd SHOR BN43.............41 F3
St Mary's Sq BRIE/ROTT BN2......58 D1
St Matthew's Rd WTHG BN11........4 C3
St Maur's Rd FERR BN12...............53 E3
St Michael's Ct WTHG BN11...........4 A5
St Michael's Pl BRI BN1...................2 D3
St Michael's Rd PTSD BN41..........43 F3
  WTHG BN11......................................4 A5
St Michael's Ter LEWES BN7.......17 F2
St Nicholas La LEWES BN7..........17 F3
St Nicholas Rd BRI BN1..................3 F5
  PTSD BN41.....................................43 F3
St Nicolas La SHOR BN43............40 D2
St Osmund Rd FERR BN12...........52 D4
St Pancras Gdns LEWES BN7......16 D4
St Pancras Gn LEWES BN7..........31 F4
St Pancras Rd LEWES BN7..........16 D4
St Patrick's Rd HOVE BN3............44 C3
St Paul's Av LAN/SOMP BN15......56 D1
St Paul's St BRIE/ROTT BN2........46 B2
St Peter's Av PEAHV BN10...........62 C5
St Peter's Cl SEAF BN25...............70 C3
St Peter's Pl BRI BN1......................3 F1
  LAN/SOMP BN15 * 57 E1
  LEWES BN7.....................................17 E4
St Peter's Rd PTSD BN41.............43 F3
  SEAF BN25......................................70 C3
St Peter's St BRI BN1.....................3 H1
St Philips Ms HOVE BN3...............44 B3
St Raphael's Rd WTHG BN11 * 54 D3

St Richards Cl FERR BN12............54 A2
St Richard's Rd PTSD BN41.........43 F3
St Swithun's Ter LEWES BN7.......17 E4
St Thomas's Rd SALV BN13.........55 F1
St Valerie Rd WTHG BN11............55 E4
St Wilfred's Pl SEAF BN25............73 F1
St Wilfred's Rd SALV BN13...........55 H1
Salisbury Rd HOVE BN3................45 E4
  SEAF BN25......................................70 C5
  WTHG BN11......................................4 E4
Saltdean Dr BRIE/ROTT BN2.......61 F4
Saltdean Park Rd
  BRIE/ROTT BN2.............................61 G4
Saltdean V BRIE/ROTT BN2.........61 H2
The Saltings LAN/SOMP BN15......39 H5
  SHOR BN43.....................................40 D4
Saltings Wy STEY/UB BN44............8 A2
Saltwood Rd SEAF BN25...............71 G4
Salvington Cl SALV BN13..............36 C3
Salvington Gdns SALV BN13........36 D4
Salvington Hl SALV BN13..............36 C1
Salvington Rd SALV BN13.............36 C3
Samphire Dr SALV BN13...............35 C5
Sandgate Cl SALV BN13................71 G3
Sandgate Rd BRI BN1...................28 A5
Sandhurst Av BRIE/ROTT BN2.....48 B1
Sandore Cl SEAF BN25.................71 E4
Sandore Rd SEAF BN25................71 E4
Sandown Av FERR BN12...............54 A5
Sandown Cl FERR BN12...............54 A4
Sandown Rd BRIE/ROTT BN2.......46 D3
  STHW BN42.....................................42 B2
Sandringham Cl HOVE BN3..........26 C4
  SEAF BN25......................................71 E2
Sandringham Ct
  LAN/SOMP BN15 * 39 H5
Sandringham Dr HOVE BN3.........26 C4
Sandringham Ms SALV BN13........36 B3
Sandwich Rd WTHG BN11............54 D4
Sanyhils Av BRI BN1.....................13 H5
Sark Gdns FERR BN12..................53 F4
Saunders Hl BRI BN1....................14 D5
Saunders Park Ri
  BRIE/ROTT BN2.............................46 C1
Saunders Park Vw
  BRIE/ROTT BN2.............................46 C1
Saxifrage Wy SALV BN13.............35 G5
Saxon Cl ANG/EP BN16.................52 B2
Saxon La SEAF BN25....................72 C1
Saxon Rd HOVE BN3.....................43 H4
  NEWHV BN9.....................................68 C1
  STEY/UB BN44..................................7 H3
Saxons SHOR BN43.......................41 F1
Saxony Rd SALV BN13...................36 A4
Scarborough Rd BRI BN1..............45 F1
School Cl STHW BN42...................42 C3
School Hl SALV BN13.....................18 C1
School La BRIE/ROTT BN2............61 G3
  STEY/UB BN44..................................7 F3
School Ri BRIE/ROTT BN2............47 E4
School Rd HOVE BN3....................44 B3
  STEY/UB BN44..................................8 A2
Scotland St BRIE/ROTT BN2..........3 K3
Scotney Cl SALV BN13..................35 H5
Scott Rd HOVE BN3.......................44 B3
Seacliffe PEAHV BN10 * 66 B1
Sea Cl FERR BN12.........................54 C3
Seadown Pde
  LAN/SOMP BN15 * 38 D5
Sea Dr FERR BN12.........................53 F5
Seafield Av FERR BN12.................54 B5
Seafield Cl SEAF BN25..................71 F3
Seafield Rd HOVE BN3..................44 D5
Seaford Rd HOVE BN3..................43 G4
  NEWHV BN9.....................................69 F1
Seagrave Cl SEAF BN25 * 69 G2
Seagrove Wy SEAF BN25.............70 D3
Seahaven Gdns SHOR BN43........40 C5
Sea La ANG/EP BN16.....................52 D5
  FERR BN12......................................53 F3
  FERR BN12......................................54 A4
Sea Lane Cl FERR BN12................53 F3
Sea Lane Gdns FERR BN12..........53 F4
Seamill Park Av WTHG BN11........57 E2
Seamill Park Crs WTHG BN11.......56 D2
Seamill Wy WTHG BN11................56 D2
Sea Pl FERR BN12..........................53 G4
Searle Av PEAHV BN10.................67 G2
Sea Rd ANG/EP BN16....................52 A5
Sea-Saw Wy BRIE/ROTT BN2.......47 F3
Seaside Av LAN/SOMP BN15........39 H5
Seaside Cl LAN/SOMP BN15.........39 H5
Seaside Rd LAN/SOMP BN15........39 H5
Seaview Av ANG/EP BN16.............52 A5
  PEAHV BN10...................................67 G3
Seaview Cl LAN/SOMP BN15........57 F1
Seaview Rd BRIE/ROTT BN2........47 H2
  NEWHV BN9.....................................65 F4

  PEAHV BN10...................................67 G3
Sea View Rd WTHG BN11...............4 A7
Sea View Wy BRIE/ROTT BN2......48 B1
Seawaves Cl ANG/EP BN16..........52 A4
Second Av HOVE BN3....................45 E5
  LAN/SOMP BN15.............................39 H4
  NEWHV BN9.....................................68 C2
  SALV BN13.......................................37 H3
Second Rd PEAHV BN10...............66 C1
Sedbury Rd LAN/SOMP BN15.......39 G2
Sefton Cl SALV BN13......................36 B4
Sefton Rd PTSD BN41....................24 D4
Segrave Cl LEWES BN7.................16 D3
Selba Dr BRIE/ROTT BN2.............29 E5
Selborne Pl HOVE BN3..................45 E5
Selborne Rd HOVE BN3.................45 E4
  WTHG BN11......................................5 J2
Selden La SALV BN13....................34 B1
  WTHG BN11......................................5 J4
Selden Pde SALV BN13 * 36 D3
Selden Rd WTHG BN11...................5 J3
Selden's Ms SALV BN13................36 D4
Selden's Wy SALV BN13................36 D4
Selham Cl BRI BN1.........................28 D1
Selham Dr BRI BN1........................28 D1
Selham Pl BRI BN1 * 28 D1
Selhurst Rd BRIE/ROTT BN2........48 C4
Selkirk Cl SALV BN13.....................54 C1
Selmeston Pl BRIE/ROTT BN2......47 F4
Selsey Cl BRI BN1..........................29 E1
  SALV BN13.......................................36 D5
Selsfield Dr BRIE/ROTT BN2.........28 D4
Semley Rd BRI BN1.......................46 A1
Senlac Rd NEWHV BN9.................68 D1
Sevelands Cl BRIE/ROTT BN2......47 F3
Seventh Av LAN/SOMP BN15........39 G2
Seville St BRIE/ROTT BN2............46 C3
Seymour Sq BRIE/ROTT BN2.......58 D1
Shadwells Cl LAN/SOMP BN15.....39 H3
Shadwells Rd LAN/SOMP BN15....39 H3
Shaftesbury Av FERR BN12..........54 C2
Shaftesbury Pl BRI BN1................46 A2
Shaftesbury Rd BRI BN1...............46 A2
Shakespeare Rd WTHG BN11........4 B3
Shakespeare St HOVE BN3..........44 C2
Shandon Gdns SALV BN13...........37 H4
Shandon Rd SALV BN13................37 H4
Shandon Wy SALV BN13...............37 H4
Shanklin Rd BRIE/ROTT BN2........46 C2
Shannon Cl PEAHV BN10.............62 D4
Sharpthorne Crs PTSD BN41........43 G1
Sheepbell Cl PTSD BN41..............25 F4
Sheepfair LEWES BN7...................16 C2
Sheep Pen La SEAF BN25............71 E5
  STEY/UB BN44..................................7 F3
Sheep Wk BRIE/ROTT BN2..........60 D4
Shelby Rd SALV BN13....................36 A4
Sheldon Ct WTHG BN11 * 4 A6
Shelldale Av PTSD BN41...............43 F3
Shelldale Crs PTSD BN41.............43 F3
Shelldale Rd PTSD BN41..............43 F2
Shelley Cl LEWES BN7..................16 D3
Shelley Rd HOVE BN3...................44 B3
  WTHG BN11......................................4 C5
Shenfield Wy BRI BN1...................28 B5
Shepham Av BRIE/ROTT BN2.......61 G4
Shepherds Cl NEWHV BN9...........64 B3
Shepherds Cot PEAHV BN10 * 63 F1
Shepherds Cft BRI BN1.................27 F3
Shepherds Md SALV BN13............19 E4
Sheppard Wy PTSD BN41.............25 E4
Shepway Pde SEAF BN25 * 70 C5
The Shepway SEAF BN25.............71 F4
Sherbourne Cl HOVE BN3............25 H4
Sherbourne Rd HOVE BN3...........25 H4
Sherbourne Wy HOVE BN3..........25 H4
Sherbrooke Cl SALV BN13............36 B4
Sheridan Rd SALV BN13................37 H5
Sheridan Ter HOVE BN3................44 C2
Shermanbury Rd SALV BN13..........4 B1
Sherrington Rd BRIE/ROTT BN2...48 D2
Sherwood Ri SEAF BN25...............70 D4
Sherwood Rd SEAF BN25.............70 D4
Shetland Ct SALV BN13.................35 H5
Shingle Rd SHOR BN43.................41 G4
Shipley Rd BRIE/ROTT BN2..........48 C3
Ship St BRI BN1...............................3 F5
  NEWHV BN9.....................................64 C5
  SHOR BN43.....................................41 G5
Ship Street Gdns BRI BN1 * 3 F5
Shirley Av HOVE BN3.....................26 D5
Shirley Cl SALV BN13.....................37 F3
  SHOR BN43.....................................42 A2
Shirley Dr HOVE BN3.....................45 E1
  SALV BN13.......................................37 F3
Shirley Rd HOVE BN3....................45 E2
Shirley St HOVE BN3.....................44 D3
Shooting Fld STEY/UB BN44...........7 F2
Shopsdam Rd LAN/SOMP BN15...57 H1

Shoreham By-Pass PTSD BN41....
  SHOR BN43.....................................
Shoreham Rd STEY/UB BN44.......
Short Brow SEAF BN25..................
Shortgate Rd BRIE/ROTT BN2......
Sidehill Dr PTSD BN41...................
Sillwood Pl BRI BN1.......................
Sillwood Rd BRI BN1......................
Sillwood St BRI BN1.......................
Sillwood Ter BRI BN1.....................
Silver Birch Dr SALV BN13............
Silverdale WTHG BN11 * ....
Silverdale Av HOVE BN3................
Silverdale Dr LAN/SOMP BN15......
Silverdale Rd HOVE BN3...............
Singleton Cl FERR BN12................
Singleton Crs FERR BN12.............
Singleton Rd BRI BN1....................
Sir George's Pl STEY/UB BN44.....
Skyline Vw PEAHV BN10...............
Slindon Av PEAHV BN10...............
Slindon Rd SALV BN13..................
Slinford Cl BRIE/ROTT BN2...........
Slonk Hill Rd SHOR BN43..............
Smugglers La STEY/UB BN44.......
Smugglers Wk FERR BN12...........
Snedrone LEWES BN7...................
Solway Av BRI BN1........................
Somerhill Av HOVE BN3................
Somerhill Rd HOVE BN3................
Somerset Cl SALV BN13................
Somerset Rd ANG/EP BN16..........
  FERR BN12......................................
Somerset St BRIE/ROTT BN2.......
Sompting Av SALV BN13...............
Sompting By-Pass SALV BN13......
Sompting Cl BRIE/ROTT BN2........
Sompting Rd SALV BN13...............
Sopers La STEY/UB BN44.............
Southall Av BRIE/ROTT BN2.........
Southampton St BRIE/ROTT BN2..
South Ash STEY/UB BN44.............
South Av BRIE/ROTT BN2.............
  FERR BN12......................................
South Beach SHOR BN43 * ....
South Coast Rd BRIE/ROTT BN2...
  PEAHV BN10...................................
Southcourt Rd SALV BN13............
Southdown Av BRI BN1..................
  LEWES BN7.....................................
  PEAHV BN10...................................
  PTSD BN41.....................................
Southdown Cl NEWHV BN9...........
Southdown Cnr SEAF BN25 * ....
Southdown Ms BRIE/ROTT BN2....
Southdown Pl BRI BN1...................
Southdown Rd BRI BN1.................
  NEWHV BN9.....................................
  PTSD BN41.....................................
  SEAF BN25......................................
  SEAF BN25......................................
  SHOR BN43.....................................
  STHW BN42.....................................
South Downs Rd LEWES BN7.......
South Downs Wy HFD BN5............
  LEWES BN7.....................................
  SHOR BN43.....................................
  STEY/UB BN44.................................
Southdown Ter STEY/UB BN44.....
Southdown View Cl SALV BN13.....
Southdown View Rd
  SALV BN13.......................................
Southdown View Wy
  SALV BN13.......................................
South Dr FERR BN12......................
Southey Rd WTHG BN11................
South Farm Rd SALV BN13...........
Southfield Rd SALV BN13..............
South La NEWHV BN9....................
South Ldg LAN/SOMP BN15 * ....
Southmount BRIE/ROTT BN2.........
Southon Cl PTSD BN41..................
Southover High St LEWES BN7.....
Southover Pl BRIE/ROTT BN2.......
Southover Rd LEWES BN7............
Southover St BRIE/ROTT BN2.......
South Rd BRI BN1..........................
  NEWHV BN9.....................................
South Road Ms BRI BN1................
Southsea Av FERR BN12...............
South Strd ANG/EP BN16..............
South St BRI BN1...........................
  BRI BN1..
  LAN/SOMP BN15.............................
  LEWES BN7.....................................
  PTSD BN41.....................................
  SALV BN13.......................................
  SEAF BN25......................................
  WTHG BN11......................................

Vw ANG/EP BN16 ...... 52 B5
lew Cl SHOR BN43 ...... 42 A3
lew Dr WTHG BN11 ...... 55 E3
lew Gdns WTHG BN11 ...... 54 D3
w Rd PEAHV BN10 ...... 63 E5
BN42 ...... 42 C2
lew Ter NEWHV BN9 * 65 E3
water Cl BRIE/ROTT BN2 ...... 46 D4
BN12 ...... 53 H2
Wy LEWES BN7 ...... 16 C3
HV BN9 ...... 68 D1
BN25 ...... 73 G2
rays SALV BN13 ...... 38 A4
rick Sq STHW BN42 ...... 42 C3
rick St STHW BN42 ...... 42 C2
vold Cl SALV BN13 ...... 36 C1
Woodlands BRI BN1 ...... 27 G3
ign Cl SEAF BN25 ...... 71 E3
arrows PEAHV BN10 ...... 63 F4
vell Cl SALV BN13 ...... 35 G5
r Av HOVE BN3 ...... 25 H4
s Fld LEWES BN7 ...... 17 G2
s La LEWES BN7 ...... 17 F2
SALV BN13 ...... 36 A2
s Gv STHW BN42 ...... 42 B3
nneys LEWES BN7 ...... 17 G2
nney ANG/EP BN16 ...... 52 A5
BN3 ...... 27 E4
rd Rd BRI BN1 ...... 16 D3
te Rd STHW BN42 ...... 42 D2
ield Av PEAHV BN10 ...... 62 B5
ield Rd BRI BN1 ...... 45 H2
Gdns BRI BN1 ...... 3 F4
S BN7 ...... 17 F3
St BRI BN1 ...... 1 D4
on Dr SALV BN13 ...... 35 H4
uare SALV BN13 * 37 H5
La SALV BN13 ...... 18 C1
d Rd BRI BN1 ...... 45 G2
BN25 ...... 70 D5
ers Hl HFD BN5 ...... 10 D1
an Cl BRI BN1 ...... 28 D1
d Av BRI BN1 ...... 45 H2
d Cl HOVE BN3 ...... 45 E1
d Rd BRI BN1 ...... 45 G2
rd Sq WTHG BN11 ...... 4 E3
pe Rd WTHG BN11 ...... 4 E3
Av PTSD BN41 ...... 24 D4
Rd BRI BN1 ...... 46 A3
V BN10 ...... 62 D4
BN41 ...... 43 E2
BN11 ...... 5 F2
BRIE/ROTT BN2 ...... 3 K4
r Av BRIE/ROTT BN2 ...... 61 G3
r Park Rd BRI BN1 ...... 28 A5
r St BRI BN1 ...... 28 B5
r Vls BRI BN1 ...... 28 B4
eld Rd LEWES BN7 ...... 16 D2
ad Crs BRIE/ROTT BN2 ...... 48 D4
ield Dr BRIE/ROTT BN2 ...... 29 F4
R HOVE BN3 ...... 43 H2
Ap BRI BN1 ...... 29 H1
BN25 ...... 70 D5
Pde LAN/SOMP BN15 * 39 G5
G BN11 * 55 E2
Rd BRI BN1 ...... 27 F4
BN3 ...... 43 G3
S BN7 ...... 17 F4
HV BN9 ...... 65 F4
BN25 ...... 69 H4
UB BN44 ...... 7 G3
...... 42 C3
G BN11 ...... 5 F2
St BRI BN1 ...... 3 G2
S BN7 ...... 17 F3
l SALV BN13 ...... 18 C2
own Rd
SOMP BN15 ...... 39 E2
a SALV BN13 ...... 18 C2
Vw SALV BN13 ...... 37 E5
Gdns BRIE/ROTT BN2 ...... 3 H5
La BRI BN1 ...... 3 G5
t BRIE/ROTT BN2 ...... 3 H6
ns Rd BRI BN1 ...... 28 B5
son Rd BRI BN1 ...... 28 A1
s Inn La LEWES BN7 * 17 E4
Rd SEAF BN25 ...... 72 D1
Gdns WTHG BN11 ...... 5 G5
C BN11 ...... 72 C1
yne SEAF BN25 * 72 C1
SOMP BN15 ...... 39 F2
g Av HOVE BN3 ...... 26 B5
V BN10 ...... 67 E2
g By-Pass
UB BN44 ...... 7 H5
g Cl FERR BN12 ...... 53 H2
SOMP BN15 ...... 39 F2
BN25 ...... 73 G1

Steyning Rd BRIE/ROTT BN2 ...... 60 D4
SEAF BN25 ...... 73 G1
SHOR BN43 ...... 22 C2
Stirling Av SEAF BN25 ...... 71 G4
Stirling Cl SEAF BN25 ...... 71 G5
Stirling Pl HOVE BN3 ...... 44 C4
Stoke Abbott Rd WTHG BN11 ...... 4 E4
Stoke Cl SEAF BN25 ...... 71 F5
Stoke Manor Cl SEAF BN25 ...... 71 F5
Stone Cl SALV BN13 ...... 36 D4
Stonecroft Cl HOVE BN3 ...... 26 A3
Stonecross Rd BRIE/ROTT BN2 ...... 29 F3
Stoneham Cl LEWES BN7 ...... 17 E1
Stoneham Rd HOVE BN3 ...... 44 B3
Stonehurst Ct BRIE/ROTT BN2 ...... 46 C4
Stonehurst Rd SALV BN13 ...... 36 D5
Stone La SALV BN13 ...... 36 D4
Stoneleigh Av BRI BN1 ...... 27 H1
Stoneleigh Cl BRI BN1 ...... 27 H1
Stonery Cl BRI BN1 ...... 25 E5
Stonery Rd PTSD BN41 ...... 25 E5
Stone St BRI BN1 ...... 2 D4
Stonewood Cl SEAF BN25 ...... 71 G5
Stoney La SHOR BN43 ...... 42 A2
Stopham Cl SALV BN13 ...... 37 E5
Storrington Cl HOVE BN3 ...... 26 A5
Storrington Ri SALV BN13 ...... 18 D3
Stour Cl SALV BN13 ...... 36 A2
Stour Rd SALV BN13 ...... 36 A2
Strand Pde FERR BN12 ...... 54 C1
The Strand BRIE/ROTT BN2 ...... 59 G2
FERR BN12 ...... 53 E5
Strathmore Cl SALV BN13 ...... 54 C1
Strathmore Rd SALV BN13 ...... 54 C1
The Street LAN/SOMP BN15 ...... 39 G2
LEWES BN7 ...... 32 A2
SALV BN14 ...... 35 E1
SHOR BN43 ...... 40 D1
STEY/UB BN44 ...... 7 H4
Stringer Wy BRI BN1 ...... 27 H4
Stuart Cl WTHG BN11 ...... 5 K1
Sudeley Pl BRIE/ROTT BN2 ...... 58 D1
Sudeley St BRIE/ROTT BN2 ...... 58 D1
Sudeley Ter BRIE/ROTT BN2 ...... 58 D1
Suffolk St HOVE BN3 ...... 44 B2
Sugden Rd WTHG BN11 ...... 5 J2
Sullington Cl BRIE/ROTT BN2 ...... 29 F3
Sullington Gdns SALV BN13 ...... 18 D3
Sullington Wy SHOR BN43 ...... 41 G2
Summer Cl PTSD BN41 ...... 43 E3
Summerdale Rd HOVE BN3 ...... 25 H5
Summerdown Cl SALV BN13 ...... 35 H5
Summerfields SALV BN13 ...... 18 C1
Summersdeane STHW BN42 ...... 42 D1
Sunningdale Cl SEAF BN25 ...... 73 E1
Sunningdale Ct FERR BN12 * 54 C1
Sunningdale Rd SALV BN13 ...... 36 B4
Sunninghill Av HOVE BN3 ...... 26 A5
Sunninghill Cl HOVE BN3 ...... 26 A5
Sunny Cl FERR BN12 ...... 54 C4
Sunnydale Av BRI BN1 ...... 28 A1
Sunnydale Cl BRI BN1 ...... 28 A1
Sunnyside Cl ANG/EP BN16 ...... 52 A1
Sunset Cl PEAHV BN10 ...... 62 D4
Sun St LEWES BN7 ...... 17 E3
Sunview Av PEAHV BN10 ...... 67 F2
Surrenden Cl BRI BN1 ...... 27 H3
Surrenden Crs BRI BN1 ...... 27 G3
Surrenden Holt BRI BN1 ...... 27 H3
Surrenden Pk BRI BN1 ...... 28 A4
Surrenden Rd BRI BN1 ...... 27 H4
Surrey Cl SEAF BN25 ...... 70 A4
Surrey Rd SEAF BN25 ...... 70 A4
Surrey St BRI BN1 ...... 3 F2
WTHG BN11 ...... 4 D6
Surry St SHOR BN43 ...... 41 F3
Sussex Border Pth BRI BN1 ...... 11 G1
PTSD BN41 ...... 24 C1
Sussex Hts BRI BN1 * 2 D5
Sussex Ms BRIE/ROTT BN2 ...... 59 E1
Sussex Pl BRIE/ROTT BN2 ...... 3 J3
Sussex Rd HOVE BN3 ...... 44 D5
LAN/SOMP BN15 ...... 40 C5
WTHG BN11 ...... 5 F3
Sussex Sq BRIE/ROTT BN2 ...... 59 E1
Sussex St BRIE/ROTT BN2 ...... 3 J4
Sussex Ter BRIE/ROTT BN2 ...... 3 J3
Sussex Wy PEAHV BN10 ...... 66 B1
Sussex Whf SHOR BN43 * 41 H4
Sutherland Rd BRIE/ROTT BN2 ...... 46 C5
Sutton Av PEAHV BN10 ...... 66 D1
SEAF BN25 ...... 70 C5
Sutton Av North PEAHV BN10 ...... 62 D5
Sutton Cl BRIE/ROTT BN2 ...... 48 C1
Sutton Croft La SEAF BN25 ...... 70 C5
Sutton Dro SEAF BN25 ...... 70 D4
Sutton Park Rd SEAF BN25 ...... 70 D5
Sutton Pl SEAF BN25 * 71 F4
Sutton Rd SEAF BN25 ...... 70 D5

Swallows Cl LAN/SOMP BN15 ...... 40 C5
Swallows Green Dr
SALV BN13 ...... 36 A5
The Swallows PEAHV BN10 ...... 62 D4
Swanborough Dr
BRIE/ROTT BN2 ...... 47 F3
Swanborough Dro LEWES BN7 ...... 32 B4
Swanborough Hollow
LEWES BN7 ...... 32 D4
Swanborough Pl
BRIE/ROTT BN2 ...... 47 F3
Swanbourne Cl
LAN/SOMP BN15 ...... 39 H2
Swandean Cl SALV BN13 ...... 36 C2
Swannee Cl PEAHV BN10 ...... 63 F4
Swillage La SALV BN13 ...... 34 A1
Swiss Gdns SHOR BN43 ...... 41 E3
Sycamore Cl BRIE/ROTT BN2 ...... 48 C2
PTSD BN41 ...... 25 G4
SALV BN13 ...... 71 G5
The Sycamores PEAHV BN10 ...... 63 F4
Sydney St BRI BN1 ...... 3 G3
Sylvan Rd LAN/SOMP BN15 ...... 38 D4
Sylvester Wy HOVE BN3 ...... 25 G4
Symbister Rd PTSD BN41 ...... 43 G3

T

Talbot Crs BRI BN1 ...... 28 D1
Talbot Ter LEWES BN7 ...... 17 E3
Talland Pde SEAF BN25 * 72 C1
Tamar Av SALV BN13 ...... 36 A2
Tamar Cl SALV BN13 ...... 36 A2
Tamarisk Wy FERR BN12 ...... 53 F5
Tamplin Ter BRIE/ROTT BN2 * 3 J2
Tamworth Rd HOVE BN3 ...... 44 B3
Tandridge Rd HOVE BN3 ...... 44 A4
Tangmere Rd BRI BN1 ...... 28 A1
Tanners Brook LEWES BN7 ...... 17 F4
Tanyard La STEY/UB BN44 ...... 7 E3
Tarmount La SHOR BN43 ...... 41 F5
Tarner Rd BRIE/ROTT BN2 ...... 3 K4
Tarragon Wy SHOR BN43 ...... 42 A1
Tarring Cl NEWHV BN9 ...... 64 D3
Tarring Ga SALV BN13 * 55 E1
Tarring Rd WTHG BN11 ...... 4 A2
Tasman Wy SALV BN13 ...... 36 A3
Taunton Rd BRIE/ROTT BN2 ...... 47 F1
Taunton Wy BRIE/ROTT BN2 ...... 47 G1
Tavistock Down BRI BN1 ...... 28 C5
Tavy Cl SALV BN13 ...... 36 A4
Taw Cl SALV BN13 ...... 36 B3
Teg Cl PTSD BN41 ...... 25 C5
Telgarth Rd FERR BN12 ...... 53 E5
Telscombe Cliffs Wy
PEAHV BN10 ...... 66 B1
Telscombe Cl PEAHV BN10 ...... 63 F3
Telscombe Pk PEAHV BN10 ...... 63 G3
Telscombe Rd PEAHV BN10 ...... 63 G3
The Templars SALV BN13 ...... 38 A3
Temple Gdns HOVE BN3 ...... 2 C1
Temple St BRI BN1 ...... 2 C4
Ten Acres WTHG BN11 ...... 56 C2
Tenantry Down Rd
BRIE/ROTT BN2 ...... 47 E3
Tenantry Rd BRIE/ROTT BN2 ...... 46 D2
Tennis Rd HOVE BN3 ...... 44 A4
Tennyson Rd WTHG BN11 ...... 4 D1
Terminus Pl BRI BN1 ...... 3 F1
Terminus Rd BRI BN1 ...... 3 F1
Terminus St BRI BN1 ...... 3 F1
The Terrace FERR BN12 * 54 A3
LAN/SOMP BN15 ...... 57 C1
Terringes Av SALV BN13 ...... 36 C5
Teville Ga WTHG BN11 ...... 4 E2
Teville Pl WTHG BN11 ...... 4 D2
Teville Rd WTHG BN11 ...... 4 D2
Thackeray Rd SALV BN13 ...... 56 B1
Thakeham Cl ANG/EP BN16 ...... 52 B2
FERR BN12 ...... 53 G3
Thakeham Dr FERR BN12 ...... 53 G3
Thalassa Rd WTHG BN11 ...... 56 D2
Thames Cl BRIE/ROTT BN2 ...... 3 K4
Thames Wy SALV BN13 ...... 36 B3
The Thatch Ct
LAN/SOMP BN15 * 39 H2
Thesiger Cl WTHG BN11 ...... 56 C1
Thesiger Rd WTHG BN11 ...... 56 C1
Third Av HOVE BN3 ...... 44 D5
LAN/SOMP BN15 ...... 39 G3
NEWHV BN9 ...... 68 C2
SALV BN13 ...... 37 H3
Third Rd PEAHV BN10 ...... 66 C1
Thirlmere Crs LAN/SOMP BN15 ...... 38 D5
Thomas St LEWES BN7 ...... 17 G2

Thompson Rd BRI BN1 ...... 46 C1
NEWHV BN9 ...... 65 F3
Thomson Cl SALV BN13 ...... 35 H4
Thornbush Crs PTSD BN41 ...... 25 F4
Thorndean Rd BRIE/ROTT BN2 ...... 28 D4
Thornhill Av BRI BN1 ...... 14 A5
Thornhill Cl HOVE BN3 ...... 26 A5
Thornhill Ri PTSD BN41 ...... 25 E3
Thornhill Wy PTSD BN41 ...... 25 E4
Thorn Rd WTHG BN11 ...... 4 C6
Thornscroft STEY/UB BN44 ...... 7 F2
Thurlow Rd WTHG BN11 ...... 5 H2
Thyme Cl SHOR BN43 ...... 42 A1
Ticehurst Rd BRIE/ROTT BN2 ...... 47 F5
Tichborne St BRI BN1 ...... 3 G4
Tidy St BRI BN1 ...... 3 G3
Tilbury Pl BRIE/ROTT BN2 ...... 3 J4
Tilbury Wy BRIE/ROTT BN2 ...... 3 K3
Tilgate Cl BRIE/ROTT BN2 ...... 46 D4
Tillstone Cl BRIE/ROTT BN2 ...... 28 D5
Tillstone St BRIE/ROTT BN2 ...... 3 K5
Timber Cl SALV BN13 ...... 36 A5
Timber Yd Cots LEWES BN7 ...... 17 G3
Tintern Cl BRI BN1 ...... 46 B1
Tisbury Rd HOVE BN3 ...... 44 D4
Titch Hl LAN/SOMP BN15 ...... 20 C3
Titian Rd HOVE BN3 ...... 44 B3
Titnore La FERR BN12 ...... 35 G4
Titnore Wy SALV BN13 ...... 35 G5
Tivoli Crs BRI BN1 ...... 45 F1
Tivoli Crs North BRI BN1 ...... 27 F5
Tivoli Pl BRI BN1 ...... 27 F5
Tivoli Rd BRI BN1 ...... 27 F5
Tollgate PEAHV BN10 ...... 62 D4
Tongdean Av HOVE BN3 ...... 27 E4
Tongdean La BRI BN1 ...... 27 F3
Tongdean Ri BRI BN1 ...... 27 E3
Tongdean Rd HOVE BN3 ...... 26 D4
Toomey Rd STEY/UB BN44 ...... 7 F1
Torcross Cl BRIE/ROTT BN2 ...... 47 G2
Toronto Cl SALV BN13 ...... 36 A4
Toronto Ter BRIE/ROTT BN2 ...... 3 K3
LEWES BN7 ...... 17 E3
Torrance Cl HOVE BN3 ...... 44 B2
Torridge Cl SALV BN13 ...... 36 A4
Tor Rd PEAHV BN10 ...... 63 E4
Tor Rd West PEAHV BN10 ...... 62 D3
Totland Rd BRIE/ROTT BN2 ...... 46 D3
Tottington Wy SHOR BN43 ...... 41 H1
Towergate BRI BN1 ...... 27 G5
Tower Rd BRIE/ROTT BN2 ...... 46 C4
LAN/SOMP BN15 ...... 39 F5
WTHG BN11 ...... 5 G3
Towers Rd STEY/UB BN44 ...... 8 B2
Trafalgar Cl PEAHV BN10 ...... 63 E4
Trafalgar Ct BRI BN1 ...... 3 H2
Trafalgar Ga BRIE/ROTT BN2 ...... 59 F2
Trafalgar La BRI BN1 ...... 3 G2
Trafalgar Pl BRI BN1 ...... 3 G2
Trafalgar Rd PTSD BN41 ...... 43 F2
Trafalgar St BRI BN1 ...... 3 G2
Trafalgar Ter BRI BN1 * 3 G2
Transit Rd NEWHV BN9 ...... 68 D1
Tredcroft Rd HOVE BN3 ...... 26 D5
Tree Tops BRIE/ROTT BN2 ...... 48 C2
Treharne Cl SALV BN13 ...... 36 B3
Tremola Av BRIE/ROTT BN2 ...... 61 G3
Trent Cl LAN/SOMP BN15 ...... 39 E4
Trent Rd FERR BN12 ...... 54 C3
Trevor Cl WTHG BN11 ...... 4 D4
Treyford Cl BRIE/ROTT BN2 ...... 48 C1
Trinity St BRIE/ROTT BN2 ...... 46 B1
Tristram Cl LAN/SOMP BN15 ...... 38 C3
Troon Cl SEAF BN25 ...... 69 G2
Truleigh Cl BRIE/ROTT BN2 ...... 48 D3
Truleigh Dr PTSD BN41 ...... 24 D3
Truleigh Rd STEY/UB BN44 ...... 8 B2
Truleigh Wy SHOR BN43 ...... 41 G2
Truro Cl WTHG BN11 * 55 E4
Tudor Cl BRIE/ROTT BN2 * 60 D3
HOVE BN3 ...... 26 B5
SALV BN13 ...... 18 C1
SEAF BN25 ...... 70 B4
Tudor Dr STEY/UB BN44 ...... 8 A1
Tumulus Rd BRIE/ROTT BN2 ...... 61 G3
Tunsgate STEY/UB BN44 ...... 7 F3
Turner Rd SALV BN13 ...... 38 A4
Turnpike Cl PEAHV BN10 ...... 63 E5
Turton Cl BRIE/ROTT BN2 ...... 46 D5
Tuscan Cl PEAHV BN10 * 66 B1
Twineham Cl BRIE/ROTT BN2 ...... 47 F3
Twitten Cl STHW BN42 ...... 42 C3
Twittenside STEY/UB BN44 * 8 B3
The Twitten STHW BN42 ...... 42 C3
Twitten Wy SALV BN13 ...... 55 E1
Twyford Cl SALV BN13 ...... 36 C4
Twyford Gdns SALV BN13 ...... 36 C4
Twyford Rd BRI BN1 ...... 28 D1
SALV BN13 ...... 36 C4

Tye Cl BRIE/ROTT BN2 .... **61** H5
Tyedean Rd PEAHV BN10 .... **62** B5
Tye Vw PEAHV BN10 .... **62** B5
Tyne Cl SALV BN13 .... **36** A3
The Tynings LAN/SOMP BN15 ...... **39** G5

U

Uckfield Cl BRIE/ROTT BN2 .... **47** F4
Ullswater Rd LAN/SOMP BN15 ..... **38** D5
Underdown Rd STHW BN42 .... **42** C2
Undermill Rd STEY/UB BN44 .... **8** B2
Union Pl WTHG BN11 .... **5** F4
Union Rd BRIE/ROTT BN2 .... **3** J1
Union St BRI BN1 .... **3** G5
Uplands Av SALV BN13 .... **36** D1
Uplands Rd BRI BN1 .... **28** C5
Upper Abbey Rd
    BRIE/ROTT BN2 .... **58** D1
Upper Bannings Rd
    BRIE/ROTT BN2 .... **62** A2
Upper Bedford St
    BRIE/ROTT BN2 .... **58** C1
Upper Belgrave Rd SEAF BN25 .... **70** D3
Upper Bevendean Av
    BRIE/ROTT BN2 .... **47** E1
Upper Boundstone La
    LAN/SOMP BN15 .... **39** F3
Upper Brighton Rd SALV BN13 ..... **37** H3
    SALV BN13 .... **38** B3
Upper Chalvington Pl
    BRIE/ROTT BN2 .... **47** E5
Upper Chyngton Gdns
    SEAF BN25 .... **71** F4
Upper Dr ANG/EP BN16 .... **52** B5
The Upper Dr HOVE BN3 .... **45** E2
Upper Gardner St BRI BN1 .... **3** G3
Upper Gloucester Rd BRI BN1 ...... **3** F2
Upper Hamilton Rd BRI BN1 .... **45** G2
Upper High St WTHG BN11 .... **5** G2
Upper Hollingdean Rd BRI BN1 ..... **46** B1
Upper Kingston La STHW BN42 ..... **42** B1
Upper Lewes Rd
    BRIE/ROTT BN2 .... **46** B3
Upper Market St HOVE BN3 .... **2** B4
Upper North St BRI BN1 .... **2** D3
Upper Park Pl BRIE/ROTT BN2 ..... **3** K4
Upper Rock Gdns
    BRIE/ROTT BN2 .... **3** K5
Upper St James's St
    BRIE/ROTT BN2 .... **3** K6
Upper Sherwood Rd
    SEAF BN25 .... **70** D4
Upper Shoreham Rd
    SHOR BN43 .... **40** D2
Upper Sudeley St
    BRIE/ROTT BN2 .... **58** D1
Upper Valley Rd NEWHV BN9 ...... **68** B2
Upper Wellington Rd
    BRIE/ROTT BN2 .... **46** C3
Upper West Dr FERR BN12 .... **53** E4
Upper West La
    LAN/SOMP BN15 .... **39** G3
Upper Winfield Av BRI BN1 .... **27** H1
Upton Av STHW BN42 .... **42** C1
Upton Gdns SALV BN13 .... **54** D1
Upton Rd SALV BN13 .... **54** D1

V

Vale Av BRI BN1 .... **13** G5
    SALV BN13 .... **18** D5
Vale Cl SEAF BN25 .... **71** F3
Vale Dr SALV BN13 .... **18** D5
Vale Gdns PTSD BN41 .... **43** F3
Valence Rd LEWES BN7 .... **16** D3
Valencia Rd WTHG BN11 .... **55** E2
Valentine Cl SALV BN13 .... **37** F3
Valerie Cl PTSD BN41 .... **25** F5
Vale Rd BRIE/ROTT BN2 .... **61** H2
    PTSD BN41 .... **43** G3
    SEAF BN25 .... **70** D4
The Vale BRIE/ROTT BN2 .... **48** C5
Vale Wk SALV BN13 .... **18** D5
Vallance Gdns HOVE BN3 .... **44** C4
Vallance Rd HOVE BN3 .... **44** C4
Valley Cl BRI BN1 .... **27** E3
    NEWHV BN9 .... **64** B5
Valley Dene NEWHV BN9 .... **68** B1
Valley Dr BRI BN1 .... **27** E3
    SEAF BN25 .... **71** E3
Valley Gdns SALV BN13 .... **37** E1
Valley Ri SEAF BN25 .... **70** D4
Valley Rd LAN/SOMP BN15 .... **39** E2
    LEWES BN7 .... **16** C4

NEWHV BN9 .... **68** B1
PEAHV BN10 .... **63** E3
PTSD BN41 .... **25** E5
Vancouver Cl SALV BN13 .... **36** B4
Vancouver Rd SALV BN13 .... **36** A4
Vanguard Wy SEAF BN25 .... **73** E2
Varey Rd SALV BN13 .... **35** H4
Varndean Cl BRI BN1 .... **27** G4
Varndean Dr BRI BN1 .... **27** G4
Varndean Gdns BRI BN1 .... **27** G4
Varndean Holt BRI BN1 .... **27** H4
Varndean Rd BRI BN1 .... **27** G4
Ventnor Vls HOVE BN3 .... **44** D4
Vere Rd BRI BN1 .... **46** A2
Vermont Dr ANG/EP BN16 .... **52** A4
Vermont Wy ANG/EP BN16 .... **52** A4
Vernon Av BRIE/ROTT BN2 .... **48** A1
    PEAHV BN10 .... **67** F2
Vernon Gdns BRI BN1 .... **2** D2
Vernon Ter BRI BN1 .... **2** D2
Veronica Cl ANG/EP BN16 .... **52** A5
Veronica Wy BRIE/ROTT BN2 ...... **3** K6
Verralls Wk LEWES BN7 .... **17** E4
Viaduct Rd BRI BN1 .... **46** A3
Vicarage Cl NEWHV BN9 .... **65** E3
    SEAF BN25 .... **70** D5
Vicarage Flds SALV BN13 .... **36** B3
Vicarage La BRIE/ROTT BN2 .... **60** D4
    STEY/UB BN44 .... **7** F3
Vicarage Ter BRIE/ROTT BN2 ...... **60** D4
Victor Cl SEAF BN25 .... **70** B3
Victoria Av PEAHV BN10 .... **67** E2
Victoria Gv HOVE BN3 .... **45** E4
Victoria Ms BRIE/ROTT BN2 * **60** D4
Victoria Park Gdns WTHG BN11 .... **4** C3
Victoria Pl BRI BN1 .... **2** D3
Victoria Rd BRI BN1 .... **2** D3
    PTSD BN41 .... **43** F2
    SHOR BN43 .... **41** E3
    STHW BN42 .... **42** B3
    WTHG BN11 .... **4** D3
Victoria St BRI BN1 .... **2** D3
Victory Ms BRIE/ROTT BN2 .... **59** G2
View Rd PEAHV BN10 .... **63** E5
Viking Cl SEAF BN25 .... **69** G2
The Village Barn BRI BN1 .... **13** G5
Village Cl PTSD BN41 .... **25** F5
Village Wy BRI BN1 .... **30** A1
Villiers Cl BRIE/ROTT BN2 .... **48** C2
Vincent Cl LAN/SOMP BN15 .... **39** F4
Vine Pl BRI BN1 .... **2** E3
Vineries Cl SALV BN13 .... **37** E4
Vines Cross Rd BRIE/ROTT BN2 ... **47** F3
Vine St BRI BN1 .... **3** H3

W

Wadhurst Dr FERR BN12 .... **53** H5
Wadhurst Ri BRIE/ROTT BN2 .... **59** F1
Waite Cl LEWES BN7 .... **17** F2
Wakefield Rd BRIE/ROTT BN2 ...... **46** B2
Waldegrave Rd BRI BN1 .... **27** H5
Waldron Av BRI BN1 .... **28** D1
Waldron Pl BRI BN1 * **28** D1
Waldshut Rd LEWES BN7 .... **16** C1
Walesbeech Rd BRIE/ROTT BN2 .. **61** H5
The Walkway ANG/EP BN16 .... **52** A1
Wallace Av WTHG BN11 .... **54** D3
Wallace Ms WTHG BN11 * **54** D4
Wallace Pde FERR BN12 * **54** D3
Wallands Crs LEWES BN7 .... **17** E2
Walmer Crs BRIE/ROTT BN2 .... **47** H1
Walmer Rd SEAF BN25 .... **71** G4
Walnut Cl BRI BN1 .... **27** G4
Walnut Ldg SALV BN13 * **4** C1
Walnut Tree Wy SALV BN13 .... **35** H5
Walpole Av FERR BN12 .... **54** B3
Walpole Rd BRIE/ROTT BN2 .... **58** C1
Walpole Ter BRIE/ROTT BN2 .... **46** D5
Walsingham Rd HOVE BN3 .... **44** B4
Walton Bank BRI BN1 .... **29** E2
Walton Cl SALV BN13 .... **36** D4
Walton Ldg SALV BN13 .... **36** D4
Wanderdown Cl
    BRIE/ROTT BN2 .... **60** C1
Wanderdown Dr
    BRIE/ROTT BN2 .... **60** C1
Wanderdown Rd
    BRIE/ROTT BN2 .... **60** B1
Wanderdown Wy
    BRIE/ROTT BN2 .... **60** C1
Wantley Rd SALV BN13 .... **37** E1
Warbleton Cl BRIE/ROTT BN2 ...... **47** E5
Warenne Rd HOVE BN3 .... **25** G4
Warleigh Rd BRI BN1 .... **46** A2
Warmdene Av BRI BN1 .... **27** H1
Warmdene Rd BRI BN1 .... **27** H1

Warmdene Wy BRI BN1 .... **27** H1
Warner Rd SALV BN13 .... **56** B1
Warnham Cl FERR BN12 .... **54** C4
Warnham Ms FERR BN12 * **54** C4
Warnham Ri BRI BN1 .... **28** A2
Warnham Rd FERR BN12 .... **54** B3
Warren Av BRIE/ROTT BN2 .... **48** A1
Warren Cl BRIE/ROTT BN2 .... **47** H2
    LEWES BN7 .... **16** D4
    SALV BN13 .... **37** F3
Warren Dr LEWES BN7 .... **16** C4
Warren Farm Pl SALV BN13 .... **37** E2
Warren Gdns SALV BN13 .... **37** F3
Warren Ri BRIE/ROTT BN2 .... **47** H2
Warren Rd BRIE/ROTT BN2 .... **47** E3
    SALV BN13 .... **37** F3
The Warren FERR BN12 .... **53** F5
Warren Wy BRIE/ROTT BN2 .... **48** B2
    PEAHV BN10 .... **62** C4
Warr Gn LEWES BN7 .... **16** D1
Warrior Cl PTSD BN41 .... **25** F5
Warwick Gdns WTHG BN11 .... **5** G5
Warwick La WTHG BN11 * **5** G5
Warwick Mt BRIE/ROTT BN2 * **58** C1
Warwick Pl WTHG BN11 .... **5** H4
Warwick Rd SEAF BN25 * **70** C5
    WTHG BN11 .... **5** H5
Warwick St WTHG BN11 .... **5** F5
Washington St BRIE/ROTT BN2 .... **3** K2
Waterdyke Av STHW BN42 .... **42** C3
Waterford Cl PEAHV BN10 .... **63** E3
Watergate La LEWES BN7 .... **17** E4
Waterhall Rd BRI BN1 .... **27** E1
Water La ANG/EP BN16 .... **34** C3
Waterloo Pl LEWES BN7 .... **17** F3
Waterloo St HOVE BN3 .... **2** B5
Watersfield Rd SALV BN13 .... **37** F5
Watling Cl STHW BN42 .... **42** C3
Watling Rd STHW BN42 .... **42** C3
Waverley Crs BRI BN1 .... **46** B1
Wavertree Rd FERR BN12 .... **54** B2
Wayfield Av HOVE BN3 .... **44** A1
Wayfield Cl HOVE BN3 .... **44** A1
Wayland Av BRI BN1 .... **27** E3
Wayland Hts BRI BN1 .... **27** E3
Wayside BRI BN1 .... **27** F1
    LAN/SOMP BN15 * **39** E5
Wayside Av SALV BN13 .... **36** B3
The Way ANG/EP BN16 .... **52** A5
Weald Av HOVE BN3 .... **44** B1
Weald Cl LEWES BN7 * **17** E2
Weald Dyke SHOR BN43 .... **41** F4
Wear Cl SALV BN13 .... **36** A3
Wear Rd SALV BN13 .... **36** A3
Weavers Hl ANG/EP BN16 .... **34** A4
Weavers Ring ANG/EP BN16 .... **34** A5
Welbeck Av HOVE BN3 .... **44** A4
Welesmere Rd BRIE/ROTT BN2 ... **61** E2
Welland Cl SALV BN13 .... **36** B2
Welland Rd SALV BN13 .... **36** B2
Wellesley Av FERR BN12 .... **54** B3
Wellgreen La LEWES BN7 .... **32** B2
Well House Pl LEWES BN7 .... **17** E4
Wellingham La SALV BN13 .... **36** C1
Wellington Pk SEAF BN25 .... **71** E5
Wellington Rd BRIE/ROTT BN2 .... **46** B3
    NEWHV BN9 .... **65** E3
    PEAHV BN10 .... **67** G2
    PTSD BN41 .... **43** F4
Wellington St BRIE/ROTT BN2 ..... **46** C3
    LEWES BN7 .... **17** F3
Wells Ct WTHG BN11 * **55** E4
Wembley Av LAN/SOMP BN15 ..... **39** F4
Wembley Gdns
    LAN/SOMP BN15 .... **39** F4
Wenban Rd WTHG BN11 .... **4** E3
Wenceling Cots
    LAN/SOMP BN15 .... **40** C5
Wendale Dr PEAHV BN10 .... **63** F3
Went Hill Pk SEAF BN25 .... **71** E5
Wentworth Cl SALV BN13 .... **36** D2
Wentworth Ct ANG/EP BN16 * **52** A4
Wentworth St BRIE/ROTT BN2 ..... **3** J6
West Av LAN/SOMP BN15 .... **40** A5
    WTHG BN11 .... **55** E4
West Beach Rd SHOR BN43 .... **40** D5
Westbourne Av SALV BN13 .... **4** E1
Westbourne Gdns HOVE BN3 ...... **44** C4
Westbourne Pl HOVE BN3 .... **44** C4
Westbourne St HOVE BN3 .... **44** C3
Westbourne Vls HOVE BN3 .... **44** B4
Westbrook BRIE/ROTT BN2 * **61** G3
Westbrooke WTHG BN11 .... **4** E4
Westbrook Wy STHW BN42 .... **42** D3
West Buildings WTHG BN11 .... **4** E6
Westcourt Pl SALV BN13 .... **4** D1
Westcourt Rd SALV BN13 .... **4** D2
Westdean Av NEWHV BN9 .... **68** D3
West Dean Ri SEAF BN25 .... **71** E4

Westdean Rd SALV BN13 .... **...**
Westdene Dr BRI BN1 .... **...**
Westdown Rd SEAF BN25 .... **...**
West Dr BRIE/ROTT BN2 .... **...**
    FERR BN12 .... **...**
West End Wy LAN/SOMP BN15 .... **...**
Westergate Cl FERR BN12 .... **...**
Westergate Rd BRIE/ROTT BN2 ... **...**
Western Cl LAN/SOMP BN15 .... **...**
Western Esp PTSD BN41 .... **...**
Western Ldg LAN/SOMP BN15 * ... **...**
Western Pl WTHG BN11 .... **...**
Western Rd HOVE BN3 .... **...**
    LAN/SOMP BN15 .... **...**
    LEWES BN7 .... **...**
    NEWHV BN9 .... **...**
    SHOR BN43 .... **...**
Western Rd North
    LAN/SOMP BN15 .... **...**
Western Rw WTHG BN11 .... **...**
Western St BRI BN1 .... **...**
Western Ter BRI BN1 .... **...**
    LAN/SOMP BN15 * .... **...**
Westfield Av ANG/EP BN16 .... **...**
    BRIE/ROTT BN2 .... **...**
Westfield Av North
    BRIE/ROTT BN2 .... **...**
Westfield Av South
    BRIE/ROTT BN2 .... **...**
Westfield Cl BRI BN1 .... **...**
Westfield Crs BRI BN1 .... **...**
Westfield Ri BRIE/ROTT BN2 .... **...**
West Hl SALV BN13 .... **...**
West Hill Cl SALV BN13 * .... **...**
West Hill Pl BRI BN1 .... **...**
West Hill Rd BRI BN1 .... **...**
West Hill St BRI BN1 .... **...**
Westlake Cl SALV BN13 .... **...**
Westland Av SALV BN13 .... **...**
Westlands FERR BN12 .... **...**
West La LAN/SOMP BN15 .... **...**
Westmeston Av
    BRIE/ROTT BN2 .... **...**
Westmount Cl STHW BN42 .... **...**
West Onslow Cl FERR BN12 * ...... **...**
West Pde WTHG BN11 .... **...**
Westpark La FERR BN12 .... **...**
West Quay NEWHV BN9 .... **...**
West Rd PTSD BN41 .... **...**
West St BRI BN1 .... **...**
    BRIE/ROTT BN2 .... **...**
    LAN/SOMP BN15 .... **...**
    PTSD BN41 .... **...**
    SEAF BN25 .... **...**
    SHOR BN43 .... **...**
    WTHG BN11 .... **...**
West Tyne SALV BN13 .... **...**
West Vw HOVE BN3 * .... **...**
    SEAF BN25 .... **...**
West View Ct SEAF BN25 * .... **...**
Westview Ter SALV BN13 .... **...**
West Wy HOVE BN3 .... **...**
    LAN/SOMP BN15 .... **...**
    SALV BN13 .... **...**
Westway Cl PTSD BN41 .... **...**
Westway Gdns PTSD BN41 .... **...**
Wharf Rd HOVE BN3 .... **...**
Wheatfield Wy BRIE/ROTT BN2 ... **...**
Wheatland Cl PEAHV BN10 .... **...**
Wheatsheaf Gdns LEWES BN7 ..... **...**
Whichelo Pl BRIE/ROTT BN2 .... **...**
Whippingham Rd
    BRIE/ROTT BN2 .... **...**
Whippingham St
    BRIE/ROTT BN2 .... **...**
Whitebeam Rd SALV BN13 .... **...**
Whitecross St BRI BN1 .... **...**
Whitehawk Cl BRIE/ROTT BN2 ..... **...**
Whitehawk Crs BRIE/ROTT BN2 ... **...**
Whitehawk Hill Rd
    BRIE/ROTT BN2 .... **...**
Whitehawk Rd BRIE/ROTT BN2 .... **...**
Whitehawk Wy BRIE/ROTT BN2 ... **...**
White House Pl SALV BN13 .... **...**
Whitelot Cl STHW BN42 .... **...**
Whitelot Wy STHW BN42 .... **...**
Whiterock Pl STHW BN42 .... **...**
White St BRIE/ROTT BN2 .... **...**
White Styles Rd
    LAN/SOMP BN15 .... **...**
Whitethorn Dr BRI BN1 .... **...**
White Wy LEWES BN7 .... **...**
Whiteway Cl SEAF BN25 .... **...**
Whiteway La BRIE/ROTT BN2 ...... **...**
Whittingehame Gdns BRI BN1 ...... **...**
Whylands Av SALV BN13 .... **...**
Whylands Cl SALV BN13 .... **...**
Whylands Crs SALV BN13 .... **...**
Wickhurst Cl PTSD BN41 .... **...**

irst Ri *PTSD* BN41	24	D4
irst Rd *PTSD* BN41	24	D5
ids Av *BRIE/ROTT* BN2	61	H4
ombe Wy		
/ROTT BN2	29	E5
ater Cl *LAN/SOMP* BN15	40	C5
ater Ct *SHOR* BN43 *	40	D5
re Cl *BRI* BN1	46	B1
re Rd *SALV* BN13	37	H4
y Av *HOVE* BN3	45	E2
y Crs *HOVE* BN3	45	F3
y Gdns *HOVE* BN3	45	E2
y Gv *HOVE* BN3	45	E4
y Rd *HOVE* BN3	45	E4
y Vls *HOVE* BN3	45	E3
Av *STHW* BN42	42	C1
ark Cl *BRIE/ROTT* BN2	29	E4
Rd *HOVE* BN3	43	H2
son Cl *ANG/EP* BN16	52	A1
/ROTT BN2	60	D2
son Wy *SEAF* BN25	70	C4
Olders Rd *ANG/EP* BN16	52	A1
s Rd *SHOR* BN43	41	H2
St *BRIE/ROTT* BN2	3	H4
BN41	43	F3
don Rd *BRIE/ROTT* BN2	47	E1
brook Rd *SALV* BN13	56	B1
Cl *BRIE/ROTT* BN2	48	C2
SOMP* BN15	40	C5
/UB BN44	7	C2
Ct *WTHG* BN11	55	E2
Crs *SALV* BN13	36	A5
Dr *SEAF* BN25	71	C3
low Est *NEWHV* BN9 *	65	E5
hayne Av *ANG/EP* BN16	52	A1
hayne Cl *ANG/EP* BN16	52	A5
hayne Crs *ANG/EP* BN16	52	A1
llows *BRIE/ROTT* BN2 *	46	B2
SOMP* BN15 *	39	C5
BN13 *	18	C1
BN25 *	70	C5
Wk *NEWHV* BN9	64	C5
gton Cl *BRI* BN1	28	A2
gton Pde *BRI* BN1	27	H2

Wilmington Rd *NEWHV* BN9	68	B2
SEAF BN25	70	B4
Wilmington Wy *BRI* BN1	27	H2
Wilmot Rd *SHOR* BN43	42	A2
Wilson Av *BRIE/ROTT* BN2	59	F1
Winchelsea Cl *SEAF* BN25	71	F3
Winchelsea Gdns *WTHG* BN11	54	D4
Winchester Rd *WTHG* BN11	4	B5
Winchester St *BRI* BN1	46	A2
Wincombe Rd *BRI* BN1	45	F1
Windermere Ct *FERR* BN12 *	53	H3
Windermere Crs *FERR* BN12	36	B5
Windlesham Av *HOVE* BN3	2	C2
Windlesham Cl *PTSD* BN41	43	E1
Windlesham Gdns		
ANG/EP BN16	52	A3
BRI BN1	2	D2
SHOR BN43	41	F2
Windlesham Rd *BRI* BN1	2	D2
SHOR BN43	41	F2
Windmill Cl *ANG/EP* BN16	52	A1
HOVE BN3	26	B5
STEY/UB BN44	8	B2
Windmill Dr *BRI* BN1	27	E1
Windmill Rd *STHW* BN42	42	C1
Windmill St *BRIE/ROTT* BN2	3	K4
Windmill Ter *BRIE/ROTT* BN2	3	K3
Windmill Vw *BRI* BN1	28	B1
Windover Crs *LEWES* BN7	16	C2
Windrush Cl *SALV* BN13	36	A2
Windsor Cl *HOVE* BN3	26	C4
SEAF BN25	69	H2
Windsor Rd *WTHG* BN11	5	K3
Windsor St *BRI* BN1	3	F4
Windsor Wy *LAN/SOMP* BN15	40	B4
Winfield Av *BRI* BN1	27	H1
Winfield Cl *BRI* BN1	27	H2
PTSD BN41	25	E4
Winston Rd *LAN/SOMP* BN15	57	E2
Winterbourne Cl *LEWES* BN7	16	D4
SALV BN13	35	H5
Winterbourne Hollow		
LEWES BN7	16	D4
Winterbourne La *LEWES* BN7	16	C4

Winterbourne Ms *LEWES* BN7	16	D4
Winterbourne Wy *SALV* BN13	35	H5
Winterton Wy *SHOR* BN43	41	H4
Winton Av *BRIE/ROTT* BN2	61	G3
Winton Pl *WTHG* BN11	4	E1
Wish Rd *HOVE* BN3	44	A4
Wiston Av *SALV* BN13	37	F5
Wiston Cl *SALV* BN13	37	F5
Wiston Rd *BRIE/ROTT* BN2	47	F3
Wiston Wy *BRIE/ROTT* BN2	47	F3
Withdean Av *BRI* BN1	27	F5
FERR BN12	53	H5
Withdean Cl *BRI* BN1	27	F4
Withdean Court Av *BRI* BN1	27	F4
Withdean Crs *BRI* BN1	27	C4
Withdean Ri *BRI* BN1	27	F4
Withdean Rd *BRI* BN1	27	F5
Withyham Av *BRIE/ROTT* BN2	61	C3
Wivelsfield Rd *BRIE/ROTT* BN2	61	G2
Woburn Pl *BRI* BN1	29	F2
Wolseley Rd *BRI* BN1	28	D1
PTSD BN41	43	E2
Wolstonbury Rd *HOVE* BN3	45	G3
Wolverstone Dr *BRI* BN1	28	C5
Woodard Rd *LAN/SOMP* BN15	39	H3
Woodards Vw *SHOR* BN43	40	D5
Woodbourne Av *BRI* BN1	27	H5
Woodbridge Pk *ANG/EP* BN16	52	A4
Woodhouse Cl *HOVE* BN3	44	A3
Woodhouse Rd *HOVE* BN3	44	A3
Woodland Av *HOVE* BN3	26	D3
SALV BN13	36	D1
Woodland Cl *HOVE* BN3	26	D5
Woodland Dr *HOVE* BN3	26	D5
Woodlands *HOVE* BN3	27	E5
Woodlands Cl *ANG/EP* BN16	34	A3
PEAHV BN10	62	D4
SALV BN13	35	F1
The Woodlands *BRI* BN1	27	G2
Woodland Wk *BRIE/ROTT* BN2	60	B1
Woodland Wy *BRI* BN1	27	H3
Woodlea Rd *SALV* BN13	55	E1
Woodmancote Rd *SALV* BN13	55	F1
Woodpecker Wy *SALV* BN13	36	A5

Woodruff Av *HOVE* BN3	27	E5
Woodside Av *BRI* BN1	27	F5
Woodside Rd *SALV* BN13	4	B1
Woods Wy *FERR* BN12	54	A2
Woodview *SHOR* BN43	41	F1
Woodview Cl *BRI* BN1	28	D1
Woodview Ct *SHOR* BN43 *	41	F1
Worcester Ct *WTHG* BN11 *	55	E4
Worcester Vls *HOVE* BN3	45	C3
Wordsworth Rd *WTHG* BN11	4	B5
Wordsworth St *HOVE* BN3	44	C4
Wychwood Gdns *WTHG* BN11	56	D2
Wyke Av *WTHG* BN11	5	G5
Wykeham Cl *STEY/UB* BN44	7	F3
Wykeham Rd *WTHG* BN11	4	C4
Wykeham Ter *BRI* BN1 *	2	E4
Wyndham St *BRIE/ROTT* BN2	3	K6
Wynnes Ms *HOVE* BN3	44	C3

Y

Yardley St *BRI* BN1	46	A2
Yarrow Rd *LEWES* BN7	16	D2
Yeoman Rd *SALV* BN13	35	H5
Yeoman Wy *SALV* BN13	53	H1
York Av *HOVE* BN3	52	C4
York Gv *BRI* BN1	45	H3
York Hi *BRI* BN1	3	C1
York Pl *BRI* BN1	3	H2
York Rd *HOVE* BN3	2	C4
PEAHV BN10	67	G2
WTHG BN11	5	G5
York Vls *BRI* BN1	45	H3
Youngsmere Cl *BRI* BN1	28	B1

Z

Zion Gdns *BRI* BN1	3	F4

dex - featured places

mary Department		
BN1	27	G5
ositive		
erground Theatre		
/ROTT BN2	58	C1
ton House Hospital		
E BN3	44	B4
otel Seattle		
/ROTT BN2	59	F2
owling		
G BN11	4	E6
RC Primary School		
BN25	73	H4
f Cleves House		
eum		
ES BN7	17	E4
na Swimming Pool		
G BN11	5	H5
len Foot &		
th Clinic		
/ROTT BN2	3	H5
ton Hotel		
G BN11	5	C5
re School		
G BN11	4	E4
bly Hall		
G BN11	4	E4
r J&I School		
N1	27	H4
heatre		
BN25	72	C1
Hotel		
G BN11	4	C7
ys College		
E BN3	45	E3
wer Industrial Estate		
/ROTT BN2	59	F1
d Junior School		
BN41	43	G2
ey Hotel		
E BN3	4	D6
st Western		
nton Hotel		
E BN3	2	B5
dean Primary School		
ROTT BN2	29	F5

Blatchington Mill School		
HOVE BN3	26	C5
Blatchington Mill School &		
Sixth Form College		
HOVE BN3	44	C1
Blatchington Road		
Industrial Estate		
SEAF BN25	70	C5
Booth Museum of		
Natural History		
HOVE BN3	45	F2
Bowden House School		
SEAF BN25	70	C4
Bramber Castle		
STEY/UB BN44	7	H4
Bramber Road First School		
SALV BN13	38	A4
Breaky Bottom Vineyard		
LEWES BN7	50	C3
Bridge Industrial Estate		
NEWHV BN9	64	D5
Brighton Business Centre		
BRI BN1	45	H2
The Brighton Centre		
BRI BN1	2	E5
Brighton College of Technology		
BRIE/ROTT BN2	3	J1
Brighton County Court		
BRIE/ROTT BN2	3	H4
Brighton Fishing Museum		
BRI BN1	3	F6
Brighton General Hospital		
BRIE/ROTT BN2	46	D3
Brighton & Hove Albion FC		
(Withdean Stadium)		
BRI BN1	27	F4
Brighton & Hove Golf Club		
BRI BN1	11	H5
Brighton & Hove		
Greyhound Stadium		
HOVE BN3	44	C1
Brighton & Hove High School		
HOVE BN3	45	E2
Brighton & Hove		
High School GDST		
BRI BN1	2	C3

Brighton Hove & Sussex		
Sixth Form College		
HOVE BN3	45	G2
Brighton Media Centre		
BRI BN1	3	F5
Brighton Museum & Art Gallery		
BRI BN1	3	H4
Brighton Pier		
BRIE/ROTT BN2	3	H7
Brighton Racecourse		
BRIE/ROTT BN2	47	E3
Brighton RFC		
BRI BN1	26	D1
Brighton University		
LEWES BN7	16	D1
Brighton Youth Centre		
BRIE/ROTT BN2	3	K5
Brightwell Industrial Estate		
NEWHV BN9	69	E1
British Engineerium -		
Museum of Steam &		
Mechanical Antiquities		
HOVE BN3	26	D5
Broadwater and Worthing		
Cemetery		
SALV BN13	37	G5
Broadwater CE F&M School		
SALV BN13	37	G5
Broadwater Industrial Estate		
SALV BN13	38	B4
Broadwater Manor School		
SALV BN13	37	H5
Brooklands Trading Estate		
SALV BN13	4	B2
Bross Estate		
NEWHV BN9	65	E5
Buckingham Middle School		
SHOR BN43	41	F2
Cardinal Newman School		
HOVE BN3	45	F2
Carlton Hill Primary School		
BRIE/ROTT BN2	3	J4
Castledean School		
BRI BN1	28	C5
Cavendish Hotel		
WTHG BN11	4	D7

Centenary		
Industrial Estate		
BRI BN1	46	B1
Chapel Royal		
BRI BN1	3	G5
Charter Medical Centre		
HOVE BN3	2	B1
Chesswood Middle School		
WTHG BN11	5	H1
Child Clinic		
BRIE/ROTT BN2	3	H4
Churchill Square		
Shopping Centre		
BRI BN1	2	E5
Cineworld		
BRIE/ROTT BN2	59	F2
Cissbury Ring		
SALV BN13	19	F2
City College of		
Brighton & Hove		
BRI BN1	3	H2
Clapham & Patching CE		
Primary School		
SALV BN13	35	E1
Clarks Industrial Estate		
HOVE BN3	44	D2
Cliffe Business Centre		
LEWES BN7	17	G3
Cliffe Industrial Estate		
RING/NEW BN8	17	H4
Coldean Primary School		
BRI BN1	14	D5
Connaught Theatre & Cinema		
WTHG BN11	5	F4
Conway Court Clinic		
HOVE BN3	44	D2
Coombe Road Primary School		
BRIE/ROTT BN2	46	D1
Corn Exchange Theatre		
BRI BN1	3	G4
Corsica Hall Education		
Training Centre		
SEAF BN25	72	D1
Cottesmore St Marys RC		
Primary School		
HOVE BN3	45	F2

The Courtlands Hotel
HOVE BN3 ....45 E4
Cradle Hill Community
Primary School
SEAF BN25 ....70 D3
Cradle Hill Industrial Estate
SEAF BN25 ....71 F3
Cyril Richings Business Centre
SHOR BN43 ....41 H3
David Lloyd Health &
Fitness Centre
BRIE/ROTT BN2 ....59 E2
Davigdor Infant School
HOVE BN3 ....2 A2
Davison CE High
School for Girls
WTHG BN11 ....5 K2
D-Day Museum
SHOR BN43 ....40 D3
Deacon Trading Estate
SALV BN13 ....38 B5
Deepdene School
HOVE BN3 ....43 H3
Denton Community School
NEWHV BN9 ....65 E4
The De Vere Grand Hotel
BRI BN1 ....2 D5
Devil's Dyke
BRI BN1 ....11 G1
Dharma School
BRI BN1 ....28 A1
Dolphin House Clinic for Adults
BRI BN1 ....3 G4
Dolphin Industrial Estate
SHOR BN43 ....42 A3
Dome Cinema
WTHG BN11 ....5 G6
Downlands Business Park
SALV BN13 ....38 A2
Downsbrook Middle School
SALV BN13 ....38 A5
Downsbrook Trading Estate
SALV BN13 ....38 A4
Downs Crematorium
BRIE/ROTT BN2 ....46 D2
Downs Infant School
BRI BN1 ....46 A2
Downs Junior School
BRI BN1 ....46 A1
Downs Leisure Centre
SEAF BN25 ....71 E4
Downs Park School
PTSD BN41 ....25 F5
The Dr Jan De Winter Clinic for
Cancer Prevention Advice
BRI BN1 ....3 G5
Duke of York's Premier
Picture House Cinema
BRI BN1 ....46 A3
Durrington First School
SALV BN13 ....36 C3
Durrington Health Centre
SALV BN13 ....36 B4
Durrington High School
SALV BN13 ....36 C5
East Brighton Golf Club
BRIE/ROTT BN2 ....59 F1
East Preston CP School
ANG/EP BN16 ....52 A3
East Sussex County
Music School
LEWES BN7 ....17 E4
East Worthing Industrial Estate
SALV BN13 ....38 B5
Elm Grove County First School
WTHG BN11 ....54 D2
Elm Grove Primary School
BRIE/ROTT BN2 ....46 C3
English Bowling Association
WTHG BN11 ....5 H4
English Martyr Catholic
Primary School
FERR BN12 ....36 B5
Environment Agency
WTHG BN11 ....5 F5
Euro Business Park
NEWHV BN9 ....64 D4
Evolution Health Centre
BRI BN1 ....2 D3
Fairlight Primary School
BRIE/ROTT BN2 ....46 C2
Fairway Trading Estate
BRIE/ROTT BN2 ....29 E3
Falmer High School
BRI BN1 ....29 G2
Ferring CE Primary School
FERR BN12 ....53 F3
Ferring FC
FERR BN12 ....53 E3

Ferryfield Industrial Estate
NEWHV BN9 ....69 E1
Field Place First School
FERR BN12 ....54 B1
Findon Manor Hotel
SALV BN13 ....18 C1
Fishersgate First School
PTSD BN41 ....43 E3
The Fold School
HOVE BN3 ....43 H3
Freshbrook County
First School
LAN/SOMP BN15 ....39 G4
Freshfield Industrial Estate
BRIE/ROTT BN2 ....46 C5
Garcia Trading Estate
SALV BN13 ....54 D2
Gardner Arts Centre Cinema
BRI BN1 ....15 G5
Gemini Business Centre
HOVE BN3 ....44 C2
George II Statue
BRI BN1 ....3 G4
Georgian House Business Centre
BRIE/ROTT BN2 ....3 H5
Glebe Middle School
STHW BN42 ....42 B3
Goldstone Primary School
HOVE BN3 ....44 A1
Goldstone Retail Park
HOVE BN3 ....44 D2
Goring CE First School
FERR BN12 ....54 A3
Goring CC
FERR BN12 ....53 G3
Granville Hotel
BRI BN1 ....2 D5
Grays School
NEWHV BN9 ....68 D2
Guildbourne Shopping Centre
WTHG BN11 ....5 G5
Ham Bridge Trading Estate
SALV BN13 ....56 C1
Ham Business Centre
SHOR BN43 ....41 G3
Hamilton Lodge School
BRIE/ROTT BN2 ....46 D5
Hangleton County J&I School
HOVE BN3 ....26 A5
Harveys Brewery
LEWES BN7 ....17 F3
The Hawthorns First School
SALV BN13 ....36 A5
Hazel Cottage Clinic
BRIE/ROTT BN2 ....48 A2
Hazelwood Trading Estate
SALV BN13 ....56 B1
Heene CE First School
WTHG BN11 ....4 C3
Herbert Hone Clinic
BRI BN1 ....46 B3
Herons Dale School
SHOR BN43 ....42 B1
Hertford Junior School
BRI BN1 ....28 C4
Highdown Gardens
FERR BN12 ....35 F5
Highdown Hill
FERR BN12 ....35 E5
Hill Barn Golf Club
SALV BN13 ....37 G2
Hillside Special School
PTSD BN41 ....25 E5
HM Prison
LEWES BN7 ....16 C3
Hoddern County Junior School
PEAHV BN10 ....62 D5
Hollingbury Castle
BRI BN1 ....28 C3
Hollingbury Industrial Estate
BRI BN1 ....14 B5
Hollingbury Park Golf Club
BRI BN1 ....28 B3
Holmbush First School
SHOR BN43 ....42 B1
Homecare Business Centre
LEWES BN7 ....17 G3
Home Farm Business Centre
BRI BN1 ....28 D4
Hotel du Vin
BRI BN1 ....3 F5
Hove Business Centre
HOVE BN3 ....44 D2
Hove General Hospital
HOVE BN3 ....44 C3
Hove Medical Centre
HOVE BN3 ....26 A5
Hove Museum & Art Gallery
HOVE BN3 ....44 C3

Hove Park School
HOVE BN3 ....44 C1
Hove Polyclinic
HOVE BN3 ....44 B1
Hove RFC
HOVE BN3 ....44 D1
The Hyde Business Park
BRIE/ROTT BN2 ....47 F1
Iford & Kingston CE
Primary School
LEWES BN7 ....32 B2
Imperial Hotel
HOVE BN3 ....45 E5
Innkeeper's Lodge
BRI BN1 ....27 G1
Intensive School of English
BRI BN1 ....3 F4
J D English Tuition
NEWHV BN9 ....65 F4
K-Bis Theatre School
BRI BN1 ....27 G5
Kemptown Brewery
BRIE/ROTT BN2 ....58 C1
King Alfred Leisure Centre
HOVE BN3 ....44 C5
The Kings Hotel
BRI BN1 ....2 C5
Kingsmanor Community College
SHOR BN43 ....42 A2
Kingston Buci First School
SHOR BN43 ....41 H2
Kingsway Hotel
WTHG BN11 ....4 C6
The Knoll Business Centre
HOVE BN3 ....43 H2
Komedia
BRI BN1 ....3 G3
Lady Bee Marina
Industrial Estate
PTSD BN41 ....42 C4
Lancing Business Centre
LAN/SOMP BN15 ....39 E5
Lancing College
LAN/SOMP BN15 ....22 A5
Lancing College Chapel
LAN/SOMP BN15 ....22 B5
Lancing Health Centre
LAN/SOMP BN15 ....39 G4
The Lanes
BRI BN1 ....3 G5
The Lansdown Place Hotel
HOVE BN3 ....2 A5
The Laurels County First School
SALV BN13 ....35 H4
Lewes Athletics Track
LEWES BN7 ....17 G4
Lewes Business Centre
LEWES BN7 ....17 E2
Lewes Castle & Barbican
House Museum
LEWES BN7 ....17 E3
Lewes College
LEWES BN7 ....17 F4
Lewes FC
LEWES BN7 ....17 F4
Lewes Golf Club
LEWES BN7 ....17 H4
Lewes Grammar School
LEWES BN7 ....17 E3
Lewes Leisure Centre
LEWES BN7 ....17 G4
Lewes Little Theatre
LEWES BN7 ....17 E3
Lewes New School
LEWES BN7 ....17 E2
Lewes Old Grammar School
(Seniors & Sixth Form)
LEWES BN7 ....17 E3
Lewes Sports Club
LEWES BN7 ....16 D5
Lewes Victoria Hospital
LEWES BN7 ....16 C3
Limeburners (Camping)
ANG/EP BN16 ....34 A2
Little Theatre
SEAF BN25 ....72 C1
Longhill High School
BRIE/ROTT BN2 ....60 C1
Longley Industrial Estate
BRI BN1 ....46 A3
Lyndhurst First School
WTHG BN11 ....5 K2
Malling Industrial Estate
LEWES BN7 ....17 G2
Malt House Trading Estate
SHOR BN43 ....41 H3
Manor Hall County Middle
School
STHW BN42 ....42 C2

Manor Hall First School
STHW BN42 ....
Manor House Hospital
HOVE BN3 ....
Manor Sports Ground Pavilion
SALV BN13 ....
Marine Clinic
BRIE/ROTT BN2 ....
Marlborough Business Centre
LAN/SOMP BN15 ....
Marlipins Museum
SHOR BN43 ....
Martello Tower & Seaford Muse
SEAF BN25 ....
Martlets Trading Estate
FERR BN12 ....
Meadow Road Industrial Estate
WTHG BN11 ....
Meeching Valley CP School
NEWHV BN9 ....
The Meridian Industrial Estate
PEAHV BN10 ....
Meridian Leisure Centre
PEAHV BN10 ....
Meridian Primary School
PEAHV BN10 ....
Middle Street Primary School
BRI BN1 ....
Mile Oak Clinic
PTSD BN41 ....
Mile Oak Primary School
PTSD BN41 ....
Mill Road Industrial Estate
PTSD BN41 ....
Mill View Hospital
HOVE BN3 ....
Modern Moulds
Business Centre
LAN/SOMP BN15 ....
Monk's House (NT)
LEWES BN7 ....
Montague Shopping Centre
WTHG BN11 ....
Montessori House for Children
BRI BN1 ....
Morley Street Health Centre
BRIE/ROTT BN2 ....
Moulsecoomb Health Clinic
BRIE/ROTT BN2 ....
Moulsecoomb Primary School
BRIE/ROTT BN2 ....
Mowden School
HOVE BN3 ....
Newhaven Ferry Terminal
NEWHV BN9 ....
Newhaven Health Centre
NEWHV BN9 ....
Newlands Manor School
SEAF BN25 ....
Newlands Preparatory School
SEAF BN25 ....
New Venture Theatre
BRI BN1 ....
Nore Down
NEWHV BN9 ....
Northbourne Medical Centre
SHOR BN43 ....
Northbrook College Sussex
FERR BN12 ....
SALV BN13 ....
WTHG BN11 ....
Northbrook Trading Estate
SALV BN13 ....
Northease Manor School
LEWES BN7 ....
North Lancing
First & Middle School
LAN/SOMP BN15 ....
Oakfield Middle School
LAN/SOMP BN15 ....
Oakgrove College
SALV BN13 ....
Oaklands Business Centre
WTHG BN11 ....
Odeon Cinema
BRI BN1 ....
Old Darlington Mushroom Farm
Industrial Estate
ANG/EP BN16 ....
Old Grammar School (Juniors)
LEWES BN7 ....
Old Ship Hotel
BRI BN1 ....
The Old Tollgate
Restaurant & Hotel
STEY/UB BN44 ....
The Orchards Community
Middle School
FERR BN12 ....

dy of Lourdes RC
  E/ROTT BN2 ....60 D3
dy of Sion Junior School
  HG BN11 ....4 E4
dy of Sion School
  HG BN11 ....4 D5
dean Hall School
  E/ROTT BN2 ....60 B1
ne School
  R BN12 ....36 B5
se Park & Gardens
  /SOMP BN15 ....64 D4
nd Business Centre
  /SOMP BN15 ....57 F1
iew Leisure Centre
  E BN3 ....44 A3
am High School
  BN1 ....27 H1
am House Special School
  BN1 ....27 G1
am Infant School
  BN1 ....27 G1
am Junior School
  BN1 ....27 H1
avilion Clinic
  BN1 ....2 D4
on Retail Park
  E/ROTT BN2 ....28 C5
on Theatre
  BN1 ....3 G4
VG BN11 ....5 F6
n Business Centre
  E BN3 ....43 H2
haven
  *munity School
  HV BN10 ....63 E5
haven Golf Club
  HV BN9 ....68 A1
haven Infant School
  HV BN10 ....66 D1
haven Sports Centre
  HV BN9 ....67 F1
ck Industrial Estate
  E BN3 ....45 F3
E Primary School
  ES BN7 ....17 E2
ter Gladwin
  *mary School
  D BN41 ....25 D3
ix Industrial Estate
  ES BN7 ....17 F2
t's Business Park
  VG BN11 ....4 D3
nd Business Park
  E BN3 ....44 A3
nd Road Trading Estate
  E BN3 ....43 H2
ade Community College
  D BN41 ....25 E4
  N BN42 ....24 D5
ade Health Centre
  D BN41 ....43 F3
ade Sixth Form Centre
  D BN41 ....43 E1
er Travel Inn
  BN1 ....3 F5
  HV BN9 ....65 E5
n Manor
  BN1 ....45 G1
n Park Clinic
  BN1 ....46 A1
n Park Hotel
  BN1 ....27 G5
 Regent
  *ming Complex
  BN1 ....3 G4
s Marine Hotel
  E BN3 ....44 C4
 Gateway
  ES BN7 ....17 E4
 Ruins
  ES BN7 ....17 E4
 School
  ES BN7 ....17 G4
 Hotel
  BN1 ....2 E5
 Alexandra Hospital Home
  G BN11 ....4 B5
sdown School
  BN1 ....28 C4
 Victoria Statue
  E BN3 ....45 E5
a Hotel
  E BN3 ....2 B5
h Estate
  HV BN9 ....65 E4
dustrial Estate
  HV BN9 ....65 E4

Riverbank Business Centre
  SHOR BN43 ....40 D3
Riverside Business Centre
  SHOR BN43 ....41 F3
Riverside Industrial Estate
  LEWES BN7 ....17 F2
RNIB
  HOVE BN3 ....2 B2
Rodmell CE Primary School
  LEWES BN7 ....51 G1
Roedean School
  BRIE/ROTT BN2 ....59 H2
Rottingdean FC
  BRIE/ROTT BN2 ....60 D2
Royal Pavilion
  BRI BN1 ....3 G5
The Royal Pavilion
  Townhouse Hotel
  BRI BN1 ....2 C5
Royal Sussex County Hospital
  BRIE/ROTT BN2 ....58 D1
Rudyard Kipling CP School
  BRIE/ROTT BN2 ....48 C3
Sackville Trading Estate
  HOVE BN3 ....44 C2
St Andrews CE High
  School for Boys
  SALV BN13 ....56 A1
St Andrews CE Primary
  School
  HOVE BN3 ....44 D4
St Annes School
  LEWES BN7 ....16 D4
St Aubyns School
  BRIE/ROTT BN2 ....61 E4
St Bartholomews CE
  Primary School
  BRI BN1 ....3 G1
St Bartholomews
  Tutorial College
  BRI BN1 ....3 G5
St Bernadettes RC
  Primary School
  BRI BN1 ....27 G5
St Christophers School
  HOVE BN3 ....44 B4
St Faith Clinic
  BRIE/ROTT BN2 ....59 E1
St Johns School & College
  SEAF BN25 ....70 C3
St John the Baptist
  Primary School
  SALV BN13 ....18 D1
St John the Baptist RC
  Primary School
  BRIE/ROTT BN2 ....46 D5
St Josephs Business Park
  HOVE BN3 ....44 C2
St Josephs RC Primary School
  BRI BN1 ....46 B1
St Josephs Trading Estate
  HOVE BN3 ....44 B2
St Lukes Swimming Pool
  BRIE/ROTT BN2 ....46 C4
St Lukes Terrace
  Junior School
  BRIE/ROTT BN2 ....46 C4
St Marks CE Primary School
  BRIE/ROTT BN2 ....59 E1
St Martins CE Primary School
  BRIE/ROTT BN2 ....46 C2
St Mary Magdalen
  Primary School
  BRI BN1 ....2 D3
St Marys Hall School
  BRIE/ROTT BN2 ....58 D1
St Marys RC Primary School
  PTSD BN41 ....43 F3
  WTHG BN11 ....4 C4
St Nicholas & St Mary CE
  First & Middle School
  SHOR BN43 ....41 G2
St Pancras RC Primary School
  LEWES BN7 ....16 D3
St Pauls CE Primary School
  BRI BN1 ....2 E3
St Peter's Catholic
  Primary School
  SHOR BN43 ....41 G2
St Peters Infant School
  PTSD BN41 ....43 F3
St Peters Medical Centre
  BRI BN1 ....3 H1
Saltdean Primary School
  BRIE/ROTT BN2 ....61 G3
Sandhurst School
  WTHG BN11 ....5 J4
The Seaford Business Centre
  SEAF BN25 ....70 C5

Seaford Day Hospital
  SEAF BN25 ....70 D5
Seaford Golf Club
  SEAF BN25 ....70 D2
Seaford Head
  Community College
  SEAF BN25 ....72 D1
Seaford Head Golf Club
  SEAF BN25 ....73 E2
Seaford Head Lower School
  SEAF BN25 ....72 D1
Seaford Health Centre
  SEAF BN25 ....70 C5
Seaford Primary School
  SEAF BN25 ....70 C4
Seaford RFC
  SEAF BN25 ....70 B5
Seaford Sports & Leisure Centre
  SEAF BN25 ....70 C5
Sea Life Centre
  BRIE/ROTT BN2 ....3 H6
The Seven Dials Medical Centre
  BRI BN1 ....2 E2
Shelleys Hotel
  LEWES BN7 ....17 E3
Shoreham Airport
  SHOR BN43 ....40 C3
Shoreham Beach First School
  SHOR BN43 ....41 G4
Shoreham College
  SHOR BN43 ....42 B3
Shoreham FC
  PTSD BN41 ....43 F3
Shoreham First School
  SHOR BN43 ....41 G2
Shoreham Health Centre
  SHOR BN43 ....41 F3
Somerhill Junior School
  HOVE BN3 ....2 A2
Sompting Abbots School
  LAN/SOMP BN15 ....38 C2
Southdown Junior School
  NEWHV BN9 ....68 C1
South Downs Business Park
  LEWES BN7 ....17 G2
South Downs Health Clinic
  BRI BN1 ....3 F2
South Malling CE
  Primary School
  LEWES BN7 ....17 F1
Southwick Business Centre
  STHW BN42 ....42 C3
Springfield First School
  SALV BN13 ....56 A1
Stanford Infant School
  BRI BN1 ....45 G2
Stanford Road Junior School
  BRI BN1 ....45 H2
Stanley Deason Leisure
  Centre
  BRIE/ROTT BN2 ....47 F5
Steyning Athletic Club
  STEY/UB BN44 ....7 E3
Steyning Grammar
  Upper School
  STEY/UB BN44 ....7 F3
Steyning Health Centre
  STEY/UB BN44 ....7 F3
Steyning St Andrews CE
  Primary School
  STEY/UB BN44 ....7 F3
Steyning Sports Centre
  STEY/UB BN44 ....7 E2
Steyning Town FC
  STEY/UB BN44 ....7 F2
Stonelands School
  HOVE BN3 ....44 D4
Sussex County CC
  HOVE BN3 ....45 E3
Sussex Downs College
  LEWES BN7 ....17 F4
  NEWHV BN9 ....64 D5
Sussex English
  Language School
  WTHG BN11 ....4 E5
Sussex Eye Hospital
  BRIE/ROTT BN2 ....58 D1
Sussex House Business Park
  HOVE BN3 ....44 B2
Sussex Nuffield Hospital
  BRIE/ROTT BN2 ....48 A2
  HOVE BN3 ....44 B4
The Sussex Toy & Model
  Museum
  BRI BN1 ....3 G2
Sussex University
  LEWES BN7 ....17 G2
Swandean Hospital
  SALV BN13 ....36 B2

Swandean School of English
  WTHG BN11 ....4 D4
Swedish Folk High School
  PTSD BN41 ....43 F2
Telscombe Cliffs Primary School
  PEAHV BN10 ....62 C5
Templars County Infants School
  LAN/SOMP BN15 ....38 D4
Theatre Royal
  BRI BN1 ....3 G4
Thistle Hotel
  BRI BN1 ....3 G6
Thomas A Becket First School
  SALV BN13 ....37 E5
Thomas A Becket
  Middle School
  SALV BN13 ....37 F5
Thornberry Middle School
  LAN/SOMP BN15 ....39 H5
Ticehurst Clinic
  HOVE BN3 ....44 C4
Tideway School
  NEWHV BN9 ....68 B2
Timberlaine Trading Estate
  SALV BN13 ....38 B5
Torah Academy
  HOVE BN3 ....44 C4
The Towers Convent School
  STEY/UB BN44 ....8 C3
Town Hall Museum & Art Gallery
  WTHG BN11 ....5 F4
Travelodge
  BRI BN1 ....45 H2
University of Brighton
  BRI BN1 ....28 C5
  BRI BN1 ....29 H2
  BRIE/ROTT BN2 ....3 H4
University of Sussex
  BRI BN1 ....29 H1
University of Sussex
  Sports Centre
  BRI BN1 ....29 G1
Uplands Special School
  BRI BN1 ....28 C5
Upper Beeding Primary
  School
  STEY/UB BN44 ....8 A2
Vale First & Middle School
  SALV BN13 ....18 D5
Varndean College
  BRI BN1 ....27 H4
Varndean School
  BRI BN1 ....28 A4
Victoria Road Trading Estate
  PTSD BN41 ....43 G2
Volks Electric Railway
  BRIE/ROTT BN2 ....3 K7
Wallands Primary School
  LEWES BN7 ....16 C2
Waterhall Golf Club
  BRI BN1 ....26 C1
Waytefield Clinic
  BRI BN1 ....27 H5
Welfare Centre
  HOVE BN3 ....26 A5
West Blatchington
  Junior School
  HOVE BN3 ....26 B3
Westdene Primary School
  BRI BN1 ....27 E2
Westernroad Primary School
  LEWES BN7 ....16 D3
West Hill Community Hall
  BRI BN1 ....3 F1
Westholme Clinic
  FERR BN12 ....54 B3
  WTHG BN11 ....4 C5
West Hove Golf Club
  HOVE BN3 ....25 G2
West Hove Junior School
  HOVE BN3 ....44 B3
Weston Road
  Community School
  LEWES BN7 ....17 E4
West Park CE
  Controlled School
  FERR BN12 ....54 B3
West Pier (Derelict)
  BRI BN1 ....2 D6
West Sussex College of Design
  WTHG BN11 ....5 F4
West Sussex School of English
  STEY/UB BN44 ....7 F3
Whitehawk Clinic
  BRIE/ROTT BN2 ....47 F5
Whitehawk Primary School
  BRIE/ROTT BN2 ....47 E4
Whitestyles Middle School
  LAN/SOMP BN15 ....38 D4

Acknowledgements

Schools address data provided by Education Direct.

Petrol station information supplied by Johnsons

One-way street data provided by © Tele Atlas N.V. Tele Atlas

Garden centre information provided by

Garden Centre Association Britains best garden centres

Wyevale Garden Centres

The statement on the front cover of this atlas is sourced, selected and quoted from a reader comment and feedback form received in 2004

How do I find the perfect place?